A Sound History

A VOLUME IN THE SERIES

AMERICAN POPULAR MUSIC

Edited by
Jeffrey Melnick

A Sound History

LAWRENCE GELLERT, BLACK MUSICAL PROTEST, AND WHITE DENIAL

STEVEN P. GARABEDIAN

UNIVERSITY OF MASSACHUSETTS PRESS
AMHERST AND BOSTON

Printed in the United States of America

ISBN 978-1-62534-530-1 (paper); 529-5 (hardcover)

Designed by adam b. bohannon
Set in Baskerville
Printed and bound by Books International, Inc.

Cover design by adam b. bohannon

Library of Congress Cataloging-in-Publication Data
Names: Garabedian, Steven P., author.
Title: A sound history : Lawrence Gellert, Black musical protest, and white denial / Steven P. Garabedian.
Description: Amherst : University of Massachusetts Press, 2020. | Series: American popular music | Includes bibliographical references and index.
Identifiers: LCCN 2020019282 | ISBN 9781625345295 (hardcover) | ISBN 9781625345301 (paperback) | ISBN 9781613767801 (ebook) | ISBN 9781613767795 (ebook)
Subjects: LCSH: African Americans—Music—History and criticism. | Folk Music—United States—History and criticism. | Protest songs—United States—History and criticism. | Gellert, Lawrence, 1898–1979. | Music—Historiography. | African Americans—Historiography. | Music—Political aspects—United States—History—20th century.
Classification: LCC ML3556 .G35 2020 | DDC 782.42162/96073—dc23
LC record available at https://lccn.loc.gov/2020019282

British Library Cataloguing-in-Publication Data
A CATALOG RECORD FOR THIS BOOK IS AVAILABLE FROM THE BRITISH LIBRARY.

Portions of the introduction, chapters 1–2, chapters 4–6, and the epilogue were published in a previous form in "Reds, Whites, and the Blues" in *American Quarterly* 57 (March 2005): 179–206. Used by permission of Johns Hopkins University Press. Portions of chapters 5–6 were published in a previous form in "Forgotten Manuscripts: Lawrence Gellert, Negro Songs of Protest" in *African American Review* 49, no. 4 (Winter 2016): 297–311. Used by permission of Johns Hopkins University Press. Portions of the introduction, chapters 3–6, and the epilogue were published in a previous form in "The Blues Image in the White Mind" in *Popular Music and Society* 37, no.4 (October 2014): 476–94. See www.tandfonline.com. Used by permission of Routledge, Taylor & Francis Group.

To Sean

CONTENTS

Preface
ix

Introduction
Hidden in Plain Sight
Lawrence Gellert and
"Negro Songs of Protest"
1

Chapter One
The Roads to Perdition
Lawrence Gellert's Early Biography
and Emergence
15

Chapter Two
Free Radical
Lawrence Gellert's Early Collecting
and Rise to Prominence
35

Chapter Three
"Songs about the White Man"
Black Protest and White Denial
53

Chapter Four
"The Great Red Heart
of the American Revolution"
Lawrence Gellert, the Lomaxes,
and the Leftwing Folksong Revival
81

Chapter Five
Big White Fog
Controversy and Containment in the Postwar
108

Chapter Six
Scholarly Rigors
Propaganda or Protest in the Gellert Archive?
135

Epilogue
Freedom Songs, Sixties Revivalism, and the Tragedy of White Denial
172

Notes
183

Index
211

PREFACE

Years ago, I was cautioned by a prominent figure in American folk music against investing my young scholarly career in the Gellert archive. Lawrence Gellert, I was warned, was a questionable figure with an unreliable documentary collection. "Negro Songs of Protest," as the body of music had come to be called, was tainted, a fabrication of Gellert's own hand rather than genuine folklore. I had already been involved in my Gellert research for a few years, and I was confident of its value, as were others. Still, I took the warning in good faith. All along, I have tested the Gellert trail and archive to double- and triple-corroboration. I have not been dissuaded by doubters, but I have been careful not to rest easy with first conclusions. Over time, as the reality of the Gellert archive cohered so apparently with the reality of African American cultures of resistance generally, my interest expanded. Why had this material come into doubt? How is it that the suspicions seemed to come, in fact, from Gellert's own interpretive community in the white folksong revival? Why were some allies in the cause of racial justice so sure that "Negro Songs of Protest" were a product of white propaganda rather than Black vernacular creativity?

This book is premised on the fact of Black protest and the long reality of white denial. I argue that the Gellert musical archive is sound, that Lawrence Gellert was a sincere worker in the Cultural Front of the 1930s and 1940s, and that his prominence reflects a meaningful moment of synthesis in the convergence of "red" and "Black," leftwing activism and African American cultures of opposition, that still holds lessons for those of us looking for change today. As I show, the Gellert archive is not wholly unique, as some alleged, but it is striking. What is striking as well is the trajectory of celebration to defamation that Gellert and "Negro Songs of Protest" experienced before and after World War II.

I have long been fascinated by the intersection of Black music tradition and Black social resistance. In this, I followed a path similar to Lawrence Gellert. In each case, we "discovered" what was already out there but had been historically denied, dismissed, or hidden from the dominant culture. Like so many white outsiders before and since, we became admirers of African American musical artistry and struggle in large part because we found something lacking in our own communities of origin. Black culture was a viable alternative to mass Americanism, an antidote to alienation. It seemed to hold a redemptive power for personal transformation and social change. The power was there inherent to the music, but we also projected a lot from our respective removes of race and class.

Lawrence Gellert espoused the politics of the communist movement in the so-called "Red Era" of American history, and his archive of Black vernacular song featured lyrics of explicit race and class protest. Contemporary readers might well ask what it means, then, that the "verboten" tradition of protest that he documented had a period of recognition in the 1930s and 1940s, but then went largely "off the record" in the dominant culture. The acceptance and brief popular vogue of "Negro Songs of Protest" reflected both the possibilities and foreclosures of a radical movement for social and economic justice in the United States in the critical decades surrounding World War II. Just as the channels for a trenchant critique of capitalist political economy were circumscribed in the hot and cold war years of the 1940s and 1950s, so went the grounds of acceptance for an alternative tradition of African American vernacular expression calling out systemic American racial oppression and class exploitation. In the civil rights era, racism was most often delimited as interpersonal animosity rather than national policy, and class inequality was, as always, shouldered as personal failing. Systemic critiques were dismissed by conservatives and liberals as "Old Left" dogma to avoid in the new frontier of the global superpower.

The Black freedom struggle did not begin or end with Lawrence Gellert or the Communist Left of his era. Whether as blues, jazz, rhythm and blues, gospel, soul, or hip hop, "Negro Songs of Protest" continued to proliferate from out of the seeds of oppression. But the contribution of Lawrence Gellert was fated to fall on deaf ears by the 1960s as a result of more than ten years of anticommunist repression, Cold War cultural backlash, and rising conservatism and consumerism. In this respect, the denial of "Negro Songs of Protest" speaks to much more than simply a lapse in historiography. Rather, it is symbolic of a larger denial of social class and institutionalized racism that rose to orthodoxy in American dominant culture in the postwar and remains with us today.

* * *

This book took a long time to complete, and thinking through my acknowledgments is like leafing through a scrapbook. Some of my thanks for specific points of assistance are included in the chapter endnotes. But here I will do my best to round up the cast of characters generally.

My first thanks go to faculty, staff, and students from my graduate years in American Studies at the University of Minnesota. David Roediger was a hands-on advisor who remains hands-on and so very helpful. Through all these years, he continues to read everything I bug him with and to offer feedback. Lary May was critical in my formative years of Gellert discovery and in teaching me twentieth-century American cultural history. David W. Noble taught with warmth and conviction at the U of M for more than fifty years. He was still in his long prime when I was there. Noble introduced me to US intellectual history and alerted me to "American exceptionalism" as false consciousness and nationalist dogma. His alternative textbook, *The Free and the Unfree: A Progressive History of the United States*, co-authored with Peter Carroll, predated Zinn's *A People's History* and remains a classic in its own right.

Outside of my formal graduate affiliations, Ron Cohen, Paul Garon, and Archie Green were invaluable advisors. Thanks are owed as well to Scott Barretta, Mat Callahan, David King Dunaway, Adam Gussow, Jerrold Hirsch, Aaron Leonard, Marian Levy, Judy McCulloh, Scott Nelson, Daniel Smith-Christopher, Elijah Wald, and James Wechsler. And, at the Archives of Traditional Music, past and present, thanks to Marilyn Graf, Alan Burdette, and staff generally.

This project advanced in my years at the Smithsonian Institution as a pre-doctoral fellow with affiliation at both the National Museum of American History (NMAH) and the Center for Folklife and Cultural Heritage (CFCH). My co-advisors were Pete Daniel, Charlie McGovern, and Jeff Place, all three wonderful scholar-curators with unmatched breadth and expertise. Jeff presided with encyclopedic knowledge over the musical stores at the CFCH, and Pete and Charlie curated at the NMAH. Each mentored numerous young academics, and yet still made time for one more. Pete Daniel, in particular, is renowned for organizing once-weekly Happy Hours and for hosting incredible dinner parties. I got to enjoy it all while I learned. Pete has remained a mentor in the years since my Smithsonian days.

The following individuals were kind in allowing me to interview them by phone, by email, or in person. I appreciate their time and perspectives: Penny Gellert Freeman, Donald Gellert, James Gellert, Tom Gellert, David Margolis, Michael McCue, Bob Neidich, Bill Nowlin, Joanne Reuss, Pete Seeger, Irwin Silber, Dick Weissman, and Israel "Izzy" Young.

The following libraries and archives were essential, especially in the early days before the world was digitized: American Folklife Center, Library of Congress; Archives of American Art, Smithsonian Institution; Archives of Traditional Music and Lilly Library, Indiana University Bloomington; Bancroft Library,

University of California, Berkeley; Beinecke Rare Book and Manuscript Library, Yale University; Center for Folklife and Cultural Heritage, Smithsonian Institution; Indiana University Archives, Indiana University Bloomington; National Museum of American History, Smithsonian Institution; Recorded Sound Reference Center, Library of Congress; Special Collections and Archives, George Mason University; Tamiment Library, New York University; *Tryon Daily Bulletin* archives, Tryon, North Carolina; Wilson Library, University of North Carolina at Chapel Hill.

Colleagues, staff, and students at my workplace, Marist College in Poughkeepsie, New York, have been essential to my progress and fulfillment all these years. From the first time I set foot in the School of Liberal Arts, I knew I'd found a home. My peers in the History Department, in particular, deserve special gratitude. I am a lucky individual, indeed.

At the University of Massachusetts Press, thanks to production editor Rachael DeShano, senior editor Brian Halley, and series editor Jeffrey Melnick.

Finally, this book would not exist without the inspiration and support of my parents, Pierre and Sheila Garabedian, who have always modeled the standard of how to be a good person—loving, honest, hard-working, and generous. To my family on both coasts, thank you.

The book could not have been completed without the love, intelligence, and indulgence of Kristin Bayer, who renewed my confidence and enthusiasm in the project after some hard years. Our teenagers, Sean and Raven, keep life exciting and about more than just work.

A Sound History

INTRODUCTION

Hidden in Plain Sight

LAWRENCE GELLERT AND "NEGRO SONGS OF PROTEST"

"I'm not a folklorist. I hate folklorists!" Lawrence Gellert asserted late in life. "I wasn't interested in just music" for its own sake, he insisted, but rather music "as a weapon" in the service of Black freedom and social justice.[1] Despite such claims after the fact, Lawrence Gellert did indeed, for a time as a younger man in the 1930s and 1940s, earn distinction as a chronicler of African American folk expression. And, it was the stated political nature of his work—articulated in just such characteristic fashion above—that accounted for both Gellert's rise and fall in the changing contexts of United States history.

In 1932, a Gellert collaborator and comrade-in-arms was unreserved in his praise: "These songs collected by Lawrence Gellert from plantations, chain gangs, lumber camps, and jails are of inestimable value, if they do nothing more than show that not all Negroes are shouting spirituals, cheering endowed football teams, dancing to the blues, or mouthing inter-racial oratory. Some of them are tired of being poor, and picturesque, and hungry. Terribly and bitterly tired." The statement was composed by African American literary icon Langston Hughes. Though never published, the lines were intended as part of a four-page foreword for Gellert's first songbook, *Negro Songs of Protest* from 1936.[2] In an accompanying letter penned from Tougaloo, Mississippi, Hughes hoped that the material was "not too late, and that you will like it." He commented, "I think the songs are great, and am honored to be chosen to do the foreword." The following year, while he was on a tour of the Soviet Union, Hughes went about preparations for a Russian translation of *Negro Songs of Protest*. He secured a contract with the Music Union in Moscow, arranged for a cash advance, and "did a plain English version of the songs." Providing additional assistance on this last score, he informed Gellert that he had "explained to the translator all the idioms, so that he could put them into Russian." The Soviet publication was released in 1938.[3]

Gellert spoke favorably about Hughes throughout his life, and his admiration reflected the overlapping roles each played in the leftwing Cultural Front of the Depression years. In interviews in the 1960s and 1970s, after Hughes had passed, Gellert spotlighted the writer for never "turning" on his radical past like some artists and intellectuals who found the Left in the 1930s and then "crawled off on one pretext" or another "as soon as the little prosperity came back again." The collector credited Hughes for his work in the communist movement, but he added that Hughes remained a free thinker "never under control" of the Party. Hughes's "best stuff was in the leftwing press," said Gellert. "He was a wonderful guy. Did you ever get to meet him?" asked the collector of his interviewer in 1976.[4]

Lawrence Gellert was similarly "never under control," and, like Langston Hughes, produced some of his "best stuff" as a Left radical in the 1930s. From the 1920s into the 1950s, Gellert documented Black vernacular music in the US South in written transcription and audio. A "lean, scraggly-haired New Yorker," as *Time* magazine called him, Gellert was an independent white music collector, without formal training, credentials, or affiliation.[5] "How Long, Brethren?" was one of the songs that he encountered in his fieldwork. It was a "city blues," he recalled, "right out of Charleston." Original unaccompanied sound fragments are represented among Gellert's field recordings from the 1930s, and a full transcript with musical arrangement is included in *Negro Songs of Protest*. As he printed it, the item reads:

> How long, brethren, how long,
> Must my people weep and mourn?
> How long, how long, brethren, how long?
>
> So long my people been asleep
> White folks plowin' n——r's soul down deep.
> How long, how long, brethren, how long?
>
> Too long, brethren, too long
> We just barely miserin' along
> Too long, too long, brethren, too long.

White folks ain't Jesus, he just a man,
Grabbin' biscuit out of poor n——r's hand.
Too long, too long, brethren, too long.

So long, brethren, so long
N——r keep a-singin' the same old song.
So long, so long, brethren, so long.

N——r he just patch black dirt,
The raisin' part of the white man's earth,
So long, so long, brethren, so long.[6]

For those familiar with the blues, the song may strike a chord. It bears a marked resemblance in sound and structure to the popular standard "How Long, How Long Blues," a commercial "race record" hit in 1928 for the influential piano and guitar duo of Leroy Carr and Scrapper Blackwell. On that record, the chorus and verse in part went this way:

How long, babe, how long
Has that evenin' train been gone?
How long, how long, yes baby, how long?

I stood at the station, watched my baby leaving town
Feeling disgusting, nowhere could peace be found
Well, how long, how long, baby, how long?[7]

In the commercial recording, Carr sings about romantic longing; in the Gellert transcription, the unnamed informant sings about the long struggle for Black freedom. Both items are, I hold, authentic expressions from out of African American vernacular culture. Still, the difference is significant, and so are the stakes of recognition. To that point, it is useful to note that there was already a long history behind "How Long" before even Carr and Blackwell or Gellert. In 1867, compilers William Francis Allen, Charles Pickard Ware, and Lucy McKim Garrison published "My Father, How Long?" in *Slave Songs of the United States*, the first major collection of Black folk music in the United States. They included a revealing annotation that the "negroes had been put in jail at Georgetown,

South Carolina, at the outbreak of the Rebellion" for singing the title. Lines like "We'll soon be free," they explained, were "too dangerous an assertion," and "De Lord will call us home" was "evidently thought to be a symbolic verse" that alluded to the "Yankees."[8] Clearly, Gellert's informant did not originate the theme in the documentary item, and neither did Carr and Blackwell for that matter in their blues recording.

Lawrence Gellert always explained that he happened into Black music research purely by accident. At the start of his musical awakening in the early 1920s, Gellert collected primarily out of simple curiosity. But progressive family associations and the unfolding contexts of history brought him to a new place by the next decade. In the 1930s, as the nation's political economy was in collapse, Gellert emerged to considerable prominence in the "Red Era" of the American past. Adopting the rubric of "Negro Songs of Protest" for his work, the collector showcased his song material in the print media, in two published songbooks, and on the stage.[9] Though his song archive ranged broadly, including many familiar folklore and popular items, Gellert singled out for public attention his store of Black lyrical protest. The collector was not the source of this music, but he was an important platform for discovery. Indeed, in a time of institutionalized segregation, Gellert was an agent in the emergent dominant cultural awareness of African American resistance. He was making a reputation, credited *Time*, for "collecting Negro songs that few white men have ever heard."[10]

This is a book about Black protest and white denial. It examines the rise and fall of Lawrence Gellert in the key decades bracketed by the folksong revivals of the 1930s and the 1960s. Moreover, it explores the changing politics in the nation's dominant culture that allowed for the "discovery" and then "denial" of Gellert's collection, and traditions of African American musical protest generally, in this span of history. It follows Gellert, but it is not a formal biography.[11] Broadly, this is a story of openings and closings—solidarity, struggle, and contradiction—in the defining middle decades of the American twentieth century.

Sociologist Stanley Cohen has defined "denial" as "knowing and not-knowing." His book, *States of Denial: Knowing about Atrocities and Suffering*, has reached scholars and activists in fields wide. Michelle Alexander applies Cohen's insights in *The New Jim Crow: Mass Incarceration in the Age of Colorblindness*, and I apply it here as well to issues of race, protest, and injustice. As Cohen shows, the workings of denial extend from psychology to politics, the private to the public, the individual to the collective. Cohen provides the common scientific understanding of denial as "an unconscious defense mechanism for coping with guilt, anxiety and other disturbing emotions aroused by reality. The psyche blocks off information that is literally unthinkable or unbearable." He adds, "Denial may be neither a matter of telling the truth nor intentionally telling a lie. The statement is not wholly deliberate, and the status of 'knowledge' about the truth is not wholly clear. There seem to be states of mind, or even whole cultures, in which we know and don't know at the same time." Through his examination, Cohen is unflinching in casting judgment. The point is intervention, not resignation. "The political echoes of these states of mind may be found in the mass denial so characteristic of repressive, racist and colonial states. Dominant groups seem uncannily able to shut out or ignore the injustice and suffering around them," he writes. "Acknowledgment" is the counter to denial, argues Cohen, and it must be encouraged for human progress. Cohen's work is pointed and highly generative as regards denial and the dynamics of power. I reference the term throughout this book as a marker signaling white blind spots, intransigence, and defensiveness when it has come to Black agency and resistance.[12]

The historical element in my framework of denial is "romantic racialism." George Fredrickson conceptualized the term in *The Black Image in the White Mind* in 1971. The concept is still relevant. Fredrickson identified romantic racialism as a conflicted corollary of modern racialist thinking. In the ideological and political battles leading up to and following the Civil War and Reconstruction, the notion that there was a scientific basis to presumed racial difference became the commonsense of white consciousness for parties on all sides of the "Negro problem." For those whites sympathetic to the plight of Black slaves and freed people, this could lead in peculiar directions. In the 1840s and 1850s, some anti-slavery moderates embraced a liberal humanitarianism toward people of African descent that was at once radical and conservative. In short, they adopted a doctrine that, as Fredrickson puts it, "acknowledged permanent racial differences but rejected the notion of a clearly defined racial hierarchy." Liberal romantic racialists, in other words, inverted the new racist dogma toward what they believed were sympathetic ends. They agreed that "Negroes" were innately docile, childlike, and submissive. But they lauded these very characteristics as ameliorative or, indeed, superior to the aggressive, materialistic, and coldly rational nature of Anglo-Saxon or Caucasian temperament. In an age of Western venality and spiritual decline, they charged, the "Negro" offered an inspiring symbol of self-sacrifice and redemption. He was, in fact, a "natural Christian" of disarming moral and human integrity. This viewpoint was embodied most sensationally in Harriet Beecher Stowe's fictional creation of Uncle Tom. Combining the best elements of African "racial" heritage with, as some advocates added, the finest qualities of "feminine" virtue, the Negro was not only different, but perhaps better than his white oppressor.[13]

Fredrickson concludes that the "romantic racialist view of the Negro and his role in American society, popular and even influential by 1864, occupies an anomalous position in the history of American racial thinking." It was "benevolent in intent," he writes, and "not linked to an unequivocal theory of white supremacy" in the general sense. Fredrickson stipulates, however, that "[a]s characteristically put forth by whites," romantic racialism "often revealed a mixture of cant, condescension, and sentimentality, not unlike the popular nineteenth-century view of womanly virtue, which it so closely resembled." Whether in the case of people of color or women, this kind of advocacy did not equate to egalitarianism. "It was never suggested that whites become literally like the black stereotype and sacrifice their alleged superiority in intellect and energy," stresses Fredrickson.[14]

The romantic racialist mindset allowed that one might favor Black music while still denying Black intellect or agency. It also meant that white chroniclers of African American vernacular music might project a politics of race and culture of their own making. Whether left, right, or center, white music collectors engaged in a tradition of folklore studies and folk revivalism in the twentieth century that overlapped with the long tradition of romantic racialism. People of color have been expected to sing with open hearts, but not openly speak their minds.

I am a cultural historian of the modern United States, with a special interest in domination and resistance, and a research focus on Left radicalism and African American history. Though he was never a card-carrying Communist Party member, as the old cliché would have it, Lawrence Gellert was an American "Red" over a period of years when that was both tolerated and not tolerated. An outspoken alternative thinker who was awakened to issues of racial and economic oppression during the worst years of the Great Depression, Gellert was still, at age seventy in interviews from the late 1960s, saying that "communism will succeed in the world simply because it's a superior society to capitalism."[15] He was no joiner, but he was a radical. In the folk revival ferment of the 1930s, he was one of many culture workers on the Left who came to discover American vernacular music as he came to an analysis of American injustice.

Gellert was also only one among multiple white rebel music collectors and afficionados from over the years who came to prize African American music in particular as part of this awakening. Young and earnest, these restive white Americans, mostly men from the urban and suburban North and West, sought a usable past and a meaningful present in the alternative culture of rural southern

Black America. Typically working from a remove of race, class, and regional difference, some of these white individuals became weekend music hobbyists, and some went off into the field directly to become folklorists, blues scholars, promoters, experts, activists, or any combination of the above. In the first half of the twentieth century, Black vernacular music styles (blues, jazz, and rhythm and blues on the secular side) were the primary province of everyday African American working people; in the second half of the century, Black music crossed over to mass awareness with the rock 'n' roll, folk, and blues music explosions of the 1950s and 1960s. What was gained and what was lost in this transition is another of the themes raised in this study. As historian Grace Hale has detailed it most broadly, disaffected white rebels from the dominant culture found a love for "outsider" America in the postwar. But in the disequilibrium of race and class inequality, white middle-class love could turn from empathy to fantasy. The result, argues Hales, is that "we live in an age when illusions—the idea that black culture is more authentic and middle-class whites are outsiders—rule. The romance of the outsider perpetuates a disavowal of power that damages us all."[16]

Lawrence Gellert is an expansive and enigmatic historical figure. In life, he was everywhere and nowhere, it seemed. Folk and blues revivalism, however, with its changing meanings before and after World War II, was the backdrop to his story. From the mid-1930s to the latter 1940s, a leftwing folksong movement emerged in the United States that orbited around the institutional mainspring of the Communist Party USA (CPUSA) and its liberal New Deal intersections in labor and civil rights. As this leftwing folksong revival was gaining a wider popular currency, however, it was cut short by the Cold War and the most reactionary years of US anticommunism. In 1950, Pete Seeger's group, The Weavers, scored a record contract and the first in a series of commercial hits with Lead Belly's "Goodnight Irene." By the next year, Seeger had been listed nationally as a communist, the Weavers were blacklisted, and Senator Joseph McCarthy was in the midst of his notorious ascent in Washington.

The period from 1958, with the Kingston Trio's popular hit "Tom Dooley," until 1965, when Bob Dylan "went electric" at the Newport Folk Festival, saw a resurgence of folk music discovery with a new generation of revivalists. This was the era of the "folk boom," in American dominant culture. Pete Seeger resurfaced to mainstream visibility; Bob Dylan came to the fore, first as a Woody Guthrie imitator and Seeger heir-apparent; and popular artists Joan Baez and the trio Peter, Paul, and Mary made "folk music" a household word and a viable commercial prospect. Spinning off into offshoots and hybrids, "unplugged" American roots music and personalities remained highly visible through the 1960s.

Whether these two periods, spanning two generations, constitute a single ongoing revival or separate revivals is a point of discussion in contemporary folksong historiography. The matter is significant. As editor Neil V. Rosenberg contends in *Transforming Tradition: Folk Music Revivals Examined*, there are important differences between the "great boom" after World War II, as he calls it, and the Old Left activity from before. The very term "revival," Rosenberg holds, only came "to achieve widespread currency" after "the great boom was under way." Significantly, he elaborates, it came to supplant the "semantic niche previously occupied by 'movement,'" perhaps because it "did not evoke the notion of political action" as did the former.[17] Robert Cantwell, in *When We Were Good: The Folk Revival*, underlines the point: "What is most interesting about the [postwar] revival is not its political affiliations, but the absence of them." He concludes that "for those of us whose revival began around 1958," Old Left associations "were absent and would have been, in our naive and compliant youth, a barrier to any enthusiasm for folksong."[18]

As for Lawrence Gellert, what is clear is that the collector—still very much alive and active in the 1950s and 1960s—was a notable presence in the first period, and a relative absence in the second. One can argue about the activism of the Depression and World War II years versus the activism of the postwar, the Old Left versus the New Left. But certainly, the folk boom of the 1960s had its politics, blossoming as it did in the same soil as the civil rights and anti–Vietnam War movements. In this context—especially one in which race, justice, and southern music were again an American preoccupation—where was Lawrence Gellert? More importantly, where was the archive of "Negro Songs of Protest" that had once been touted as a key index of Black freedom?

If Gellert came and went in folk revival consciousness from the 1930s to the 1960s, he was, even at the height of his success, an unstable entity. African American luminaries Langston Hughes and Sterling Brown, for instance, praised Gellert's work and shared a degree of professional and friendly acquaintance with the man, as we will see. But Gellert bickered with other figures of considerable repute, from W. C. Handy to John and Alan Lomax. In 1937, Gellert reportedly won, and then lost, a Rockefeller Foundation grant for continued field research, owing he said to his politics. In 1939, a second songbook, "*Me and My Captain*," followed his first, *Negro Songs of Protest*, but the proposed third and fourth installments never appeared. By World War II, Gellert was already so "sore at the whole folk lore racket," as he put it, that he considered turning in all of his aluminum field discs as scrap for the War Department.[19] During the Cold War in the 1950s, Gellert said his stuff was untouchable, and by the early 1960s, in the peak of the "folk boom," he was defamed as a fraud in influential circles. Gellert's archive was tainted if not outright phony, went the charge, an example of white leftwing propaganda and interference rather than Black vernacular creativity and resistance.

In 1963, the Student Nonviolent Coordinating Committee's Freedom Singers, Odetta, Joan Baez, Bob Dylan, Peter, Paul and Mary, and Mahalia Jackson, among others, crystalized the ideal of the engaged folk movement when they performed in front of the 250,000 activists assembled at the March on Washington. That same year, Irwin Silber, influential editor of the movement organ *Sing Out!* magazine and an Old Left radical from the Communist Party days, issued a public charge of fakery against Lawrence Gellert. Silber wrote:

> Frankly, as a person familiar with folk music and folklore materials for considerable time, I find it very difficult to accept the material presented by Gellert as folk songs which he really collected. Aside from the fact of documentation which would let us know where and under what circumstances, etc. the songs were collected, the fact that no one else has ever been able to collect similar songs or the same song in a different version, would tend to indicate that this material should be approached with a great deal of care. . . . I am strongly of the opinion that these songs of Lawrence Gellert are more likely his or someone else's original creation rather than material, which by any stretch of the imagination, could fall into the domain of folk songs.[20]

What had happened? At the apex of the 1960s boom, as the synthesis of vernacular music and progressive politics was inspiring countless new young people, a stigma had attached to Gellert's name that lingers today.

Through a number of academic generations, following the retrenchments after World War II, a series of scholars waged what seems an uphill battle to prompt and sustain critical interest in Gellert's considerable contribution to Black folksong research and American cultural history more generally. In the early 1950s, authors John Greenway and Russell Ames both drew on the collector's work in their respective studies of American vernacular music. Greenway employed Gellert's material in a chapter titled "Negro Songs of Protest" in his *American Folksongs of Protest* published in 1953; Ames cited Gellert's "extraordinary collection" alongside that of John and Alan Lomax as well as Howard Odum and Guy Johnson in *The Story of American Folk Song* from 1955.[21] Such efforts positing an organic cross-fertilization of traditional music and topical lyricism, however, rankled the new disciplinary proponents of academic folklore, only just gaining an institutional footing on most university campuses in the years after World War II. Moreover, they tested the limits of cultural work in the strained political climate of the domestic Cold War.

In the latter 1960s, folk music, revival, and Left specialist Richard A. Reuss conducted hours of taped interviews with Lawrence Gellert about his background, fieldwork, song collection, political commitments, and relations in the folk music community. I refer to these interviews often in this study.[22] Reuss treated Gellert in some detail in his seminal doctoral dissertation from 1971. David King Dunaway has called Reuss "the preeminent scholar of the American folksong revival." In that effort, Reuss made the invaluable first strides in Gellert studies. After a drought of neglect and suspicion, he set in motion the effort to reclaim Gellert's "Negro Songs of Protest" for a new set of researchers in the 1970s. But again, energies stalled. Reuss, himself, saw his scholarship thwarted. Though his doctoral thesis from 1971, "American Folklore and Left-Wing Politics, 1927–1957," was referenced for years as the definitive study, he could not find a publisher and ended up leaving academia. Reuss passed away in 1986 at only forty-six years of age. His dissertation was finally published in 2000.[23]

In the 1980s, Bruce Conforth took the lead as the authority on Gellert. Conforth first encountered Gellert's material while he was working as a graduate student in folklore at the Archives of Traditional Music at Indiana University in Bloomington. In the early 1970s, after hunting around some, Gellert had deposited his original field discs, notes, lyric transcriptions, correspondence, and manuscripts at the university. With this trove of previously unexamined material at hand and through subsequent primary research, Conforth produced the first extended study of Gellert's life and song archive as his master's thesis in 1984.[24] Additionally, he expanded his efforts from print to sound. Between 1973 and the early 1980s, there were three commercial albums issued from out of Gellert's extensive field recordings, all on long-playing vinyl and with accompanying documentation.[25] After four decades, those interested were afforded the opportunity for the first time to review Gellert's original documentary items. Prior to these important sound releases, as blues scholar Paul Garon reminds us, readers might have been able to dig up a copy of Gellert's lyric transcriptions and accompanying arrangements in print, but listeners were unable to make determinations based on actually hearing Gellert's sound discs from the field.[26] While Gellert was involved in the earliest of these productions in 1973, he was not involved in the latter two. Bruce Conforth was the impetus behind these historic releases in 1982 and 1984. His liner notes for the albums, and master's thesis, became source texts that piqued interest in the scholarly community. But, once again, curiosity did not translate to any major sustained follow up.

Beyond the above efforts, and until my own scholarly article in 2005 and Bruce Conforth's long-awaited *African American Folksong and American Cultural Politics: The Lawrence Gellert Story*, published in 2013, there were only passing secondary mentions of Gellert scattered within a varied field of literature. Generally, these treatments were curious and approving rather than dismissive. Nevertheless, most were brief references along the way in studies focused on other or broader subjects. Sometimes, authors simply used Gellert's material without much, if any, comment. In other instances, they raised interest, called for more investigation, and moved on.[27]

Because of parallels such as "How Long, Brethren?" / "How Long, How Long Blues" mentioned above and because of the impressive guitar-accompanied blues featured on the 1984 release *Nobody Knows My Name: Blues from South Carolina and Georgia* (the last of the Gellert LPs), blues scholars have shown a particular, if at times halting, interest in Gellert since the popular cross-over period of the 1960s. William Ferris cited Gellert's "Negro Songs of Protest" in the 1970s, as did David Evans in *Big Road Blues* in 1982. Bruce Bastin was the first to offer any kind of published profile in his highly respected regional survey, *Red River Blues: The Blues Tradition in the Southeast* from 1986. Bastin was followed with mentions by Paul Oliver in the "Bibliographical References" section at the end of the revised edition of *Blues Fell This Morning*, along with Steven Tracy, Charles Wolfe and Kip Lornell, Paul Garon, John Cowley, Francis Davis, Dutch expert Guido van Rijn, and, more currently, Elijah Wald, Adam Gussow, R. A. Lawson, and Roger House. More or less, each of these authors take Gellert as credible, but each has a larger story to tell and offers only limited coverage.[28]

Scholars of the folksong revival, in turn, built on Richard Reuss's defining contribution. In 2000, the book version of Reuss's dissertation included its original key sections on "important collector" Lawrence Gellert. Robert Cantwell made reference to Gellert in *When We Were Good*, as have historians Robbie Lieberman, Ronald Cohen, Dick Weissman, David King Dunaway, and John Szwed.[29]

There have been a number of nods to Gellert in contemporary interdisciplinary studies in American cultural history, Southern history, communist history, and African American studies. Mark Naison, Robin D. G. Kelley, James Smethurst, and Mark Solomon each mention Gellert in their histories of the communist movement and African American radicalism before World War II. Scott Nelson, David Roediger, and Grace Hale, as well, cite Gellert in their critical historical work. From abroad, scholar Mechal Sobel relates Gellert's archive of song to other vernacular currents of African American "retaliatory violence." In her study of outsider painter Bill Traylor, Sobel references Gellert's material and argues that "bitter blues" were a reality, on record and on paper.[30]

I am not certain if I first encountered Lawrence Gellert's name in Lawrence Levine's classic *Black Culture and Black Consciousness*, Robin D. G. Kelley's *Hammer and Hoe*, or Michael Denning's *The Cultural Front*. Levine's book from 1977 remains an academic standard. With no hint of uncertainty, Levine includes a few of Gellert's song texts in his sweeping foundational history. *Hammer and Hoe* helped establish Kelley as a major scholar when it was released in 1990. Kelley quotes song lyrics from Gellert's pieces in *New Masses* and also cites a report on the Scottsboro Boys defense that Gellert contributed from the field in Alabama. Michael Denning's expansive *The Cultural Front* contained the most formal and analytical treatment. In the book, Denning not only connects African American blues tradition to labor and Left history, with reference to "radical folklorist" Lawrence Gellert's "Negro Songs of Protest," but beyond that, Denning's formulation of a "political vernacular of the blues" proved pivotal to my thinking. Each of these books was central to my reading as a doctoral student in American Studies in the 1990s, but I cannot recall which came first in my Gellert consciousness. In reflecting back, whatever the source of my initial curiosity, the larger point is that the collector and his archive were there hidden in plain sight in a number of discourses all along.[31]

What is more, as I quickly realized back then, a wealth of Gellert primary sources were readily available in a public archive. Gellert's 221 field recording discs comprising 505 song items are preserved with accompanying materials as "United States, North and South Carolina, Georgia, African Americans, 1920s–1940s" at the Archives of Traditional Music (ATM) at Indiana University in Bloomington. His correspondence, assorted lyric transcriptions, unpublished manuscripts, and archival miscellany are available as "Gellert mss., 1927–1978" and "Gellert mss. II" in the Lilly Library there. Additionally, there are the hours of taped interviews with Richard Reuss (mentioned above), also housed at the ATM in Bloomington. Why wasn't anyone pursuing this material further?[32]

Lawrence Gellert was said to have passed away in 1979. Actually, he had vanished at eighty years old that June from his apartment at 148 Sullivan

Street in Manhattan. To this day, family members, friends, and police have no clear answers to this disconcerting end. Though his siblings are identifiable in the Social Security Death Index, Lawrence Gellert is not listed. Police never resolved his "missing person" case, reported a body, or established a trail of disappearance.[33]

In a further twist, the tragic Etan Patz missing child case that took place in New York City in 1979 comes into this story. Six-year-old Patz went missing only a few blocks from Gellert's apartment. Though Gellert was never a serious suspect, his eldest brother Hugo believed that Lawrence was developing clinical paranoia in his advanced age. When the police came to question him as part of a broad canvassing of the neighborhood, Lawrence may have panicked and fled, or taken his own life. Additionally, some allege that things went as far as foul play. The theory is that Lawrence was set up as a suspect for the missing child case by an unscrupulous landlord with police connections who wanted him out of his rent-controlled apartment. Greenwich Village artist David Margolis, a close friend of both Hugo and Lawrence for fifty years, believed that Gellert was a victim of such a conspiracy. On the other hand, as I was told by nephew Donald Gellert, Donald's father Otto (Lawrence's older brother by two years) believed that Lawrence fled back to the South to live out his remaining years in anonymity. Some family members suggest that Otto, in fact, helped Lawrence relocate. In a separate interview, Donald's younger brother, James, added that his "Uncle Lou" had placed an urgent phone call to two friends just days before his disappearance. For a period of time, this nephew James, who had been close to Lawrence, searched the morgues in the New York area, but to no avail. It seemed, James said, that Gellert "panicked" or "lost his mind" as a result of some "dramatic episode." He referred to the "demise of Lawrence Gellert." Whatever their respective theories, all parties involved remain baffled and saddened. In the words of nephew James, Lawrence simply "evaporated."[34]

By now, Lawrence Gellert's immediate family members and contemporaries have all died. Nevertheless, I have had the opportunity to interview or correspond with Lawrence's nephews Donald and James, as well as Bob Neidich, son of Lawrence's younger sister Billie and husband Irving. I shared email correspondence with Tom Gellert, grand-nephew of Lawrence by way of his older brother Theodor. Additionally, I maintained an active correspondence with, and interviewed as well, Israel "Izzy" Young of the Folklore Center. I interviewed artist Margolis, mentioned above, and also folksinger Pete Seeger, who offered his recollections of Gellert. In 2005, I was thrilled to be located by grand-niece Penny Gellert Freeman, as warm and brilliant a family contact as any historian could ever dream. Penny and I began an ongoing correspondence, and then I visited her and her husband, Doug Freeman, for a series of interviews in summer 2010. Penny shared family history, photographs, personal memories, and her own independent research. Incredibly, though they were unaware of the connection when they settled, Penny and Doug lived in Hendersonville, North Carolina, only a few miles from Lawrence's original base of operations in nearby Tryon.

In some ways, Lawrence Gellert's record of existence on this earth is no more or less spotty than that of anyone else. In a sense even, considering his field recordings, published writings, personal papers, and interviews, we have more, perhaps, of a Lawrence Gellert paper trail than most of us leave behind. Still, Gellert is an elusive figure. I have spent a great of time and energy delving into the gaps and mysteries surrounding his life and work.

All of this is prologue to a central set of questions guiding my interest in the man's story in the first place. If the reasons behind Gellert's continual remove from scholarly attention are more than simply "academic"—if the archive is legitimate, and the reasons for its slighting are a matter of cultural and political change as much as they are a matter of, for instance, disciplinary predilection—then what does it mean that a line of researchers in succeeding generations since World War II have found it necessary to continually renew the discussion of Gellert's "Negro Songs of Protest" after recurring periods of silence? What explains the enduring absence of this valuable material in folklore studies, blues scholarship, and African American studies? Why is it that a list of accomplished researchers, several times over, have had little long-term success in trying to reintroduce Gellert's Black songs of protest to wider recognition?

I take up these quandaries in the pages that follow. The book pursues as its general subject Black musical resistance and white dominant representation, and as its specific focus the rise and fall of Lawrence Gellert and "Negro Songs of Protest." As I conclude, the tragedy of Gellert's story, folklore collecting, and musical revivalism, generally, is the tragedy of missed opportunities and roads not followed. Ultimately, in my judgment, Lawrence Gellert was a sincere broker in the cause of racial justice and radical change; the Gellert archive is credible. But, the vindication of Gellert is about more than character rehabilitation. Rather, it is about the historical validation of a dialectic of resistance between "red" and "Black," the political Left and African American vernacular cultures of opposition, that was genuine and meaningful in the American past. I hope in my treatment to have done right by the people and music represented.

CHAPTER ONE

The Roads to Perdition

LAWRENCE GELLERT'S EARLY BIOGRAPHY AND EMERGENCE

I presume there are as many ways to become a
Negro Folk Song Collector as there are roads to perdition.

—LAWRENCE GELLERT

In 1932, Howard University's Sterling Brown spent a pleasant visit touring Boston in the company of two allies in support of the New Negro Movement of the era, radical socialite Nancy Cunard and her compatriot, one Lawrence Gellert. Already something of a sensation on both sides of the Atlantic, Cunard was the daughter of the Cunard shipping line fortune. After a failed attempt at domesticity, the heiress had jumped wholeheartedly into 1920s bohemianism. A poet and independent publisher, Cunard had by the 1930s renounced her moneyed background and committed herself to anticapitalism and racial justice. After a romance with African American jazz musician Henry Crowder, she published a provocative manifesto, "Black Man and White Ladyship," in 1931. By the following year, she had occasioned considerable "social furor," as the news media reported, when she moved into the Theresa Hotel in Harlem to pursue material for what would become a singular literary monument.[1]

Entirely self-published (with photographs, musical scores, and even a fold-out map) at an enormous expense of time and money, Cunard's massive project, *Negro: An Anthology*, was unprecedented when it was released in 1934. At eight pounds and 855 pages, it represented the largest collection ever of prose and poetry on the arts, culture, and history of the Black diaspora. With a staggering roster of some 150 contributors—including W. E. B. Du Bois, Alain Locke, Walter White, Zora Neale Hurston, Langston Hughes, Arna Bontemps, Countee Cullen, Arthur Schomburg, George Padmore, George S. Schuyler, and

E. Franklin Frazier, as well as leftwing radicals James Ford, Theodore Dreiser, Michael Gold, John Spivak, and a distinguished host of international thinkers and artists—the volume was a milestone. As Cunard opened the work, "It was necessary to make this book . . . for the recording of the struggles and achievements, the persecutions and the revolts against them, of the Negro peoples." If the writings collected within showcased the full record of Black cultural and intellectual achievement across time and space, they also reflected a clear political mandate in the view of the editor. "The Communist world-order is the solution of the race problem for the Negro," Cunard concluded in her opening. Though there were "certain sections of the Negro bourgeoisie" who still held faith in the "eventual liberality of the white man," the "more vital of the Negro race" had come to see that "it is Communism alone which throws down the barriers of race as finally as it wipes out class distinctions."[2]

Sterling Brown, who was beginning his ascendance as a towering figure in African American arts and intellect, was among the cast of writers included in the anthology. His poems "Strong Men," "Memphis Blues," and "Children of the Mississippi" were represented in the section "By Negro Poets." The third member of their touring party that day in Boston, thirty-four-year-old Lawrence Gellert, was also a contributor to the book. Gellert accompanied Cunard as she traveled the country fundraising for the Scottsboro Boys' defense campaign and gathering contributions for her proposed volume.[3] Like Brown, whose *Southern Road* was heralded as a major release by the American literati in 1932, Gellert had only recently burst onto the scene with a series of articles on rural southern African American folk music. In *Negro: An Anthology*, Gellert was accorded a prominent place. His eleven-page mini-monograph, "Negro Songs of Protest: North and South Carolina and Georgia," in the "Music" section of the book was set alongside pieces by noted authorities W. C. Handy, Zora Neale Hurston, Guy B. Johnson, and George Herzog.

That Brown, Cunard, and Gellert converged in this time period is more than incidental. Their meeting in 1932 represented the coming of age of a generation of cultural and political radicals in the darkest days of the Great Depression. The contributions of Brown and Gellert fit together comfortably in Cunard's masterwork, reflecting a shared commitment to capturing a contemporary African American vernacular of everyday poetry and resistance. Brown offered up his poem "Strong Men." The piece opens with these lines:

> They dragged you from homeland,
> They chained you in coffles,

They huddled you spoon-fashion in filthy hatches,
They sold you to give a few gentlemen ease.

They broke you in like oxen,
They scourged you,
They branded you,
They made your women breeders,
They swelled your numbers with bastards. . . .
They taught you the religion they disgraced.

You sang:

> *Keep a-inchin' along*
> *Lak a po' inch worm. . . .*

You sang:

> *Bye and bye*
> *I'm gonna lay down dis heaby load. . . .*

You sang:

> *Walk togeddeer, chillen,*
> *Dontcha git weary. . . .*
> The strong men keep a-comin' on
> The strong men git stronger.[4]

And, the poem closes with this warning:

What, from the slums
Where they have hemmed you,
What, from the tiny huts
They could not keep from you—
What reaches them
Making them ill at ease, fearful?
Today they shout prohibitions at you:
"Thou shalt not this,"
"Thou shalt not that,"

"Reserved for whites only"—
You laugh.
One thing they cannot prohibit—
    The strong men . . . comin' on,
    The strong men gittin' stronger.
    Strong men . . .
    Stronger. . . .

In the Cunard anthology, Gellert included a lyric transcription of similar spirit:

Ah's lookin' fo' no trouble, let me be
Set down white folks, stop aworryin' me
Set down white folks
Set down white folks
White folks you set down

Ah wants no ruckus, but ah ain' dat kin'
What lets you all shoe-shine on mah behin'
Set down (etc.)

Ah tells you once ah tells you 'nuf
De nex' time ah tells you ahm gwine git rough
Set down (etc.)

Come 'way f'om Georgia to git on a hog
But ah didn't come to be nobody's dog
Set down (etc.)

Cat got nine lives, use 'em all fo' he go
N——r die on'y one time, he can't die no mo'
Set down (etc.)[5]

Both items attest to the enduring Black freedom struggle in America. They trace the unceasing press of white domination and reserve the right of racial redress. Years later, in a memorial piece to Cunard, Gellert would reflect back fondly on those younger days. "I remember Sterling Brown walking with us on Boston Common," he wrote of the visit in 1932, "and writing a poem about the three of us at the cradle of American independence—an English Lady, an Hungarian immigrant's son, and a descendent of slaves." The "three of us strangely met with," he mused, but "with one and the same objective toward which we were pushing: the full equality of the black race."[6]

For Brown, of course, the fight for Black rights in America was nothing new. On the street and in the academy, African Americans, if with renewed energy since the end of World War I, had been waging a modern battle over Black self-determination in culture and politics. Still, Cunard's volume was a landmark. With the publication of *Negro: An Anthology*, certainly the largest and most comprehensive study of its kind, what scholar Lorenzo Thomas calls the "Correctionist" mission of Black historiography had reached a new height. Cunard's project reflected a significant swelling of the ranks. If the fight was not new, the arrival of a group of energetic white radicals to the cause was, indeed, an important turn.[7]

Brown published *Southern Road* in 1932, and Cunard released *Negro* in 1934. Two years later, Gellert published his own signal volume, *Negro Songs of Protest*, under the auspices of the Communist Party–affiliated American Music League, headquartered in New York City. *Negro Songs of Protest* included twenty-four lyric transcriptions and accompanying musical arrangements. The publication assembled striking statements of Black critique and rebellion likely to startle a white readership. Though transcribed in dialect, a folkloric practice not uncommon for the time, the texts were statements of affirmation rather than denigration.[8] With wit and candor, lyrics warned of the false promise of hard work and upward mobility under a racialized American political economy:

> Pickin' off de cotton,
> Hoe-in' up de corn,
> I'm de lazies' N——r sho' as yo' born.
> M-m-m-m, ain't dat de truth.
>
> If N——r work hahd,
> He worked out 'fore long,
> An' Captain only want him when he stay strong,
> M-m-m-m, ain't dat de truth.
>
> He work so hahd,
> Jes' fo' getting' ahead,
> But he were crosseye, filled Captain's pockets instead.
> M-m-m-m, ain't dat de truth.

De hahdes' workin' N——r
I ever saw,
Now goin' 'roun' beggin' can't work no mo'
M-m-m-m, ain't dat de truth.

Laborin fo' white folks,
No matter what I'm doin,'
I'm de lazies' N——r sho' as yo' born.
M-m-m-m, ain't dat de truth.

Pickin' off de cotton,
Hoe-in' up de corn,
I'm de lazies' N——r sho' as yo' born.
M-m-m-m, ain't dat de truth.

Lyrics called out gross abuse in a landscape of injustice and threatened a response:

Way down South, upon a rock quarr'l [quarry],
White folks chase N——r like chasin' a squirr'l,
In Atlanta, Georgia,
In Atlanta, Georgia.
If you don't get lynched you sho' get pinched in Atlanta, Georgia.

Jes' passin' through, didn't intend to stay.
Me an' white folks don't think de same way,
In Atlanta, Georgia,
In Atlanta, Georgia.
If you don't get lynched you sho' get pinched in Atlanta, Georgia.

Dey carry you to de jail house, make you get down on yo' knees,
Feed you nothin' except five year ol' peas,
In Atlanta, Georgia,
In Atlanta, Georgia.
If you don't get lynched you sho' get pinched in Atlanta, Georgia.

I'm goin' get me a pistol, hide behin' a tree,
Shoot ev'rybody been messin' with me,

In Atlanta, Georgia,
In Atlanta, Georgia.
If you don't get lynched you sho' get pinched in Atlanta, Georgia.

Same fo' N——r ev'ry place down South
It just done happen I'm talkin' about
Atlanta, Georgia,
Atlanta, Georgia.
If you don't get lynched you sho' get pinched in Atlanta, Georgia.

The two songs, "Pickin' Off De Cotton" and "Way Down South," are characteristic of the expressions of Black resistance collected within the book's covers. At the time, readers saw only print transcriptions with formal musical arrangements, but several of the songs—these two, for instance—were also captured in audio among the more than five hundred items in Gellert's field archive of more than two hundred recording discs. Their documentation in the heart of the Great Depression and New Deal sounded a note of revolution in terms of both the culture and politics of the modern United States.[9]

"Genuine Negro Songs, Collected by a White Man"

Lawrence Gellert was a maverick with a mission in 1936. An autodidact and self-styled bohemian radical, he had been living and working in the South documenting Black vernacular protest in written transcription and on sound recordings for some ten years. The youngest brother of prominent radical artist Hugo Gellert, Lawrence was an active proponent of the communist movement of the era. Since 1930, he had contributed articles of song lyrics and contextual commentary culled from his fieldwork to such leftwing periodicals as *New Masses* and the short-lived *Music Vanguard*. With his first book—to be followed by a second, *"Me and My Captain" (Chain Gangs): Negro Songs of Protest* in 1939—Gellert achieved considerable acclaim. *Time* magazine profiled him approvingly. The *New York Times* credited the collector for unearthing a "new genre" of Black music dealing with "the realities of Negro life." The NAACP organ, *The Crisis*, included an approving notice of *Negro Songs of Protest*, funnily enough, in its "Books by Black Authors" section. In the National Urban League's *Opportunity*, African American composer Hall Johnson contributed a glowing extended review. Johnson enthused about *Negro Songs of Protest*, a "modest little book," he wrote, that showcased "two-dozen big little songs, so lovingly collected and so sincerely offered." Hall concluded, "Here are some fine, genuine Negro songs, collected by a white man and arranged by a white man [composer Elie Siegmeister]" that "should claim and hold the attention of everybody in the world who is at all interested in how the world is getting on."[10]

From the Left press, as well, came applause. The Communist Party newspaper, the *Daily Worker*, called the release of *Negro Songs of Protest* a "landmark in American culture." Composer Lan Adomian, in *New Masses*, wrote that the book featured "some of the finest examples in Negro folk music" of the day. The collection, he concluded, represented an "indictment" against long-standing white ignorance and denial, a stark rebuke to "the slander that a nation of thirteen million people, reduced to peonage, is nothing more than a grand minstrel show."[11]

Born September 14, 1898, in Budapest, Lawrence Gellert was the fifth of six children (five sons and one daughter) in a working-class Jewish Hungarian family. The original surname was Grünbaum, but in the process of emigration and resettlement in the United States it was changed to Greenbaum and ultimately Gellert. In 1905, Lawrence's father, Adolph, emigrated to New York. The following year, he brought his wife, Catherine, and children to join him. As of 1909, when Adolph filed a Petition for Naturalization, the family was residing in the Bronx at 507 East 139th Street. Over the years, the family home moved several times locally, with addresses on the Upper East Side of Manhattan as well as in Greenwich Village, Brooklyn, and White Plains in Westchester County. In the 1920s, sons Theodor (Ted) and Otto opened what would become a prosperous family craft import business, Karavan Trading Company, with brother-in-law Irving Neidich. Though he would allow himself to be convinced to work part-time stints for the company later in life, Lawrence Gellert was not an individual suited to daily routines, however. He never formally involved himself in the family business.[12]

In the early 1920s, Gellert relocated from the winter of New York to the temperate climate of Tryon, North Carolina, located approximately forty miles south of Asheville and very near the state's southern border. He had not gone south in search of music. Rather, his interests were rest and seclusion. Suffering under the stultifying pressures of family, career, and his own unfulfilled restless ambition, Gellert was ailing physically and, by his own telling, had succumbed to a "nervous breakdown." He had wanted to be an actor but instead found himself, as he remembered it to his interviewer, working "seven days . . . eighty to ninety hours a week" as a reporter at the *Brooklyn Daily Eagle*. Additionally, it seems he chafed under the shadow of his famous older brother, already an artist of renown among the Left intelligentsia of New York. "Hugo, by that time, was a big shot, you know. Oh Christ, he was all over the place," Lawrence explained. "I didn't know what was bothering me. . . . I was known as this guy's kid brother. And, then I worked hard on this goddamn newspaper job." In the end, Gellert "quit everything," as he said, and headed out "to make a new life" on the stake of what he called his two "wealthy" businessmen brothers, Ted and Otto. He resettled 700 miles south in Tryon.[13]

In his interviews and in scattered writings, Gellert repeatedly cited 1922 as his date of arrival in the town. Specifically, in one written remembrance, he relates that he "left New York early in November," when the trees in Central Park "still clung to their greenery, despite chilling gusts of wind."[14] A series of items in the local weekly, the *Polk County News*, do certainly place Gellert in Tryon in the 1920s. By 1925, he was enough of an established community figure to warrant multiple mentions. A *News* item from September 17, 1925, reports that "Mr. Larry Goelett left the latter part of last week for New York where he will visit his parents." On October 29, the paper followed up to relate that "Larry Goelett" had returned, and on March 19, we learn that "Mr. Lawrence Goelet" was among the guests at a birthday party for "Mrs. Howard A. Shannon," wife of the *Polk County News* editor. Readers will note, of course, that Gellert's last name shows up in several variants here. This is indeed the case throughout this document trail. In *Polk County News* "society" dispatches about him, Gellert appears as Lawrence or Larry with a host of last names ranging from "Goelett" to "Goelet" to "Goellett" to "Goellet" to "Gollett." Two articles in the *News* authored by Gellert himself have the byline "Larry Goelett" and "Larry Goelet," respectively, and in one notice in the local successor paper, the *Tryon Daily Bulletin*, he is referenced as "Mr. Lawrence Goulette."[15]

Bruce Conforth, in his biography of Gellert, suggests that the name changes reflect an unstable identity. Setting aside the possibility that at least some of this was simple newspaper error, there are any number of reasons a transplant with romantic aspirations toward the stage or print might engage in self-invention. Assumed names are not uncommon among actors and writers. Additionally, Conforth questions to what extent Gellert worked, as Gellert claimed, at the local newspaper. In his interviews, Gellert talks about a "little newspaper" (never named) that needed to be put out each Thursday. Gellert laughs that he had to step in for a while when the editor—"Shannon, [I'll] never forget the Irishman"—left his wife and "ran off with a mountain girl." Conforth dismisses such newspaper work as exaggerated, sharing that he interviewed Tryon local Seth Vining Sr., "owner and publisher of the *Asheville Citizen*," who "stated unequivocally" that he had no such recollections. "Lawrence, at best," relates Conforth, "only submitted occasional reviews" according to Vining Sr.[16]

But there is corroborating data by which to credit Gellert's recollections. First, the *Asheville Citizen* was not the local paper. Rather, the *Polk County News*, a weekly in fact published every Thursday, just as Gellert notes, was the paper of record in town. Second, Seth Vining Sr. was the founder and owner of the *Tryon Daily Bulletin*, not the *Asheville Citizen*. By the time Vining Sr. started the *Daily Bulletin* in 1928, Gellert may not have been involved in the newspaper any longer in any sustained way. There is evidence, actually, of just the community scandal of the newspaper editor leaving his wife that Gellert laughed about in his interviews. "H. A. Shannon" is on the masthead as editor of the *Polk County News* starting in August 1924. His name remains through September 1925. In the September 10 issue, however, there is a notable editor's comment that, for "the first time" in Tryon history, a woman "wielded the editorial pen." The following Thursday, the editor's note reveals that "Mrs. Shannon edited the paper last week," and on the masthead for October 1, 1925, "Ruth Alexander Shannon" appears formally as editor. This is the period, prior to the advent of the *Tryon Daily Bulletin* in 1928, to which Gellert is likely referring when he recalls needing to "get the paper out" on Thursdays.[17]

By 1928, Gellert was already on the move, from Tryon north and back again. The June 17, 1926, edition of the *Polk County News* reports that "Mr. Lawrence Goellet is leaving Tryon next week for his home in White Plains, N.Y., to spend the summer with his parents." It adds that "he expects to rejoin the staff of the *New York World*, from which he has enjoyed several years leave of absence," and that "Mr. Goellet has spent four winters in Tryon, and has become so acclimated that we are counting on his presence with us next year, notwithstanding his positive assurance that he is going back to stay and work." The "four winter" reference corroborates his arrival date of winter 1922. The news blurb also suggests that Gellert worked at more than just the *Brooklyn Daily Eagle* when he lived up north. That said, Gellert's efforts to resume newspaper writing in New York may have been unsuccessful or supplanted with other business. As it happens, he did not "stay and work" in New York. A subsequent notice in the *Tryon Daily Bulletin* has him back in town visiting a friend three years later in 1929.[18]

Gellert's extended sojourns in Tryon continued into the 1930s. W. C. Handy corresponded with him at a Tryon post office box in fall 1932. F. Scott Fitzgerald, a repeat visitor in town who spent months at the local Oak Hall Hotel, remembered Gellert in 1935 as "that chap on the Tryon paper who reminded me of Carl Sandburg."[19]

As far as the claims of local newspaper work go, Gellert's credibility appears sound, but two pieces do hint at an issue where his self-invention equated to more than just name changes. In editorial comment preceding one of the two *Polk County News* articles with his byline, readers were informed that the piece's author, "Larry Goelet," was a "veteran of the late disturbance over-seas, carrying an everlasting momento [*sic*] of active service in the shape of shrapnel wounds which have been over-long in healing." Again, in the *Asheville Citizen-Times* from 1938, this fiction is repeated, describing "Lawrence Gellert" as a "composer and author, who spent some years" in Tryon "recuperating from wounds sustained in the World war."[20] Whether Gellert himself started this rumor and repeated it locally, or whether this was a fabrication or mistake of the *Polk County News* that was simply reproduced by rote later in the Asheville paper, is unclear. Bruce Conforth relates that Gellert told at least one intimate in Tryon, Alice Lightner, that he had been injured in the war. Gellert may have done so to garner romantic sympathy, or to win favor generally in town, or even to provide cover for what became his radical music collecting. At any rate, the story that Gellert had suffered combat in World War I was untrue. As we will see, he had lost an older brother, Ernest, under mysterious circumstances in the war years. But Lawrence never served.

An Elite Colony of Liberal Sentiment

Tryon proved an auspicious choice of resettlement for Gellert. In the years when he arrived, the population of the town swelled seasonally owing to its unique location in what is known as the "thermal belt" of this part of southwestern North Carolina. Situated in the foothills of the Blue Ridge Mountains, the area is protected to a great degree from temperature extremes. Tryon was opened to the railroad in 1877. With its wooded rural landscape, rolling hills, sunny skies, and affordable real estate, it came into fashion in the late nineteenth century as a resort destination for beleaguered city folk from the North and abroad. Regular seasonal residents and visitors included Lady Nancy Astor, the playwright and actor William Gillette (famous for his iconic film portrayal of Sherlock Holmes), F. Scott Fitzgerald, George Gershwin, Lefty and Nora Flynn, and actor David Niven. By the time Gellert arrived, Tryon was in vogue as an "art and music colony." Elsewhere in the state and over the border into South Carolina, the town was regarded as an anomaly, a renegade enclave in the midst of the Old South. "The homes were crowded with good books, good music, and a certain paternal and sympathetic attitude of a group," Gellert reflected, "who could admire beauty and wholesomeness without prejudice [since] it cost them nothing. Even amused and idled their time away." It could not have hurt, of course, that many of these well-heeled transplants—former Lieutenant Governor Clarence A. Lightner and family of Grosse Pointe, Michigan, as another example—commanded considerable influence. As they resettled in Tryon, they took a genuine interest in local affairs and infused this tiny corner of North Carolina with both money and prestige.[21]

Gellert claimed to have happened upon Tryon on his train ride south in search of doctor-prescribed sunshine. The collector said he maintained the town as his "center of gravity" for the next twenty-five years of his forays in the South, blending quite easily into its liberal milieu. Early on, besides the newspaper, he also busied himself with Drama Fortnightly, the new local theater company. With his sharp mind and bohemian charms, Gellert, as a family member recalled it, never had trouble situating himself at the right place at the right time. In short order, Gellert seems to have earned the friendship and support of several wealthy and influential habitués, including the Lightner's rambunctious daughter, Alice, and a former Chicago banker named William Weigel. In the years to come, these associations would prove beneficial to the idiosyncratic Lawrence Gellert. In key ways, they furnished cover and material resources that allowed for his explorations in Black folksong.[22]

With its elite colony, Tryon, as Gellert remembered it, was a relative "oasis" of liberal sentiment in the South.[23] Even so, early upon his arrival he acquired distinction as an outspoken, if affable, advocate of racial equality. This was not, in these early years, so much out of any self-conscious political initiative on Gellert's part, but rather for his apparently casual flouting of the conventional lines of race and class division in the United States. "I had no prejudice," he boasted to his interviewer in later years. "I wasn't even born in America."[24]

In Tryon, Gellert "used to have trouble with various people," he recalled, because "they saw me fraternizing with the Negroes." Locals used to deride his mode of transport as the "N——r Hurry-Up Wagon," he said, owing to his tendency to "pick up a Negro" for a ride "now and then."[25] Indeed, as late as the 1980s, he was still remembered by one white resident in the town as "spending all his time with the colored folks."[26] In the disapproving eyes of many among its native class of "Big White Folks," as Gellert adopted the term,[27] the odd newcomer's circle of relations in Tryon must have seemed to include both the very "top" and the very "bottom" of its citizenry. It was to the consternation of many, we may surmise, that he appeared untroubled by southern law and custom, and even enthusiastic about befriending the town's segregated community of Black merchants and laborers. In this respect, influential friends among the town's upper set of white transplants were likely more than a convenience. Rather, they were a crucial asset to Lawrence Gellert's unfolding ventures. Of this network of benefactors, William Weigel was perhaps the most important. As Gellert explained, "Bill" was "a Chicago gentleman with an awful lot of money." Resettled for the benefit of his infirm wife, Weigel was a man with both resources and time to spare. Over the years of their long friendship, he offered Gellert not only camaraderie, but also a place to stay, significant financing, and, more importantly, protection and access in the South. "He had tremendous influence," stated Gellert. If not for Weigel, Gellert asserted, "I'd have been run out of town."[28]

"Sing Fest for the White Folks"

At some point in the 1920s, Lawrence Gellert began collecting the songs of local African American community members. In his interviews from the 1960s, Gellert placed the start of his collecting work between 1922 and 1924. Then again, at some seventy years of age by this time, Gellert himself admitted to interviewer Reuss that "my dates are terrible." A precise dating is never finalized in their conversations. The collector's original field recordings are housed at the Archives of Traditional Music (ATM) at Indiana University, Bloomington. Of his sound recordings currently catalogued, there are 67 ten-inch discs and 154 seven-inch discs. While the ten-inch recordings are from a latter period of activity running from the early 1930s into the 1940s, the seven-inch discs have been dated by archivists to the 1920s. These fragile early aluminum discs of very low sound quality do match up, then, with the collector's recollections, but only generally. Whether the discs were recorded in the early or latter 1920s is unclear.[29]

Bruce Conforth has ventured a judgment in his recent biography. He now holds that Gellert "probably began recording in late 1924 or early 1925." Conforth asserts, therefore, that Gellert is "the first person to produce field recordings of African Americans on disc."[30] Such a conclusion may be premature, however. I further detail the matter in chapter 6. For now, I highlight a pivotal episode that took place in 1926, and thus already complicates the timeline posited above. Three times, from his first interview with Reuss to his last, Gellert tells the story of a Tryon "sing fest" fundraiser.[31] He takes obvious pride in the episode and identifies it as his critical gateway into Black music curiosity in Tryon. Newly digitized newspaper archives have only now made it possible to corroborate the event independently, backing Gellert's memories with primary source support.

Gellert narrates the concert fundraiser story in the same basic terms with each mention in his interviews. As he tells it, a resident of the Black community in Tryon came to seek his aid one day where he was staying at William Weigel's house. Weigel was out of town on a trip, and the English house servant would not allow the African American man in the front door. Gellert recalls heading out to the garden. There, he was asked if he would help mount a "sing fest for the white folks." The local country church was in disrepair, the visitor explained, and congregants thought Gellert could help in organizing a charity concert. Gellert wondered, "Why me? I'm a stranger here." He was informed, "We heard you were doing good things for our people."[32]

Gellert did help produce a successful fundraiser, and this first experience proved fortuitous. For one, it seemed to excite his innate streak of rebellion. As Gellert recounted, rather than staging the concert in the damaged Black country church as originally conceived, he surreptitiously arranged to have the concert held in the Parish House of the white Episcopal Church in Tryon. The Parish House was a frequent venue for community events and entertainment, including the Drama Fortnightly performances. In publicizing the concert, moreover, Gellert said he had posters made that simply promised an "Aggregation of Fine Singers." That evening, as the cultured set of white Tryon assembled to await the performance, they were stunned to discover that this "aggregation" was actually an ensemble made up of their own African American domestics and laborers. According to Gellert, many of the singers had in fact "begged off work early" to make the date. After a tense stand-off in which impresario Gellert was forced to address the full house to insist that the show go on, audience members allowed the Black performers to enter the white Parish House. The concert went forward to positive end. Certainly, it captured the ear of the future Black music enthusiast. "This is before I was interested in songs at all," Gellert explained to Reuss. But it was the entry point. "I had never heard anything like it," he elaborated. The concert was "all church music." Gellert was struck, however, because "that church had never rocked like that." Though he told his interviewer that he knew nothing special about music in these first years, his interest was piqued. "I was very curious, and I got acquainted with some of the boys, and we had a couple evenings together," Gellert stated. "And, then I heard something which had nothing to do with church." It was "tremendous protest."[33]

Recent research has unearthed *Polk County News* items that attest to the event. Gellert remembers the date incorrectly in his interview, initially guessing 1924.

However, the concert did happen, and much as the collector described. In the *Polk County News* from April 8, 1926, we find a "Tryon Society News" post announcing "an unusually interesting evening will be afforded at the Parish House on Tuesday evening, April 13." Gellert may have exaggerated the racial element in his storytelling, as the ensemble is characterized quite openly by the paper, in dated derogatory language, as "an aggregation of a dozen or more darkies." So the suggestion that he kept the racial identity of this "aggregation" concealed until concert night may be a stretch. Nevertheless, nowhere does the notice reveal that this choir is composed of local African American working people, which may have been what rankled white audience members, and it does confirm that the proposed event is "a recital of Spiritual Melodies, under the management of Lawrence Goellet."[34] Coverage continues in the April 15 edition. *Polk County News* readers learned that the "Recital of Negro Spirituals" had been postponed a week and was rescheduled for the upcoming Monday. More details attesting to Gellert's "sing fest" story are laid out: "This will be a very interesting program for everyone that will attend. Critics who have heard these voices say they display the old time Southern melody ringing true to the old bygone days in the early sixty's. Numbers of tickets have already been sold and the production manager, Mr. Lawrence Goelett, the 'Ziegfield' [*sic*] of Tryon, expects a capacity house to witness this rare entertainment. The report from the box office indicate brisk seat selling."[35] Finally, in a follow-up from April 22, "Old Time Singers Amuse Great Crowd," we see evidence of a successful night. The piece reports that the "recital of Spiritual Melodies given at the Parish House on Monday night pleased a large audience. These singers were brought here by Mr. Lawrence Gollett, of Tryon, N.C. Many of the old-time melodies were rendered and they presented a great display of real old time Southern harmony."[36]

In his interviews, Gellert indicates that the fundraiser was a sellout and that ticket sales generated two hundred dollars. Indeed, a "large audience" is corroborated by the news item above. Whether there was pre-concert controversy or not, however, we have no indication. Gellert seemed to relish that aspect of the story, though. He had tricked his neighbors in white Tryon, Gellert claimed, into paying "seventy-five cents to hear their own servants."[37]

A Verboten Tradition of Protest

Lawrence Gellert referred to the "sing fest" episode as formative, the turning point for his entry into Black folksong discovery. Until now, researchers had no independent evidence to detail the milestone. With these *Polk County News* items, however, Gellert's step into African American cultural inquiry comes into greater focus. It was at some point after the concert in 1926, not likely before, that Gellert began his music collecting. With his exposure after the concert to what he called "tremendous protest," Gellert had been given a rare hearing into a provocative store of Black lyrical resistance.

One of the first songs Gellert said he heard in Tryon from out of this "underground" reservoir of music—indeed, one of the tunes that was "everywhere," as he remembered it, and in fact "got [his] teeth into this"[38]—evoked the bitter relations of southern chain gangs:

> Work all de Summer
> Work all de Fall
> Gonna make dis Chris'mas
> In mah overhall
>
> Got any cawn bread
> Cawn bread save me some
> Got any cawn bread
> Buddy won' you save me some
>
> Don' min' de weather
> So de win' don' blow
> Don' min' dese chains
> So de ball don' grow
>
> Way far f'om home
> Wit hammer in mah han'
> Ahm so tire' hammerin'
> Ah cain' stan'
>
> Ah feels mah Hell arisin'
> Six feet a day
> Lord ef it keep arisin'
> Gwine wash dis damn lan' 'way[39]

As it is presented here, from Gellert's earliest published transcription in *New Masses* in 1932, "Work All the Summer" builds to a stanza of ominous warning.

Such expression may have appeared quite terrific to the white collector at the beginning of his endeavors. But it was hardly unique. In his recorded interviews, Gellert claims to have first heard the song from a local Black informant in Tryon. This first published transcription featured above, however, was reportedly collected several years later, from a county jail in South Carolina according to the annotation text that accompanies the lyric in his *New Masses* article. Moreover, there are other permutations of "Work All the Summer" in the Gellert archive. He published the song, in a slightly longer version, in 1936 in *Negro Songs of Protest.* It is also included in audio, in various forms, among both his seven-inch recordings from the 1920s and ten-inch recordings from the 1930s.[40] The audio recordings are noteworthy. In melody, phrasing, and lyric structure, they suggest a marked correspondence between "Work All the Summer" and the commercial blues standard, "Sitting on Top of the World," first made famous by The Mississippi Sheiks in 1930.[41] The commercial history of this well-known title is long and varied. It begins in the Black southern string band tradition of the Delta-based Sheiks and goes on to include country and bluegrass luminaries Bob Wills and Bill Monroe; bluesman Chester "Howlin' Wolf" Burnett; and rock performers Bob Dylan, Cream, and The Grateful Dead. What is important to note is that verses and lyric fragments associated with the tune were well incorporated into rural southern vernacular tradition, Black and white, by the time Gellert was first afforded a hearing in the 1920s. If the lines of protest he encountered among African American singers were unlikely to appear on commercial record, they were nonetheless prevalent, he asserted, in local circles on the ground.

In his early years in Tryon, Lawrence Gellert was coming to discover the expansive lines of transmission and variation that characterize vernacular culture as it is passed from person to person, town to town, and region to region. In terms of Black music, the kind of protest to which he was only gleaning the surface at first was subject even to another layer of complexity. Such expression was, as Sterling Brown referred to it, a "verboten" tradition with respect to the dominant culture. As Brown elaborated, "Where there is some protection or guaranteed secrecy" a host of "verboten songs come to light" from out of the vernacular cultures of—he offered some examples—miners, sharecroppers, and blues people. These were "songs brewed in bitterness," he explained, "not the double-talk of the slave seculars, but the naked truth of desperate men telling what is on their brooding minds." Never meant for outside listening, they constituted an alternate stream, parallel and sometimes overlapping, of Black musical tradition that had, with due cause, gone largely without recognition in the dominant culture. In Brown's estimation, it was the rare outsider who achieved the necessary level of trust to get at such material. Only when "the white captain is far enough away, do prisoners confide these songs," he wrote, in reference to the common approach to fieldwork among white collectors who favored Black convicts in isolated southern penitentiaries for their recording efforts.[42]

For Gellert, this Black musical "culture of opposition"[43] was an inspiration. It put the lie to prevailing currents of white racism that denigrated Black agency, and he set about an independent study to investigate its practice. To this effort, another early experience was formative. "I lived with this Weigel," Gellert remembered. "I was sitting on his porch," and along came a "Negro chain gang . . . widening the road. I hear a guy there singing. . . . This guy was singing a protest song. I mean just like that." As the collector recounted, however, "As soon as I came on the scene, the same music, but some words about 'a cat and a basket,' you know. Just nothing." Curious, Gellert again "removed" himself out of range, and then "crept back behind a bush." As he discovered, the man was "back again" with the previous lyrics. "Fucking white man," the leader sang, "me working in the sun, and he's sitting in the shade . . . laziest man God ever made."[44]

The episode is telling. At work in the field before Lawrence Gellert, white academics Howard Odum and Guy B. Johnson, in their book *The Negro and His Songs* published in 1925, recounted a similar incident with a Black road crew near a white homeowner's residence.[45] In this case, the laborers might have avoided the more intense protest sentiment of the Gellert encounter precisely because the white interloper did not conceal himself. Still, a comparable "white man" refrain is clearly recognizable. As the white observer sat visibly present, struggling to write down the words he heard, the crew sang:

> White man settin' on wall,
> White man settin' on wall,
> White man settin' on wall all day long,
> Wastin' his time, wastin' his time.

Odum and Johnson included the story in order to emphasize the accomplished improvisatory element of Black music-making. They shied away from any social commentary, though their parting comment did register a degree of racial anxiety. "That the 'white man' immediately moved on need not be taken as evidence that he appreciated the song any the less," they remarked, "but perhaps the incident reminded him of other times when the words he sought were indistinct, or it may recall to others with vividness similar Negro songs about the white man."[46]

The "white man" cycle of song lyrics to which Gellert as well as Odum and Johnson were a party had a wide currency among Black workers in the South. As Lawrence Levine reports in *Black Culture and Black Consciousness*, a "visitor in Florida" recorded an "identical experience" to that of these collectors. "When Negro workers in a lumber camp became aware" that a white stranger was "attempting to copy down their songs," he summarizes of an account from 1945, "they became silent for several minutes and then chanted these lines: 'White man dar, settin' on de lawg / Wastin' his time, jes wastin' his time.'"[47]

Such evidence hints at what must have been the dynamic variability of Black songs of protest in the South. Still, these kinds of adroit cultural politics were lost, it appears, on many white collectors in Gellert's time and before. As Benjamin Filene has written, for instance, "The main collector to study African American songs in the early 1900s, Howard Odum, depicted them as the manifestations of a bizarre alien culture. With doctorates in both sociology and psychology, Odum gathered songs less to preserve an American heritage than to discover what made those strange Negroes tick." Historian Marybeth Hamilton similarly stresses Odum's "scientific" pretentions in the context of the time, explaining that Odum began his music fieldwork "in the same spirit that physical anthropologists of the day took up calipers—to provide hard and objective proof of black inferiority." Odum's only major early contemporary, John A. Lomax, did prioritize preservation over science in his song collecting. But Lomax was similarly a conservative racialist. In a classic essay from 1917, Lomax posited "self-pity" as "the theme that, perhaps above all others," dominated Black folksong. He wondered why, though, since racial oppression in the way of slavery had "been a thing of the past these many years, and, after all, as a part of the race history, formed but a brief interlude—an episode—between many generations of barbaric freedom and the present status of liberty in a civilized land." Both Odum and Lomax were "Jim Crow" southerners who presumed a superiority of insight on their neighbors across the color line. As historian Jerrod Hirsch puts it, John Lomax "maintained a distinction between the civilized and the savage, and placed southern blacks on the other side of that line."[48]

Gellert, in his early years in the South, appears to have had no prior knowledge of Black music or history. He had not studied folklore and had little direct experience of any kind with people of color. Nevertheless, it seems that he was inclined to probe the deeper workings of an African American musical infrapolitics in a way that his white predecessors and contemporaries in Black folklore did not. Political scientist James C. Scott formulated the concept of "infrapolitics" to broad application in *Domination and the Arts of Resistance: Hidden Transcripts.* Scott writes that the "circumspect struggle waged daily by subordinate groups is, like infrared rays, beyond the visible end of the spectrum. That it should be invisible . . . is in large part by design—a tactical choice born of a prudent awareness of the balance of power." Robin D. G. Kelley has shown the value of such a theorization for African American history, particularly as it relates to the US South under Jim Crow. In the 1930s, Gellert collected in some of the political battlegrounds that Kelley examines in *Hammer and Hoe: Alabama Communists during the Great Depression.* Kelley references Gellert song material in the book as well as a report from Gellert in Birmingham to Louis Coleman of the Communist Party's International Labor Defense in New York City. As the intersection with Black radical history in Kelley's research suggests, Gellert happened upon the same Black musical culture as his white peers in folksong research. But he had an alternative orientation, and he pursued an infrapolitics that they did not.[49]

CHAPTER TWO

Free Radical

LAWRENCE GELLERT'S EARLY COLLECTING AND RISE TO PROMINENCE

He is a poetic figure who has spent twenty years in the South gathering folksongs: he has a thousand of them. He looks like a native Southerner and "passes" as such when he is there.

—EARL CONRAD ON LAWRENCE GELLERT, *JIM CROW AMERICA*, 1947

Lawrence Gellert embraced his early encounters with Black vernacular protest as a privileged glimpse behind the veil, to use W. E. B. Du Bois's oft-referenced metaphor from *The Souls of Black Folk.* Upon his arrival in Tryon, his white neighbors had issued the familiar cliché that Black southerners were "a happy and contented lot." But, as Gellert quickly determined, the "official dictum of the South" precluded otherwise, backed as it was with lynch law, political suppression, and economic domination. In Gellert's understanding, all was not as it seemed. "Hence the mask of the docile, amicable, treadmilling clown, the Negro must appear in if he is to survive," he wrote in his preface to *Negro Songs of Protest.* The job of a credible folklorist, he believed, was to penetrate such racial masquerade. "Long and painstakingly I cultivated and cemented confidences with individual Negroes," he asserted. Without similar efforts "any attempt to get to the core of the living folk lore is foredoomed to failure."[1] As it would happen, Gellert did, indeed, come to ridicule the mass of white folklore research on Black music on just these grounds. "Countless plantation memories have appeared on the book stalls from pens of nostalgic spinsters," he charged. These "plantation memories," he alleged, were "about as authentic Negro folk lore as next week's installment of the Amos and Andy broadcast series."[2]

To what should we attribute this alternative perspective? How exactly did Gellert stumble onto this underground culture of Black vernacular resistance? What were the dynamics behind his "safe" status among Black singer-informants? The answers are varied and complex. They involve Gellert's apparently innate rebel proclivities; his fortuitous landing in the liberalized enclave of Tryon; and his developing political consciousness and contacts with respect to the Communist Party in the United States and its organizing drives in the American South, in particular. What becomes clear in Gellert's recollections and writings is that Black folksong collecting was never a simple matter.

Gaining a Hearing in Black Culture

Lawrence Gellert's initial access to Black vernacular culture generally in Tryon appears to have been relatively straightforward, though. At the beginning, the collector traded favors for songs from local African American residents. Following the successful Black "singfest," Gellert recounted, "Negroes used to come up for this and that" from him. "They wanted a pair of shoes. They wanted a hat. They wanted a nickel or a dime." In exchange, the nascent collector solicited songs. At first, he used shorthand to take down simple written transcriptions of lyrics. Eventually, he employed methods for producing sound recordings. Gellert was a frequent visitor to the Lightner home in Tryon in the 1920s. Clarence A. Lightner and his wife, Frances, had relocated from Michigan where the former had been lieutenant governor. Their daughter, Alice, was a kindred spirit who shared Gellert's interests in the arts and politics. She was also supportive of his early endeavors in Black music collecting. After he expressed some curiosity, she made a gift for him of the family's manual table phonograph. Gellert experimented at rigging the machine with a reversed megaphone. As Black residents came to see him for favors at his adopted residence with benefactor William Weigel, Gellert would bring out his recording equipment. In return for his efforts, he said, "They used to sing for me right on the front porch there." The singers would "blow into" the megaphone "until they got white in the face," Gellert explained, and the stylus would cut a fragile groove into an aluminum blank. As word got out about the operation, these singers "brought other people" up to the porch. The newer contacts, in turn, would recommend additional family and friends.[3]

After a time, Gellert was afforded a network of folk informants throughout the area. "I had a list as long as your arm," he claimed, as singers would tell him to "look up a cousin here" and "a nephew there." Over the next years, his interest intensified, and he upgraded his recording set-up. At some point in 1933 or 1934, Gellert was able to acquire a Presto electrified portable disc cutter. The Presto Recording Corporation had just begun marketing this industry-standard technology, and Gellert was eager to employ it in his expanding fieldwork. Additionally, at some point in the 1920s, he had arranged for a makeshift mobile facility to be built onto the frame of a Velie brand automobile. With these advanced means, his projects in field recording were expanded considerably. He visited individuals, work gangs, and prisoners throughout various regions of the Southeast—in the western Carolinas and in Georgia primarily—but ventured even farther at times to Alabama, Mississippi, Louisiana, and Texas, as well as the Georgia Sea Islands and the West Indies.[4]

As far as many of his white neighbors knew, Gellert was part of a longstanding and, as it was perceived by this point in the twentieth century, benign tradition of white musical connoisseurship in the South. Even Weigel, who accompanied him on many field trips, assumed quite naturally that Gellert was collecting "beautiful" Negro spirituals. "He didn't know what I was doing," the collector recalled. "He had no idea what kind of songs I was gathering." It was a good thing. William Weigel may have been highly literate, with a mind for the arts and for world travel.[5] But Gellert explained that he "was not sympathetic at all" to the cause of Black equality, nor did he have any interest in Black music. His ventures with the colorful Lawrence Gellert were merely a source of amusement. When the collector would visit southern prisons, Weigel provided letters of introduction attesting to his high standing and influential friends, the governor of South Carolina among them. Just as often, Weigel might come along for the ride. In those cases, Gellert would have Weigel entertain the warden for a period of hours with a bottle of liquor or a walk around the grounds. Gellert made it clear that he "didn't want no white sons of bitches around," and at times he would have to assure anxious guards that he would be safe in the jailhouse alone among the Black prisoners. On other occasions, Gellert collected from prisoners out of doors. As he described it, he would park his Velie touring car alongside a country road and wait for an approaching gang of prisoners on work detail. With his Presto recording equipment secured away in his hutch, Gellert would conceal a microphone on the roadside and record the gang as it passed, or while on break if possible. In many cases, he said, the accompanying white officials were entirely unaware of his activities; they simply waved at him as they came across his car.[6]

Routinely, Gellert employed gestures meant to curry favor with informants. A standard practice, for instance, was to have Weigel furnish Gellert with cigarettes that he would hand out to ease relations. Moreover, as a letter from Camp Hill, Alabama, suggests, Gellert kept up with his informant network from afar. In 1935, one A. L. White wrote Gellert that his health was "just fine" and that he was "glad to hear from you all." White was, perhaps, a local Black sharecropper, one even who might have come into contact with Gellert through the organizing struggles of the Communist-sponsored Share Croppers Union in Tallapoosa County in the early 1930s. He thanked "Mr. and Mrs. Larry" (the latter unspecified, as Gellert was never legally married) for "the clothing that you all send here" and indicated that he would distribute pieces throughout the community. Significantly, he closed the letter mentioning thirty songs "that I will send." While Gellert's apparent donation of clothing could have been entirely unrelated to his music collecting, this passing reference suggests a connection. In the field of Black folksong, sympathetic dealings between fieldworker and informant could be the difference between song or silence. "Mister, I been on this chain gang for nine months and I don't have a penny to send my folks a postcard," said a prisoner in another typical outing that Gellert recalled. "I'll sing you a song for a postcard."[7]

Stumbling into Black Folksong Collecting

Lawrence Gellert frequently remarked later in life on the random luck of his "stumble" into Black folksong with his relocation south in the 1920s.[8] In the broad view, a number of factors contributed to Gellert's notable success. First, Gellert was in a fortuitous setting at the outset of his efforts. As local historian Michael McCue states, Tryon was likely the "most promising place in the South" for such work. The town was hardly exempt from the southern race system, of course, but it was distinct. As it was only founded in the latter part of the nineteenth century, there was not a local history of slavery among white and Black families. Roots did not run deep in the soil in this respect, and there was a relatively prosperous and proud Black community. Many African American residents were business owners or employees in Black-owned service enterprises (blacksmithing, retail, or trash disposal, among others) rather than strictly farmers and laborers for hire. Like many of their white neighbors, they were newcomers from elsewhere in the South. This made for a kind of "melting pot" citizenry, as McCue puts it, of "folks from other places."[9]

One young person who experienced Tryon's virtues and vices was Nina Simone, born Eunice Waymon in 1933. Gellert was already in touch with Black music and the Black community by this point, but throughout their respective lifetimes neither Gellert nor Simone expressed awareness of their overlap during Simone's childhood. Each drew from the same bifurcated culture of the town, however. It was a racial environment both exceptional and unexceptional. In her autobiography, in one of her cup-half-full moments, Simone grants that Tryon "was the south," but with a difference. As a "resort town Tryon had developed in an uncommon way," she elaborates. "For instance there wasn't a black side of town: it was more like a series of circles around the centre [*sic*] with blacks or whites living in these circles. And a few blacks, a few, lived almost in the centre, almost in the white areas." When the Waymon family moved to the town in 1929, she states, "My parents were very happy. Daddy was working for himself at last and Mom had a big new house to settle into. . . . Relations between the black and white community were always very cordial." Then again, as she never let slide when it came to reality checks in America, Simone added that "of course there was no policy of racial justice in Tryon, it was just an easygoing small town with a council which existed only to ensure nothing happened to spoil the peaceful life the white folks led."[10]

Simone's biographer, Nadine Cohodas, relates that Black and white Tryonites lived in "checkerboard clusters." It was "an arrangement that fostered, depending on one's viewpoint, an inchoate integration or an imperfect segregation." Housing, employment, and social life was integrated, but only to a degree, and one of the most important community institutions, the school system, was in full observance of Jim Crow. African American children, young Nina Simone included, went to the Tryon Colored School, which was grossly under-resourced and certainly not any more "separate but equal" than neighboring segregated southern communities. Simone appreciated her teachers and was an accomplished student. In looking back later in life, though, she was overcome with the gloom of feeling "trapped and scorned in a hostile world" growing up in Jim Crow Tryon.[11]

This experience of entrapment under systemic race injustice is underlined by two local histories. In these decades, the Reverend Scotland Harris, a respected African American minister, accepted a white associate's invitation to a Sunday service at the Episcopal Church of the Holy Cross. This was the same location where Gellert caused a stir a few years later with his Black "sing fest" in the adjoining Parish House. Harris's attendance with his family at the all-white church occasioned similar uproar. "It was a social barrier that was crossed," explained Harris's granddaughter. Shortly after, Harris was quietly informed that he should leave town. "His departure highlighted the precariousness of Black life in Tryon, its residents ever mindful that in more hostile communities such a moment could easily explode into violence," writes Cohodas. The trauma did explode into more open destruction in 1940 at Simone's Tryon

Colored School. That summer, the African American principal, so desperate after for so long pleading for funds for his substandard institution, burned down the school and was sent to prison for arson. When arrested, the principal said he did it so that the Black pupils under his care "could have a nice brick building like other schools."[12]

Tryon under Jim Crow was a distinct locality that can be credited as the town that took notice of Nina Simone's childhood musical genius; as the town where her teacher, Muriel Mazzanovich ("Miss Mazzy," or "my white mama"), nurtured Simone's ambitions to be a classical concert pianist; and as the town that raised scholarship funds to send Simone to the Julliard School of Music in New York. But it was also a town under white domination, and it was a town where some African Americans resisted. In adulthood, Simone frequently repeated the painful account of a Miss Mazzy piano recital when she was eleven years old. With the event full and about to commence with all of the etiquette of traditional European concert decorum, Simone saw her parents being moved from the front to the rear of the space so that two white audience members could take their places. Simone refused to perform until her parents were reseated "where she could see them," and white organizers yielded. As Nadine Cohodas adds, about the same time, Black residents in the county founded their first NAACP branch.[13]

Tryon was not a utopia, but it was likely a unique factor in Gellert's early success in Black folksong research. Alongside of location, Gellert's reputation as a racial progressive was crucial. In this respect, his status and growing song archive were self-reinforcing. When the collector's network of informants failed him on a recording trip, he could draw on his growing store of protest lyrics in order to invoke a context of safety for his Black contact. Gellert could present himself as a sympathetic "initiate" into African American culture. The collector related the details of one such occasion in a revealing story set in Atlanta at some point in the late 1920s or the early 1930s:

> I went to the Negro YMCA, and I told them what I was doing. And, the guy there was very flossy about it. He said, "We don't have that kind of thing. . . . who wants them kind of songs? We're a respectable organization." But, I told him, look, I wasn't looking for him to sing any of the songs. I just wanted a lead to where I could get [some] . . . "Well," he said, "if you want some nice old spirituals, I'll tell you where . . ." So, I went to the people that he told me about. But, they were different than he thought they were.[14]

As the story continues, Gellert was directed to a party. He finally got a singer alone and began the sensitive process of prodding for material. "I was in a room with him," remembered Gellert, and the man asked, "What kind of songs do you want?" Gellert answered that he was not interested in spirituals. He lied, in fact, that he had "plenty of those already." Rather, he wanted secular songs, "devil's tunes or reels," he said for illustration. The singer was still guarded or unclear on the matter, however. He inquired, "Like what?" At that point, Gellert began to offer up lines from out of his collection. "Well, I'd start off harmlessly, you know. And, in a stanza or so, it'd be really something." In such cases, the collector indicated, informants would shake their heads and marvel, "Where'd you get that song?" Through the exchange, he explained, "you'd get a little closer to the guy, little by little, and eventually" could uncover some rich results.[15]

In the session recounted above, Gellert said he took down the lines for "Went to Atlanta" (see Epilogue for full transcription). Certainly, the song could raise eyebrows. The delicate negotiations with the unnamed African American singer that led to the performance reflect how Gellert's store of lyrics and sympathetic status could win informant confidence and yield new material. Under the right conditions, his song archive reflected back favorably on his reputation. His reputation, in turn, led to contacts and songs. Even in the most ostensibly discouraging of circumstances, then, Gellert had means by which to inch his way into African American vernacular culture.

In sizing up his collection, Gellert always maintained that he had a strict interest in only verboten songs rather than in the whole of African American music or American folklore generally. As those who have examined his full archive have clarified, however, it is not the case, as Gellert insisted, that he "never got a song that wasn't protest."[16] A fair portion of the collector's musical archive consists of work songs, popular blues, and other common stock that do not feature any pronounced lyrics of social critique. Nevertheless, Gellert seemed to search out such music, and he appeared proudest of that contribution. His songbooks and early articles showcased a provocative range of expression with respect to Black life in the post-Reconstruction United States. Among his published examples of Black songs of protest, there are items about class exploitation in the South ("Went to Atlanta," "Pickin' Off De Cotton," "Told My Captain," and "Ah's De Man"); items naming lynching and questioning the false promise of Christian deliverance ("Sistren and Brethren" and "How Long, Brethren?"); items calling out the nation's lie of white superiority ("Ain't It Hard—To Be a N——r" and "Cause I'm a N——r"); and items calling for armed Black resistance ("Work All de Summer," "Stan' Boys Stand," and "Work Ox"). As we will see, some of these songs were collected in part or in passing by other folklorists, but no other collector assembled them under explicit label and in the express service of racial justice.

A "White War Correspondent" in the "Racial Fight" in America

Looking back, Gellert asserted that he "had more contacts than any folksong collector ever had down there." His informants, he elaborated, felt that "they were going to do themselves and their own people some good" in recording songs for him. They would stress, "You got to promise . . . that you're going to show it to people that are influential." As is clear, word about Gellert's mission traveled quickly. He recalled: "There were people in Tryon, and when I started off on trips . . . they'd give me names of people to look up along the road. And, when somebody gave me a name . . . by the time I got there, he'd already gotten word to him that 'a white man was gonna come there' and 'you needn't be afraid of him.'"[17] In Gellert's appraisal, it was his iconoclastic reputation combined with a unique local setting in Tryon—a "northern island in a southern ocean," he said—that accounted for the quality of his archive. Additionally, what was also likely a factor was his developing political leanings and associations as regards the communist Left of the United States in the 1920s and 1930s.[18]

With a distinct mission in political revolution rather than folklore preservation, Gellert developed his talents as a white collector of Black folksong in the South. By the time he published *Negro Songs of Protest* in 1936, he was an experienced fieldworker with a tested set of methods, a network of informants, a preferred list of touring stops, and a definite mission in Black music research. In the preface to his songbook, he informed readers:

> For more than a dozen years I lived alternately in Tryon, N.C., and Greenville, S.C. I enjoyed the friendship and protection of influential whites. And with impunity I haunted the Negro quarters. . . . Repeatedly from these vantage points I invaded the Black Belt. Armed with a mechanical phonograph, a sawed off megaphone and a bundle of blank aluminum records (my recording outfit) I trekked, railroaded and hitch-hiked the length and breadth of the deep South. . . . Through Georgia, the Carolinas, way over in Mississippi and Louisiana even, in city slums, on isolated farms out in the sticks, on chain gangs, lumber and turpentine

> work camps, I gathered more than 300 songs of the black folk—songs that reveal for the first time the full heroic stature of the Negro dwarfing for all time the traditional mean estimate of him. . . . These songs are still in the making. . . . They embody the living voice of the otherwise inarticulate resentment against injustice—a part of the unrest that is stirring the South. They speak, now mildly, now sarcastically, now angrily—but always in a firm and earnest manner. And they will be heard![19]

Years later, Gellert reflected, "I have calluses on my sitter and stander and walker and talker." Such injuries "prove," he elaborated, "that Negro song 'collecting' is a misnomer, an over-simplification. It includes salesmanship, diplomacy, espionage, smuggling, and the study of the highest law of self-preservation."[20] As he indicates, ingenuity and deception were necessary elements of Gellert's field methodology over the years.

In his book *Jim Crow America*, published in 1947, leftwing journalist Earl Conrad included a revealing passage on the collector. In the year before, heightened political tensions surrounding the gubernatorial race and postwar race relations in Georgia fanned the flames of violence. In Walton County, two African American men (one a recently returned veteran) and their wives suffered a heinous quadruple lynching near the town of Monroe. The episode was reported nationally, and civil rights organizations mounted campaigns to investigate.[21] Conrad closed *Jim Crow America* with a chapter that referenced the gruesome incident. "I received a telephone call from an old friend, Lawrence Gellert," he wrote. "He is a poetic figure who has spent twenty years in the South gathering folksongs: he has a thousand of them." As Conrad explained, Gellert had called to enlist aid in an investigation of the Monroe lynchings, and "so I arranged," he stated, "with the Civil Rights Congress for his dispatch to Georgia." With his position at the venerable *Chicago Defender* newspaper, Conrad had considerable influence. Moreover, he had his own skills and expertise as a professional journalist and writer. Still, Gellert was a unique asset in the effort to gather covert intelligence from local whites on the deeper conspiracy and community reaction to the case. For years, Conrad suggested, Gellert had made a career out of crossing the color line on behalf of racial justice. "He looks like a native Southerner and 'passes' as such when he is there," Conrad stated. "He spent two weeks in the vicinity of Monroe passing as a cotton farmer desirous of buying cotton land. He listened to the comments on the lynching, and since his ears catch up folk talk and hold it there like a basin catching rain water, he came away with a unique record."[22]

Gellert published his record from the field in *New Masses* in 1946. The piece was presented as reportage from the street. There was no exposition and instead just the presentation of a selection of direct quotations from locals of various identity. Gellert's "passing" as a white southerner was apparently convincing enough to solicit numerous responses. In his article, he presented statements from a "Postmaster," a "Big Farmer," and a "Courthouse Loafer," among others. A "Cotton Buyer" was unabashed in connecting the lynching to Black service in World War II: "If n—— rs [*sic*] think things have changed because of this war, the last war or by Christ any other war, then they got to be taught the same lesson over and over. It's entirely up to them if they want the killings to go on." Only one passerby was recorded to have refused Gellert's queries, a "4 Year Old Child," as Gellert noted it. The child told him, "I can't even say hello to you because my mamma said you never know who you're talking to."[23]

Gellert's political commitments and propensity for the dramatic arts found an effective outlet in the field of Black folksong. Additionally, his training in the newspaper business made him a comrade-in-arms. Indeed, more than a conventional folklorist or an antiquarian song collector, Gellert's means and motivations in Black music research were closely akin to those of crusading white political journalists of the era such as Conrad, or John L. Spivak. Like Gellert, Spivak was among the contributors to Nancy Cunard's *Negro: An Anthology* in 1934. Two years before, in his explosive *Georgia Nigger*, Spivak fictionalized what was in reality a scathing investigation of corruption and brutality issuing from criminal justice officials, politicians, and local planters in the Georgia penal system. The book included documentation and photographs of Black prisoners "hog-tied," on "the rack," and in stocks. It stirred controversy, and a federal indictment was set in motion against Spivak on behalf of the Georgia State Prison Commissioner. As a newspaper report from the time indicates, the author was charged with impersonating a federal officer "in order to photograph the torture of Negro prisoners and obtain official records from the prison commission."[24]

In his song collecting, Gellert sought to record and publicize African American sentiment where it had otherwise been suppressed. In his dealings with local whites in the South, he worked as an infiltrator, a subversive informer. He assumed the manners and dress of his white peers, as Conrad illustrated in the case of the Monroe lynching, and recorded the unvarnished views of sheriffs, prison authorities, politicians, planters, and citizens for a broader public of critical readers. Like Spivak, in his exposés on corruption and torture in southern prison farms and chain gangs, Gellert manipulated the trust of his white "neighbors." He broke the codes of the racial South and used the private confidences of white authority against that authority in a forward assault on southern brutality and hypocrisy. At the start of *Jim Crow America*, Earl Conrad identified himself for readers as a "white war correspondent" in the monumental "racial fight" ongoing in America. "I work in Harlem, but wear no battledress—just a reporter's everyday suit of clothes," he asserted. "Yet what I tell you about in this book is war correspondence just as surely as the dispatches that came from Tarawa and Normandy . . . and, whenever I can," he added, "I take pot shots at 'the enemy.'"[25]

In a similar fashion, Gellert's own "war" in Black music research was more than an aesthetic or an academic battle. Rather, it was a full-scale political campaign against racial stereotyping and Black victimization, white oppression and ruling class exploitation. Like Conrad, Gellert made a career out of taking "pot shots at the enemy." Wherever and whenever he could in his forays in the South, he sought to expose the treachery of white power and, in the converse spirit, to document the musical voice of African American resistance.

Gellert's racial passing could cut both ways, however. During World War II, the collector deployed his technical skills on behalf of Pepsi-Cola's audio letter public service campaign. Soldiers were offered the chance to record "The Voice of Your Man in Service" discs to be sent home, and Gellert had the know-how to operate the portable technology.[26] At the same time, he investigated disaffection among African American personnel. Gellert visited military bases in Texas, Mississippi, Florida, and Georgia. On one occasion on the trip, Gellert "grabbed a bus circling Keesler Field in Mississippi," he related in "Jim Crow in Khaki," a *New Masses* article from 1946. "I was already aboard and seated when I discovered it was the Negro bus. When the vehicle approached the exit, lights were turned on and an MP came aboard to check passes. When he saw me he laughed, leaned out of the window and called a local policeman." Amused that the fair-skinned stranger had, possibly, made an embarrassing error, he yelled for the other official to come "see what we got here on the n—— bus," as Gellert reported it. "The yokel swaggered over, took a long look at me. 'Hell,' he said. 'I'll be Goddamned if you ain't the whitest-lookin' n—— I ever saw. But you couldn't fool me. I can smell 'em every time.'" Later, as the bus moved on, the scene was cause for a great laugh among Gellert's fellow passengers, who according to his account knew better.[27] In his latter-day recollections, Gellert wrote that he had "been chased by sheriffs in the country and brass buttons and blue coats in towns, jeered at and cussed by respectable white folks everywhere" for his relations in Black America and causes in progressive justice.[28] Though his whiteness afforded a degree of freedom and protection surely not available to peers of color who might have sought to pursue similar avenues of activity in the South, Gellert's security was never entirely assured. His efforts in Black music collecting represented more than a romantic foray into traditional ballad hunting. Rather, they were a determined step into the political arena.

In his interviews, Gellert remembered that he was "caught between two fires" in the South. His fieldwork only became more difficult as historic racial tensions were aggravated between white and Black, North and South, in the political climate of the 1930s. "It was like being in an occupied country," he said, "especially later, after the Scottsboro business," which commenced in 1931 and really intensified in the middle years of the decade. On his trips, white authorities wanted to know what exactly Gellert was doing consorting in the African American community. "I had a bunch of records taken from me," he complained about one incident. "They made life miserable for me there." From the other side, too, relations were not always hospitable. Without a local contact or some advance word relating his activities, Black residents in the rural communities he frequented on his travels were hardly without their own suspicions. An exchange during one such trip outside of Tryon stuck in the collector's memories as emblematic. "You'd be out in the woods, fifty miles from a town to see one person, and you'd run into a little Negro ghetto," Gellert recalled. After quizzing the white visitor as to whether he was some kind of a traveling salesman or a debt collector, African American locals would finally wonder with exasperation, Gellert said, "What the Hell do you want?" His answer on this occasion—"Nothing. I just wanta sorta say hello"—did little to ease the situation. He received a response that was as humorous as it was final: "Well, you done said hello. Short visits make long friends. So, goodbye White Folks."[29]

A Radical Awakening

As Gellert refined his skills and sensitivity in Black song collecting, he also came to discover his own political values. Gellert came of age with the radical generation of the Great Depression. His own development toward a leftwing political consciousness maps, in suggestive ways, the rise of the Communist Party of the interwar period. Under the wing of his older brother Hugo, Gellert crossed paths with several key luminaries of the American Old Left in the years surrounding World War I. "I used to go to the old *Masses*" in Greenwich Village "and sweep out the floor," he remembered of these younger days before he went

South. "I had John Reed tap me on the head. . . . I remember Floyd Dell, he said, 'Geez, the girls are going to like you someday.' . . . Max Eastman, to me, Jesus, was a God. He was a great big beautiful guy. I was a kid." At the time, Gellert was still a teenager. He was not politicized, he stressed to his interviewer, and spent his days in such company "without knowing what the Hell it was all about."[30] There were significant progressive influences in Gellert's background, however. As we have seen, Hugo, the eldest sibling, had already established himself quite prominently among the community of radical artists, activists, and intellectuals in New York City. Hugo's turn to the left, like that of his youngest brother, Lawrence, was impacted by the tragic case of another sibling, Ernest Gellert. Situated in age between the two of them, Ernest was a self-proclaimed radical socialist and an early conscientious objector to World War I. In 1918, his story became a cause-célèbre within the Left when he died under mysterious circumstances in military confinement. Though the Army claimed it was suicide, family members were always convinced that Ernest was murdered by authorities for his political convictions. The loss left a deep scar.[31]

The passing of his brother may have predisposed Lawrence toward a suspicion of state authority. Still, by his own account, Gellert primarily internalized and isolated the incident as a young adult. He did not connect it with a critique of state militarism and capitalist political economy, or the socialist Left's denunciation of the Great War as an imperialist conflict. In a similar fashion, Gellert's racial views in these years were probably also somewhat unformed and amorphous. In his interviews, the collector liked to repeat two stories of his youthful encounters with race. As a child back in Budapest, he said, there was a "Negro doorman" at the local Hotel Europa. His mystique was such that Hungarians from miles around "would bring babies to touch him for good luck," Gellert recalled. The second story took place after the family had resettled in the United States. On this occasion, Gellert's mother sent him to answer a call at the front door. Upon seeing a man of color inquiring in their yet-to-be new language of English, she told Gellert, in German, to turn him away. Both were surprised, however, to hear the caller protest in perfect German himself. And, Gellert's mother exclaimed (this time in Hungarian), "This Black can talk German!" She was left further aghast, at this point, when the man responded again. "Madam," he informed her in Hungarian, "I just came from Budapest." Both experiences left a positive impression. But what is important to note is that Gellert cited these as his only personal experiences with people of color prior to his move to the South. Though he may have been kindly disposed toward "Negroes" or particularly undisturbed by racial barriers, as he always claimed,

Gellert's racial viewpoints were grounded on thin soil. Gellert, early on, did not link his self-defined cultural tolerance with any kind of political analysis or larger racial awareness. Indeed, his positions on race were likely as abstract as those of the Communist Party going into the 1920s.[32]

At the outset of his explorations in Black music, Gellert approached African American vernacular protest with little more than personal intrigue. "To me, it was fascinating," he said. Black singers were "putting something over on me and all the white people." As he became more sensitive to the brutal racial economy of the South, however, this personal fascination turned to political outrage and, ultimately, a radical political outlook. In "the thirties," politics "was in the air," Gellert asserted. "I used to come North [from Tryon] . . . just to get in on the May First parades. . . . We thought the revolution was around the corner." As he expressed it, Gellert's firsthand witness to Black racial oppression in the American South was a precipitating factor in his politicization generally. "What I saw in the South . . . anybody would have" rebelled against, he said, "unless he got infected with the virus," that is. He elaborated, "You get to be an extremist down there. Either you condone the whole business, and you say, 'The son-of-a-bitches deserve it.' Or, you go completely the other way, and you see the injustice of the whole thing . . . as human beings, you know, to be treated like that."[33]

Gellert's own political awakening to the systemic nature of Black oppression and exploitation under American capitalism provides a fitting analogue to the Communist Party's own rise to consciousness in the early decades of the twentieth century. From its inception through much of the 1920s, the CPUSA floundered with regard to its racial policy for the United States. There was a tireless and exceedingly accomplished tiny Black cadre within the Party ranks, Cyril Briggs and Richard B. Moore among the first in Harlem, for instance. But, their influence, and even their own viewpoints, in this era remained tentative. The question of "universal" class solidarity continually circumscribed the debate on the primacy of race in the matter of social revolution. Undue attention to issues of racism or sexism was seen as divisive, and it was denounced by Party ideologues as a strategy of capitalist subversion meant to fracture the international proletariat. In the 1920s, the Communist Party had to compete for support in the Black community against the rising enthusiasm for Garveyism or the more established leadership of the traditional Black intelligentsia. As historians have shown, it found little success in reaching the mass of African Americans on the street until–in Harlem, for an important example—it began to organize around everyday concerns such as police brutality, discriminatory city services, tenant evictions, and unemployment. Things started to change between 1928 and 1930.

In those formative years, the Communist International raised and subsequently adopted the Black Belt policy of African American self-determination in the South. The advent of the infamous Scottsboro trial and conviction in 1931 accelerated the momentum even further. With the arrival of the Communist-sponsored International Labor Defense (ILD) on the case, the "Scottsboro Boys" defense campaign became a national and international sensation. There was a marked shift in attitudes in the early 1930s; the Communist Party began to draw widespread name recognition and increased enthusiasm for its racial progressivism from African Americans for the first time in the United States. I take a closer look at some of this history below. But here, I merely try to raise it to draw out the provocative overlap of emergence between Communist Party policy on the matter of race and the rising political consciousness of Lawrence Gellert.[34]

As he came to stake out his views on race and social justice in the United States, Gellert, as we have seen, also started to formalize and expand his efforts in Black music collecting. He only really began to undertake a formal study of American folkloristics in this period. "It took me past the middle Thirties," he commented, "to realize exactly in what direction I was heading. . . . Then I started to read about folklore." Before that, "I wasn't interested."[35]

With his song collecting and political activism, Gellert charted a dual course among centers of labor and radical foment in the 1930s and 1940s. In the South, he worked in some measure with the ILD in Birmingham, and with noted Communist organizers Boris Israel and Nat Ross. As he also said, he was "driven out" of the Camp Hill area in Tallapoosa County, Alabama, for trying to collect "Negro Songs of Protest" in the midst of the violent organizing struggles of the Communist-sponsored Share Croppers Union (SCU). Still, readers should not get the wrong idea. Lawrence Gellert was never a Communist Party member or disciplined day-to-day organizer. Rather, he moved in and out of the Party's orbit in his lifetime. Late in his interviews, perhaps after a period of increased familiarity and comfort with his interviewer, Reuss, Gellert talked at some length about CP cultural policy and infrastructure. He recounted his dealings with the Party's American cultural commissar V. J. Jerome, as well as its Black vice presidential and presidential candidate James Ford in New York City. He was careful, however, to qualify his involvement with the institutional Left when it came to these topics. "I didn't organize very much," he said. "My political [involvement]—it was a romantic sort of a thing. So, when it came to the point where it got to be really dangerous, you know, I wasn't quite that that dedicated. The others were. These guys were fantastic." Though his political views may have been strident, Gellert's Party activism was inconsistent. Music-collecting and writing, more than direct organizing among workers, were the thrust of his attention. He was more comfortable in the "cultural front" than on the streets of Communist struggle.[36]

At some point before or in 1930, Gellert began sending song transcriptions and accompanying contextual commentary to Hugo, then among the contributing editors at *New Masses*. An original sheaf of notes bundled with string is housed among the Hugo Gellert Papers at the Smithsonian Institution's Archives of American Art. The pages consist of typed lyric transcriptions as well as handwritten annotation text and musical notation. Much of this content is clearly identifiable as the draft material that became Gellert's earliest publications in *New Masses* and in Cunard's *Negro: An Anthology*.[37] Hugo encouraged his brother to send more, and he passed the material on to the journal's famous editor, Mike Gold, the leading proponent of "proletarian literature" in the United States. Gold was a longtime family friend, and he was enthusiastic about these examples of an indigenous Black working-class culture of opposition. As Gellert tells it, Gold was in fact responsible for the name "Negro Songs of Protest" when Gellert's first article appeared in *New Masses* in 1930.[38] From this initial publication, interest spread within political and artistic circles of the era. The collector intensified his efforts, and the work "just grew," as he said later. For the next ten years and into the 1940s and 1950s, Gellert's name, song material, and writings surfaced frequently. "In the thirties, there wasn't a night when these songs weren't sung somewhere in the United States," he boasted to his interviewer. "They had a tremendous vogue."[39] Whatever the relative truth of such a claim, Gellert was a presence. The *New Masses* and its successor *Masses and Mainstream* regularly featured his submissions; the arts and entertainment columns of national newspapers followed his activities; his song archive served as the basis for Helen Tamiris's *How Long Brethren* in 1937, the longest-running stage success of the Federal Dance Theater in New York City; and, in the winter of that same year, he was awarded a Rockefeller Grant in support of his continued fieldwork in the South.[40]

From the start, however, the opportunities for a vociferous independent political collector of Black folksong were never assured. Gellert's endeavors were frequently plagued by false starts and acrimony. At the very beginning of his recognition in New York, for instance, Lawrence Gellert accepted a contract to pursue his work from none other than legendary composer, publisher, and bandleader W. C. Handy, the "Father of the Blues." As the arrangement specified, Gellert was to continue his song collecting in the South and forward this material to Handy at his Broadway publishing company, Handy Brothers Music Co. Inc. Gellert must have seen the deal as quite promising, and he came north for a meeting. Things then proceeded from a distance between the two. A letter from Handy to Gellert in Tryon, North Carolina, from 1932 shows considerable professional familiarity. In an effort toward easing the fieldwork, Handy had furnished Gellert with an electrified dictation machine. He opened his letter by saying that he was "very glad to hear" from the collector but regretted "to learn that the Dictaphone does not work." Apparently Gellert had already sent a field report of some sort by this time. Handy asked, "Will you kindly advise again the name of the person who wrote the music, since this is very important?" And he concluded with statements indicating that some sort of book deal was in the works. "There is no doubt about this collection being large enough for one volume," he wrote; "in fact, I think it is a little too much material if explanations, forewords, etc., are to included." In a subsequent letter from 1933, Handy again mentioned the "manuscript." He offered praise for Gellert's work and commented that "the book" would be "a wonderful contribution to American Negro music and just the type of work that many music lovers will appreciate. My lawyer, Mr. E. Abbe Niles has some very good connections with the book publishers and has offered some very valuable suggestions."[41]

However, the relationship turned sour and ultimately ended without fruition. As Gellert told one part of the story, the ersatz portable recording machine that Handy had provided never worked from the start. It was a "goddamn little busted down machine," he said, and the first time he plugged it in to record, it "blew out all the lights" at a chain gang encampment in the field in Marietta, Georgia. The incident led to trouble for the collector. "Holy Jesus," Gellert recalled, "the boss of the gang said, 'Look, you come in here to learn about chain gang songs—I ought to put you on the goddamn gang and you [can] start singing them firsthand.'" In addition to the faulty equipment he blamed on Handy, Gellert was unhappy with the terms of their business agreement. "Black slaves never had such a contract," he quipped. He claimed that he was "tied hand, foot, mouth . . . and, one of the stipulations was that I was going to return in good condition this terrible old Dictaphone machine." After the confrontation at the prison camp, though, Gellert could not get the equipment back from the prison official. "Handy used to write me regularly," he explained, asking, "Where's my machine? Where are my songs? I'm going to sue you." As Gellert summed up the entire experience rather sarcastically, W. C. Handy was "the first one [that] got in touch with me about the songs because he definitely knew that the folksongs would make great commercials."

The composer was "not at all politically conscious," Gellert said. Ultimately, he "was a snob, a real snob."[42]

In hindsight, the exchange with Handy is portentous. The collector's harsh attitudes toward such leading lights in his chosen field of endeavor may have kept him honest, as perhaps he thought about it, but they were hardly helpful in terms of professional advancement. In 1936, as Gellert entered the publishing world with *Negro Songs of Protest*, author Max Margulies in *Daily Worker* told of the material's difficult path to release. He wrote:

> When Gellert arrived in New York, he tried hard to bring the "Negro Songs of Protest" before the largest possible number of people. A nationally known radio station offered him a contract if he would incorporate the songs into a series of sketches a la "Amos 'n' Andy." The director of a famous choir offered to add them to his repertoire if Gellert would permit him to convert them into "spirituals." A prominent composer of Tin Pan Alley tried to interest Gellert in making foxtrots of the songs. A famous publishing house thought that Gellert's songs would interfere with its text book circulation in the South. A famous music publishing house suggested that the title "Protest" be omitted. A famous poet connected with a publishing house, thought: how wonderful! Perhaps if slavery had lasted a little longer, we would have witnessed even a greater flowering, etc.

Finally, Margulies ended, the American Music League had seen to publish "a complete volume of these songs" that was "faithfully rendered, as nearly exactly as sung into the recording machine." But if the book's "appearance" marked "a landmark in American culture," as he contended, it certainly did not seal the end of an ongoing debate in dominant culture and consciousness concerning African American music and struggle.[43]

CHAPTER THREE

"Songs about the White Man"

BLACK PROTEST AND WHITE DENIAL

This chapter, therefore, which in logic should be a survey of books and sources, becomes of sheer necessity an arraignment of American historians and an indictment of their ideals. . . . It simply shows that with sufficient general agreement and determination among the dominant classes, the truth of history may be utterly distorted and contradicted and changed to any convenient fairy tale that the masters of men wish.

—W. E. B. DU BOIS, "THE PROPAGANDA OF HISTORY," *BLACK RECONSTRUCTION IN AMERICA*, 1935

Lawrence Gellert was not alone when he began collecting African American vernacular song in the 1920s. Gellert entered a tradition of white inquiry that extended back to the liberal anti-slavery collectors of the nineteenth century and then into the twentieth century with conservative predecessor-peers John Lomax and Howard Odum. This line of white researchers—spanning in time and politics from left to right—shared a common orientation in what George Fredrickson termed "romantic racialism."[1] Whether they were advocates for racial change or defenders of the racial status quo, they heard something revealing in Black music and they set out to interpret this difference for readers in the dominant culture. In this, two modern social constructions came together. As Patrick Mullen details it in *The Man Who Adores the Negro: Race and American Folklore*, "blackness" and "folkness" originated in eighteenth-century Enlightenment thought, but gained a joint currency with nineteenth- and twentieth-century industrialization in the West. "The folk were originally conceived as rural, isolated, uneducated white Europeans with strong connections to an imagined romantic past that modern educated people had lost," explains Mullen. "But it did not take long before the folk and the racial primitive became associated as similarly inferior yet romantic classes."[2]

In the 1920s, the audience for projects in Black folklore greatly increased as the emergent African American genre of the blues took hold in its first commercial ascendance, Americans danced to a "Jazz Age," and Black arts and activism achieved mass visibility in the Harlem Renaissance, or "New Negro Renaissance," as Sterling Brown preferred the term. Additional parties entered into the field of white scholarship on Black music. Most notably, Texas-born Dorothy Scarborough published *On the Trail of Negro Folk Songs* in 1925, and North Carolina–born Newman Ivey White published *American Negro Folk Songs* in 1928. Both were English professors and represented the literary current of folklore studies in American academia. In this period, John Lomax, a pioneer in this literary school, maintained his status as a premier authority in American folksong, but he was largely preoccupied with making a living; he worked in banking until the economic collapse of the Great Depression and the untimely passing of his first wife launched him back into "ballad hunting" in the 1930s.[3] Meanwhile, Howard Odum, now paired with sociologist Guy B. Johnson, his assistant at the University of North Carolina at Chapel Hill, published two books, *The Negro and His Songs: A Study of Typical Negro Songs in the South* in 1925 and *Negro Workaday Songs* in 1926.

At this time, Lawrence Gellert had not yet published and was only just starting in Black folksong research. He would come to work the same terrain as this first-generation of folklore authority. Yet where they heard primitivism, plantation nostalgia, racial pathology, or—most tellingly, as Lomax put it—Black "self-pity," Gellert heard Black resistance. The white scholars of influence in the 1920s established a body of literature that reads today in dialogue with the broader historic tradition of "black misrepresentation." As a fellow white outsider in African American culture, Gellert was both of this tradition and resolutely opposed to it.

In *Negro Workaday Songs*, Odum and Johnson offered a provocative aside in their chapter "Construction Camps and Gangs." They acknowledged:

> There are a good many songs about the white man and the captain, excellent samples of which have already been cited in this chapter. Some were given in *The Negro and His Songs* and many more are to be found. Indeed, songs about the white man may well constitute a separate chapter in a later volume. A stock joke among the older Negroes used to be that of telling how the white man always brought "n—— out behind." The modern

> singer, albeit not always in a joking mood, still thrusts "at" his "captain" or "boss" or "white man."[4]

A year later, in an article titled "Double Meaning in the Popular Negro Blues," published in the *Journal of Abnormal and Social Psychology* no less, Guy Johnson made similar mention. Johnson highlighted the new "race record" sensation from out of African American vernacular culture, commenting that listeners "who are acquainted with the popular blues songs of to-day [*sic*] . . . have doubtless often had occasion to suspect that these songs are not always what they seem." Johnson devoted the article to "the presence of double meanings of a sex nature" in Black lyricism, but he issued an annotation to further the aside from Odum and Johnson above. In a footnote on other possible streams of double meaning, Johnson wrote, "There are, for example, many hidden references to the white man in the Negro's songs. This is an interesting field of research in which little has been done."[5]

Though both Odum and Johnson clearly registered the reality of "songs about the white man," neither pursued what they identified as this under-researched topic, nor did they contribute any "later volume" as they indicated they might in *Negro Workaday Songs*. This body of song conveyed lyrical "thrusts" against white captains, bosses, and others, Odum and Johnson related. "Songs about the white man," as they formulated it, then, were in fact songs of Black protest. Odum and Johnson, therefore, had the hint of African American expressive resistance, but they did not investigate further.

Sterling Brown characterized Black songs of protest as a "verboten tradition" only surfacing when there was some sense of "protection or guaranteed secrecy." In Brown's estimation, Lawrence Gellert was one of the rare outsiders to gain a hearing.[6] In his early fieldwork in the South, Gellert won trust by trading favors and through a renegade local reputation. But, we may surmise, it was not just that Gellert was "safe" that brought him to verboten songs; it was that Gellert was ready to hear. Gellert's peers in white research on Black folksong, conversely, appeared not ready. Their denial of Black expressive protest reflected disciplinary strictures, conservative political outlooks, and, underlying all that, a deeper racial denial of African American agency and equality. Unlike his contemporaries, Gellert had no credentials, training, or formal academic affiliations. He was not a southerner with a long southern memory, and he was not politicized at first in any formal way. As an iconoclast with "underdog" tendencies, however, Gellert professed a sympathetic curiosity that impelled him forward.

White Discovery and Black Misrepresentation

It is a peculiar fact, yet one not surprising, that the earliest figures afforded scholarly authority on secular Black folksong were white men, and southern white men at that. In 1911, Howard Odum published his influential "Folk-Song and Folk-Poetry as Found in the Secular Songs of the Southern Negroes" in the *Journal of American Folklore*. John Lomax followed with his own widely held classic, "Self-Pity in Negro Folk-Songs," in *The Nation* in 1917. Neither periodical could be characterized as narrowly "southern" or "conservative." These early pieces—devoted for the first time specifically to secular Black vernacular music as opposed to the spirituals of nineteenth-century renown—were received by a readership, North and South, as definitive statements by learned scholars. Ethnomusicologist David Evans writes that Odum and Lomax were alone in taking the next step from documentation to analysis. As Evans stipulates, though, this analysis issued from white observers at a distinct racial remove. The result, he writes, was "a stereotyped view of black secular society," highly partial subjective interpretation valued in a broad white interpretive community as highly astute objective expertise.[7]

One wonders, unfortunately, how it could have been otherwise in an era in which white distortion was a locus of oppression in American culture. In *Beyond Blackface: African Americans and the Creation of American Popular Culture, 1890–1930*, contributing essayist Stephanie Dunson offers useful terminology for this tradition of white distortion. Dunson calls it "black misrepresentation," and she historicizes it as more than just demeaning stagecraft owing originally to blackface minstrelsy in the 1830s and 1840s. Black misrepresentation, rather, was about a more enduring "erasure of black identity" and the wholesale eviction of "black people from their own skin." It reflected a larger "cultural system of privileging representation over reality" and the "systems of power and oppression that allow such privileging to become the standard."[8]

In an exchange reported in "Self-Pity in Negro Folk-Songs," Lomax is advised by "a white overseer of a river bottom plantation" on the dynamics of Black music. "A n——r sings about just two things," the man told the folklorist, "what he eats and his woman."[9] In their pioneering articles, Lomax, and Odum before him, transmuted core elements of the historic "black image in the white mind" into the modern field of music collecting and interpretation. Odum's and Lomax's scientific pretensions reflected the impulses of contemporary folklore and anthropology as they were beginning to professionalize in the United States at the turn of the century, but their scholarship read within a figurative tableau that had evolved in the decades before and after the Civil War. In *Love and Theft: Blackface*

Minstrelsy and the American Working Class, Eric Lott identifies "blackness" as a "construct and exhibition" of white racial subjectivity. He traces its emergence with the popular rise of blackface minstrelsy in the antebellum era. Cedric Robinson, in *Black Marxism: The Making of the Black Radical Tradition*, trains attention on historiography. In order to effectively disenfranchise and dispossess African Americans after the abolition of racial slavery, he argues, white Americans found renewed cause in the invention of the "Negro" in the period of backlash and retrenchment following Reconstruction. Part of a wider tradition of historical suppression, this program centered on the denial of a usable African past and the affirmation of innate Black primitivism and inferiority. At the turn of the century and into the trend of scholarship in the 1920s, these slanders were disseminated with the prestige of objective authority. They pervaded the highest reaches of academia and the lowest depths of popular culture. In law, norms, and custom, they reinforced an inequitable racial order in the United States that would only begin to come under assault again, finally, in the 1950s and 1960s.[10]

Aside from certain severely limited public roles, people of color in the late nineteenth and early twentieth centuries were denied opportunities to speak for themselves in the national arena. As they gained a hard-won footing in popular entertainment, for instance, Black Americans continually encountered a racist dominant culture that allowed for only strictly regulated forms of expressive and representational agency. Onstage and off, the costs for transgression could be grave. To step out from behind the "mask" was to risk not merely commercial failure or social censure but, as well, the extreme of white terror. According to records begun at the Tuskegee Institute in 1882, some 3,417 lynchings of Black Americans occurred in the United States between the 1880s and the mid-1940s. "Not until 1952 did a year pass without a single recorded lynching," writes author Philip Dray in *At the Hands of Persons Unknown: The Lynching of Black America*. Dray adds, moreover, that the consensus holds that these records can hardly be considered "anywhere close to comprehensive." Indeed, staff at the Equal Justice Initiative, a leading organization now documenting this history, have reassessed the total to over 4,000 between 1877 and 1950, and they continue to recover local atrocities once disappeared from record.[11]

White Denial and the Fiction of Self-Pity

In his essay from 1917, Lomax posed the question "And what does he sing about—the negro of the kitchen, the washtub, the field, and the levee—the millions little touched by education?" The initial part of his answer highlights a host of racial fictions dating back to nineteenth-century Black misrepresentation: "Among a variety of topics, most prominent are his woman, his preacher, his adventures with the law, his 'possum and greens and sweet potatoes, his mule, his 'forty-four gatlin' gun,' his boss, and, as a final solution for the trials and perplexities of this world, the golden streets of the New Jerusalem and the comforts and ease of Heaven." Lomax went on, however, to stress an additional point, one of more direct and lasting significance. He continued: "But with all this variety of topics, a prevailing mood is one of introspection—self-pity is the theme that, perhaps above all others, dominates his singing. Why this should be true is difficult to say. There surely exists no merrier-hearted race than the negro, especially in his natural home, the warm climate of the South. The negro's loud laugh may sometimes speak the empty mind, but at the same time it reveals a nature upon which trouble and want sit but lightly."[12] In this passage, Lomax introduced the central thesis that both informed his title and guided his musical analysis. The theme of "self-pity" above all else, he argued, characterized the essential logic and lyricism of Black vernacular music. Too often, I contend, the fiction of self-pity blinded white authorities to the fact of Black protest.[13]

As his choice of title for *The Nation* piece indicates, Lomax was determined in his association of Black folksong and Black self-pity. He heard Black melancholy throughout much of the core of African American vernacular music. It went back as far as the spirituals, he reported, and continued to pervade the seculars of more recent origin too, as he illustrated with examples such as the following:

> Well, my mamma sick an' my papa dead, papa dead,
> Well, my mamma sick an' my papa dead, papa dead,
> An' I ain't got nobody to pity po' me, po' me.
>
> I sometimes stops an' wonder how strange it seem to be
> Dat I don't bodder nobody, an' yet dey always talkin' 'bout po' me;
> Po' me, po' me, always talkin' 'bout po' me.[14]

In the course of his study, Lomax cast Black self-pity as a racial problem, but one that reflected back in a single direction only. Lomax theorized:

> It is credible, at least, that the negro's self-pity is based on his feeling of race inferiority—a feeling of which he may well be only sub-consciously aware. The race problem is one which is insistently present. Neighbors

> with the white man, living side by side, coming into daily contact, made equal by law while yet unequal in fact, differing widely in inheritance and instinct—the conditions of life must appear to the negro totally unfair. And it seems further credible that he has come to lump the troubles for which he himself is largely to blame along with the inevitable hardships of his situation until he has grown to regard himself as the victim of hard luck, generally abused by everybody; and, at least in many instances, he seems not averse to nursing his gloom a little.

As the collector ventured, Black self-pity could derive from a variety of sources, including "hard times," the "faithlessness of a sweetheart," or "death and bereavement." Still, it was far from inevitable. The "thrift and energy of many members of his race," Lomax wrote for instance, showed economic insecurity "to be unnecessary" for the Negro. Similarly, the infidelity of a "sweetheart" was only fitting, he admonished, when lovers were "too faithless" themselves "to deserve a better fate." Finally, mortality was the "common fate of all," he remarked, and certainly, therefore, no cause for wanton despair in a reasoned mind. For Lomax, it seemed, the burden of Black troubles was largely unwarranted. Rather more engendered by nature than circumstance alone, "Negro" self-pity developed from out of the bitter divide between Black inadequacy and white achievement. This pervasive sense of "race inferiority"—whether recognized consciously or not, as he posited—clouded the whole of African American folksong.[15]

Black melancholy, then, appeared almost endemic in the account of John Lomax. It trapped African Americans in a cycle of defeatism and self-destruction that impeded race advancement and equality. Howard Odum hinted at a similar judgment in his own Black folksong research. In his article from 1911, he lamented a brief set of lyrics on the issue of color:

> I wouldn't have yellow gal,
> Tell you de reason why:
> Her neck so long, 'fraid she never die.
>
> I wouldn't have a black gal,
> Tell you de reason why:
> Her hair so kinky, she break every comb I buy.[16]

As Odum expressed it, "The negro does not mind that his comment" in such lyricism "may be injurious to personal feelings or race opinion." In this conclusion, without questioning the ultimate source of such expression or the meaning and tone of their performance in the hearing of a white listener, the collector displaced the onus of racism from white to Black, as a problem from within rather than outside of the African American community. Lomax concurred in this shared judgment. The issue of internalized prejudice, he wrote in "Self-Pity in Negro Folk-Songs," was a "deeply tragic note" of Black folk culture. "Over and over, from many angles," he concluded, "the negro expresses his feeling of a race inferiority, and sings of what seems to be to his mind his badge of shame—his color."[17]

Lomax and Odum depicted African American life and culture in terms of blight and pathology in their formative articles. With their insistence on the primacy of racial self-pity, neither authority could see Black protest in their early folk-song research because neither could, in the first sense even, see Black agency and equality in the past or present of human civilization. At base, their work rehearsed a long tradition of white scholarly distortion. At heart, it reflected a deep investment of white racial denial. In fact, lyrics of Black derision, dissatisfaction, and resistance were embedded right from the start in this foundational scholarship.

In the opening pages of "Folk-Song and Folk-Poetry" in 1911—indeed, at the point of only the sixth song in his catalogue of 115 items in the article—Odum registered the same passing awareness of an expressive tradition of African American racial commentary that he and Guy Johnson repeated in *Negro Workaday Songs* fifteen years later. "There are apparently a good many sayings current among the negroes about the whites," Odum informed his readers. "Few of these, however, are heard by any save the negroes themselves." The author continued that the same held true in the musical field. The "songs of this nature," he explained, "would scarcely be sung where the whites could hear them." Evidently, Odum was able to hear at least two, however. In his study, the collector presented a pair of items from out of this circumspect Black oral tradition.[18]

Odum began with the shorter of the lyric transcriptions, "When He Gits Old—Old An' Gray." The song was "a reply," he wrote, "to the accusation that the negroes are nothing more than apes or monkeys." As he was told, it probably "originated with a bright negro's retort behind the back of a white" who had previously used this kind of fraught racial language. The lines read:

> When he gits old, old and gray,
> When he gits old, old and gray,
> Then white folks looks like monkeys,
> When dey gits old, old an' gray.

Odum related that "the song struck a responsive note as well as appealed to the negro" as a fitting response for such an instance. "In fact," he added with a wink, "it must be admitted to be a good rejoinder." But there was a more serious side to which the folklorist alluded in his closing remarks. Even in the case of what appeared a rather humorous jibe, Odum stated that the "subtle and sulky manner in which it is sung is a powerful comment on the negro's growing sense of race feeling. Whether there are other verses to this comment on the aged whites has not been ascertained."[19]

The second song in Odum's discussion was more extensive, and certainly more direct in its import. The author stated that "Ain't It Hard To Be A N——r" was "composed of two popular rhymes about the negro and the white man, together with other verses composed to make an agreeable song and to make suitable rhymes and combinations." He printed the following transcription:

Ain't it hard, ain't it hard,
Ain't it hard to be a n——r, n——r, n——r?
Ain't it hard, ain't it hard,
For you can't git yo' money when it's due.

Well, it make no difference,
How you make out yo' time;
White man sho' bring a
N——r out behin'.

N——r an' white man
Playin' seven-ups;
N——r win de money–
Skeered to pick 'em up.

If a n——r git 'rested,
An' can't pay his fine,
They sho' send him out
To the county gang.

A n——r went to a white man,
An' asked him for work;
White man told n——,
"Yes, git out o' yo' shirt."

N——r got out o' his shirt
An' went to work;
When pay-day come;
White man say he ain't work 'nuf.

If you work all the week,
An' work all the time,
White man sho' to bring
N——r out behin'.

With its opening refrain and succeeding verses, this song illustrates in stark detail some of the expressive currents of Black vernacular protest. Without humor or hyperbole, mask or mediation, the lyrics identify the causes and conditions of Black oppression. It is not "race inferiority," as Odum and Lomax might have speculated for instance, that "bring[s] a n——r out behin'" in the opinion of this singer. Rather, it is a rigged social and economic system, backed always with the threat of racial terror.[20]

In his explanatory comments to the title, Odum observed that "Ain't It Hard To Be A N——r" was "now well known" in the field of folklore, and indeed, the song appears in multiple established collections from over the years.[21] The general sentiment "Ain't it Hard?" as well, he wrote, was "one that is common in negro life and song." One might assume that such remarks showed cause for further inquiry into the well of oral tradition "current among the negroes about the whites," but Odum pursued no such ends. The adjoining analysis that accompanied "Ain't It Hard To Be A N——r" in the 1911 article evaded the issue. In his examination of the song, the folklorist neglected content in favor of technique. "The above song illustrates the method of making song out of rhymes, fragments, sayings, and improvised rhymes," he wrote. As the statement reflects, Odum approached his subject as a study in Black folk lyricism, identifying the varied sources of individual stanzas and concluding that "this mixed assortment of verses and sentiments made a most attractive song when sung to a common tune." Even the line "white man sho' bring n——r out behin'"—which he reported "incorporates the exact sentiment of an old ex-slave" who asserted the continuity of white oppression "in slavery and out of slavery"—occasioned no further commentary. On the whole, the impression left by the analysis is one of Black whimsy over Black intent. "The effort to make a complete song is easily felt as one reads the words," Odum concluded. "The tune may be one that the singer happens to think of; it matters little which he chooses." This musical dismissal rings in a broader harmony with the author's underlying defamation of African American character and consciousness throughout the article.[22]

If Odum turned his examination of "Ain't It Hard" into a purely technical exercise, he minimized "When He Gits Old" in a different way. As he left the song, the folklorist wondered about the reach of such racial satire in underground Black culture when he mentioned "a growing sense of race feeling." Still, he contained any anxiety that such a parting note may have sparked within the frame of his overall assessment. "When He Gits Old—Old An' Gray" is featured very briefly in his study; it is only a fragment compared against his sizable catalogue of song texts. Additionally, as Odum suggested with his friendly acknowledgment of it as a "good rejoinder," it is treated as rather a harmless ribbing than meaningful protest. In the final analysis, the collector trivialized the significance of this telling lyrical glimpse. He intimated that it extended only so far as a racial statement by narrowing its target specifically to "aged whites." Additionally, he made clear that fieldwork had yet to uncover any further verses on the topic or other similar expressions. In the end, Odum indicated, this song was aimed narrowly, toward older white people only, not at racial stereotyping or the absurdities of anti-Black racism.[23]

With his stated thesis on Black self-pity, John Lomax echoed this obliviousness. Though he did not provide titles in his article, Lomax closed his essay with the same song, "Ain't It Hard To Be A N——r," that appeared in Odum's study. His transcription was basically identical, though he did print an additional stanza:

> White folks go to college,
> N——s to de fiel';
> White folks learn to read an' write,
> N——s learn to steal.
> Well, it make no diff'ence how you make out yo' time,
> White man sho' to bring an n——r out behin'.

As Lomax heard it, such lyrics documented an encompassing "phase of the negro's mind." Certainly, not all Black folksongs were "songs of gloom," he elaborated, but many were. Simply, he summed up, "The hard fact remains that race differences cannot be blinked; and it is the present, not the mystic future, with which the individual negro is concerned each day."[24]

In several other song samples in this section, Lomax considered this bitter present. He heard "resentment against social distinctions" and even "a threat to reverse conditions," for instance, in a set of lyrics about racial segregation:

Well, I'm goin' to buy me a little railroad of my own,
Ain't goin' to let nobody ride but de chocolate to de bone.
Well, I'm goin' to buy me a hotel of my own,
Ain't goin' to let nobody eat but de chocolate to de bone.
She's long an' tall an' chocolate to de bone,
She make you a married man, den leave yo' home.

Then again, he heard the more "cheerful side" of the coin in another sample:

N——s gettin' mo' like white fo'ks,
Mo' like white fo'ks eve'y day.
N——s learnin' Greek an' Latin,
N——s wearin' silk an' satin,
N——s gettin' mo' like white fo'ks eve'y day.

But finally, the "advantages, real or fancied, taken by the dominant race" resurfaced as an inescapable theme:

White folks always a-braggin', Lawd, Lawd, Lawd,
How a n——r ain't nothin' but a waggin, Lawd, Lawd, Lawd.
Ought for ought an' figger for figger,
All for white man an' nothin' for n——.
N——r an' white man playin' seben-up, O my hon,
N——r win de money but 'fraid to pick it up, O my hon.[25]

For the collector, racial protest was not at issue in these song texts. Rather, "race inferiority" and the consequent collective self-pity that followed were more the spirit and substance of meaning. While Lomax showed some recognition of Black resentment and even "threat" in the first example above, the potency of the lines in this transcription was softened by its overall context of presentation in the article. For one thing, the notion of an inverted racial order in the United States appears somewhat grandiose in the racialized perspective of his writing; it likely struck his intended readership as humorous fancy more than anything else. By the same token, the assertive initial lines in this first sample were leavened by the unrelated closing quip about a lover "long an' tall an' chocolate to de bone."

In the two other examples, possible openings in interpretation were effectively closed. The "cheerful" lyrics about "N——s getting' mo' like white fo'ks eve'y day" might not have appeared so sanguine in their culture of origin as they did in Lomax's interpretive framing in the article. Issuing from within the African American community, these lines could have instead signaled satire with respect to white bourgeois pretension, or derision with respect to Black middle-class striving, or both, with the additional threat of an impending racial comeuppance. It is difficult to take Lomax on faith as a reliable mediator in this regard. Similarly, the excerpt with the line "White fo'ks always a-braggin'" seems to also suggest an alternative reading. To another listener, these lyrics might have been received as a frustrated comment on white hypocrisy and economic injustice rather than Black self-pity. Lomax's text here includes a fragment that both he and Odum cite in their transcriptions of "Ain't It Hard." Like that item, the song can be seen to open outward as opposed to inward in its racial import. By juxtaposing white "bragging" with Black impoverishment, it ties African American sorrow to white exploitation as opposed to Black inadequacy. In so doing, it offers an enlightened critique of the race problem in these collectors' era, and hints at the content and currents of a vernacular culture of resistance on the other side of the color line.

The "present, not the mystic future" may indeed have been the primary concern of "the individual negro," as Lomax put it, in the difficult period after the fall of Reconstruction and the consolidation of Jim Crow at the turn of the century. But folklorists Lomax and Odum seemed hard-pressed in their writings to locate their African American subjects in anything but a distant, exotic, or otherwise other-worldly plane. Their judgments on Black folk people and culture read rife with the gaps and contradictions of white denial. Despite Lomax's insistence on race issues as the contemporary basis of Black self-pity, for instance, there were no possibilities for present solutions included among his featured song evidence. Rather, the modern race question came down to the old formula of earthly suffering and deferred spiritual delivery. "Writers about negro spirituals have long surmised that the prevalence of heaven as a topic of his songs is the outgrowth of his state of slavery," the author explained. "Certain it is that the Biblical imagery relating to heaven has a strong hold on the negro mind. The very problem of social equality he expects to see solved hereafter." In the analysis of John Lomax, it was religious faith, not unceasing hard work and everyday struggle, that ultimately characterized the whole of Black action in response to racial inequality. The "expectation of heaven," he concluded, "may be said to be the negro's antidote for the self-pity he feels for his present state."[26]

In his rich intellectual history of folklore studies in *Romancing the Folk*,

Benjamin Filene writes that Howard Odum's "encounter with African American music did not open him up to black society." Rather, Odum seemed to take a definite step forward in the documentation and promotion of Black vernacular music as "an important part of America's heritage," while at the same time keeping a foot firmly in the past in his presumption of "black singers as exotic beings on the margins of society."[27] Indeed, Odum's own period language is clear. "Little need be said concerning social and political equality," he opined in *Social and Mental Traits of the Negro* in 1910. "There is no absolute race equality in any sense of the word. Those who would assist the Negro should remember this and not exact too much of him, either in demanding his results or offering him the complete ideal of the whites."[28]

Historian Jerrold Hirsch has similarly dissected John Lomax's racial footing. Hirsch identifies Lomax as a conservative romantic nationalist who synthesized the consciousness of Old South nostalgists and Anglo ballad traditionalists. But Lomax also bucked the status quo. In his classic work in the early 1900s (*Cowboy Songs and Other Frontier Ballads* in 1910, and the "Self-Pity" article in 1917, most notably), the folklorist revised the musical definition of the "ballad" to include cowboy songs and, eventually, Black seculars. In short, Lomax established that ballads need not be as old as England, nor as white. Lomax did not intend a full assault on the prevailing scholarly consensus. He was merely trying to extend the grounds of inclusion for ballad research in the modern United States. If Anglo ballads were survivals from a long-gone Elizabethan ancestry, then the cowboy songs of the American Southwest were a proud contemporary offshoot. As Lomax saw it, they were indigenous manifestations of Anglo-Saxon "virtue" that had been transplanted in the frontier context into an ideal rugged "Americanism."[29]

Lomax's musical passions registered an underlying conservative nationalism. In effect, Lomax's idealized nation was a democratic white republic, a "Herrenvolk democracy" of fraternal intraracial class unity. George Fredrickson attributes the term to Pierre L. van den Berghe. "Herrenvolk democracies," the sociologist proposed in 1967, are "regimes like those of the United States or South Africa that are democratic for the master race but tyrannical for the subordinate groups."[30] Lomax saw the cowboy songs of the rural West as the essence of American spirit, and he sought to redeem the nation from its wayward industrial course through the promotion of this folk heritage.[31]

Black Southerners, in the accounting of Odum and Lomax, were naturally expressive, and Black vernacular music was organic and unself-conscious. If we recall "romantic racialism" in its original liberal political orientation as a "doctrine which acknowledged permanent racial differences but rejected the notion of a clearly defined racial hierarchy," then we can see the concept inverted in the case of Odum and Lomax. Each articulated a conservative variant of romantic racialism that diverged from its one-time liberal impetus. In line with the racialist thinking that emerged in the nineteenth century, the collectors subscribed to an ideology of inherent biological difference that posited natural Black simplicity and emotionality against natural white rationality and self-discipline. Whereas romantic racialism had once been the province of a northern liberal intelligentsia advocating for the end of racial slavery, in the hands Odum and Lomax, it was the expression of Jim Crow Southerners representing a historic status quo of white supremacy. Odum and Lomax celebrated Blacks for a unique endowment of creative ability, and they expanded American folklore studies in the early 1900s from white to Black, the sacred to the secular. But they were unwilling to ascribe any larger virtue to their work with respect to Black racial equality.[32]

These two collectors of genteel academic orientation were disposed against anti-Black violence in the maintenance of white supremacy, but they were supremacists nonetheless. They sought to preserve segregation in the South by correcting for its most extreme permutations. The "goal," as Jerrold Hirsch summarizes, was to "eliminate the most glaring injustices" of the system, "not to challenge segregation itself."[33] The ideology behind this music research was "characterized by the belief that Blacks have a place in the South—a defined and subordinate place befitting an inferior race—and are fine as long as they know and stay in their place."[34]

The great scholar-activist W. E. B. Du Bois was a relative peer in the generation of Odum and Lomax. These three individuals shared a basic inheritance coming of age in the late nineteenth century after the collapse of Reconstruction and in the rise of Jim Crow. Their very different experiences on opposite sides of the color line informed their divergent paths in the field of Black culture and history. In the closing chapter of his towering *Black Reconstruction in America* from 1935, Du Bois issued a stark indictment of "the propaganda of history" that characterized dominant studies of the Civil War and Reconstruction in the United States in his time. "One fact and one alone explains the attitude of most recent writers," he charged, "they cannot conceive Negroes as men; in their minds the word 'Negro' connotes 'inferiority' and 'stupidity' lightened only by unreasoning gayety and humor."[35]

For writers Odum and Lomax, and their peers and readers, Black misrepresentation was common sense and learned discourse. Odum and Lomax conveyed an ethos of anti-modern romanticism that overlapped with a racialized southern conservatism. This ethos assigned key symbolic value to an idealized rural Black folk. At stake was an imaginary past, a sentimental planter pastoral where the human and the natural world existed in harmony and superior white masters reigned over contented Black inferiors. On the possibility of Black agency and protest, interpretation was foreclosed by the oppressive logic of romantic racialism.[36]

New Negro and Old Fictions

In "The Concept of the New Negro and the Realities of Black Culture," a valuable essay from 1971 that prefigured portions of his major study, *Black Culture and Black Consciousness*, historian Lawrence Levine identified a problematic historiographic convention. The concept of Black resistance as *new* in the latter twentieth century, he wrote, was "predicated on the assumption that Negroes before World War II had internalized the white man's image of themselves so that they believed that they were somehow inferior and deserving of their fate and consequently did not protest in any effective way." Levine devoted a good part of his career to correcting that record. Black resistance, "old" and "new," he showed, was ongoing in North American history. Black vernacular music, he argued, was an essential source for apprehending this reality. "Certainly, if nothing else," he pressed, "black song makes it difficult to believe that Negroes internalized their situation so completely, accepted the values of the larger society so totally, or manifested so pervasive an apathy as we have been led to believe."[37]

Levine's first example of what he called the "selective myopia" of the canon of early white representation was John Lomax's mishandling of "Ain't It Hard" from the 1917 article. In multiple instances, Lomax and peers misinterpreted satire as light-hearted humor, allegory as nonsense, protest as "self-pity." Resistance was trivialized as personal resentment, and "double meaning" was sensationalized and effectively neutralized for any larger political resonance. It was "doubtless easier," explained Levine on this latter issue, for early white authorities "to admit the existence of double meaning" in only "sexual relations, since that merely confirmed their image of the low moral state of the Negro." Lomax and Odum were joined by other white scholars in the 1920s in a continuing myopia that reaffirmed the old fictions of the Negro at precisely the time when white distortions were coming under scrutiny by leaders in the New Negro Renaissance. Demands for Black self-determination and self-representation were pressing in the decade after World War I. Yet the old racialism held fast in some quarters.[38]

A trend of book-length studies by white scholars on African American folksong emerged for the first time in the United States in the 1920s. There had been scattered published collections and analyses previously, *Slave Songs of the United States* in 1867 and Henry Edward Krehbiel's *Afro-American Folksongs: A Study in Racial and National Music* in 1914, for instance. Unlike the outpouring of monographs in the 1920s, however, which encompassed nineteenth-century spirituals to twentieth-century seculars (work songs and the blues), these prior studies prioritized "slave songs" of religious origin over other realms of Black folksong. As for protest, *Slave Songs* did, of course, include anti-slavery lyrics characteristic of its abolitionist impetus. But the racialism that elevated "civilized" spirituals as against "barbaric" shouts, nonetheless, meant that a "selective myopia" of an alternate sort conditioned what may and may not have been included.

Krehbiel's *Afro-American Folksongs*, as well, reflected liberal politics and racialist blind spots. Based in New York, Krehbiel was a leading American musicologist and critic. Citing W. E. B. Du Bois and Booker T. Washington, pulling no punches when it came to describing the brutalities of slavery, and making a case in the book for the value of African Americans as privileged contributors to a US national culture, Krehbiel clearly self-identified as a friend to the Black community. Still, some of the old racialism prevailed as the author privileged sacred music above secular songs and rehearsed the familiar trope of Black "native musical capacity." Incredibly, Krehbiel also issued a premise that all that need be said had already been said as regards Black folk lyricism. His interest was music, not words, and though this was an innovative turn for the time, one can hardly agree that in 1914, in the long nadir of Jim Crow segregation and enforced silence, "practically the entire sum of what it is essential to know about the social, literary and psychological side of the folksongs of the American negroes" had been covered in terms of lyric collection and analysis. Krehbiel did devote a chapter to traditions of Black satirical "taunt songs" tracing from African ancestry to slavery in the West, and his point stressed the function of words as a "weapon." But his song evidence was oriented around lyrics of in-group back-biting rather than subversive social commentary. Notably, on the issue of protest elsewhere in the book, Krehbiel made a claim echoed similarly by other white authorities over the decades. He wrote, "There are surprisingly few references to the servitude of the blacks in their folksongs which can be traced to ante-bellum [*sic*] days." A half-century later, leading scholars in the popular blues crossover period of the 1960s were still making the same claim, this time about the "surprising" lack of blues songs about racism in the performances they documented in fieldwork or in the commercial record.[39]

Krehbiel's book remained a standard text for years, but in the 1920s white curiosity about Black music intensified and a host of new studies arrived. Odum and Johnson's *The Negro and His Songs: A Study of Typical Negro Songs in the South* and Dorothy Scarborough's *On the Trail of Negro Folk-Songs* both appeared in 1925. Scarborough cited Odum's original 1911 article multiple times in her book, and the following year, in *Negro Workaday Songs*, Odum and Johnson cited Scarborough's *On the Trail* as "one of the most important contributions yet made" in their selected bibliography. Newman White referenced all of this literature in his study from 1928.[40]

Each of these authors identified their southern roots as a key to their Black expertise. Of the books in this class, Scarborough's was the least "academic" in pretention, the most personalized and sentimental in tone. Scholar Marybeth Hamilton writes that Scarborough may have been a young, single professional permanently relocated to New York City as a professor at Columbia University by the 1920s, but that she "built a career" in the persona of "a Southern lady." Ironically, Scarborough found it necessary to escape the gender chauvinism of her southern home to make her way as a career woman. Yet she romanticized the racial chauvinism attendant to the "old plantation of days before the war."[41] Scarborough came from a family of Confederates and slave owners, and she professed a connection to Black vernacular music that extended from childhood. "I have had this active interest as a collector for about ten years, but in reality I suppose I began in my cradle," she explained in *On the Trail.* As most of her years had "been spent in the South," Scarborough felt that she had been afforded ample "opportunity to know colored people as a race and as individuals." She was confident, therefore, in her abilities to discover and document Black folk music. Indeed, her own past was "all mixed up with Negro songs," she commented. "How many memories of my childhood and youth," she exclaimed, "are associated with loved black faces!"[42]

Scarborough's Black folksong collecting was a means of transport by which she could imagine herself out of modern-day New York into a "simpler" landscape of white gentility and non-threatening "old-time" Negroes. The likelihood of her hearing Black folk protest in this cultural project appears slim. Scarborough did, indeed, include some items of interest, but they were not taken seriously as expressions of resistance in her overall treatment. "'Twas On De Bluff," "Old Bee Make De Honeycomb," "The Monkey And The Baboon," and "Stand, Boys, Stand (Ruckus Bound To Happen)" and a scattering of recognizable lines in her "Work-Songs" chapter especially are misread or minimized in the book.[43] Two representative cases, "Ain't It Hard To Be A N——r?" and "Run, N——, Run," are instructive.

"Ain't It Hard" we have already encountered from Odum and Lomax, and it is transcribed in Scarborough identically and with a credit to Odum's 1911 article. Like these previous auditors, Scarborough disarms the song's statement of racial injustice. In her annotation, she muses, "Freedom as well as slavery has its perplexities and complications, and work has not become rosy for the Negro now, simply because he is paid wages instead of clothes and keep. He works for somebody else much as he did in earlier times, if his folk-songs are to be believed." The "if" reflects an odd degree of equivocation, and of course enslaved people may have been surprised to hear that they were "paid" commensurately for a lifetime of labor with "clothes and keep." Beyond all this, however, the song is immediately preceded by "Way Down in Old Virginia," about a slave who "couldn't stay away" from a kind master and mistress on the old plantation. Certainly, in the judgment of Scarborough, slavery had its upside.[44]

Like "Ain't It Hard," the song "Run, N——, Run" is common fare in multiple folklore collections, from *Slave Songs of the United States* in 1867 to White's *American Negro Folk-Songs* in 1928.[45] In *On the Trail*, Scarborough presents the following standard verses:

Run, n—— run; de patter-roller catch you;
Run, n——, run, it's almost day.
Run, n——, run, de patter-roller catch you;
Run, n——, run, and try to get away.

Dis n—— run, he run his best,
Stuck his head in a hornet's nest,
Jumped de fence and run fru de paster;
White man run, but n—— run faster.

Run, n——, run,
The patter-roller'll catch you;
Run, n——, run,
It's almost day.

Dat n—— run,
Dat n—— flew,
Dat n—— lost
His Sunday shoe.

Run, n——, run,
The patter-roller'll catch you;
Run, n——, run,
And try to get away.

Dat n—— run,
Dat n—— flew,
Dat n—— tore
His shirt in two.[46]

Sterling Brown commented how the lyrics of "Run, N——, Run" can "flash us back" to the brutal "social reality" of "the dread patrollers" that policed runaways, and Lawrence Levine wrote of how the song addressed "the white patrols and the whippings that continually harassed" enslaved people and "affected their lives profoundly." Scarborough, by comparison, includes the lyrics, but not the sympathies. This desperate song about freedom from bondage is framed in Scarborough's handling as a lively and entertaining tune. Scarborough relates that she remembers her mother singing the item, "one of the oldest of the plantation songs," and she informers her readers, "The darkies sang many amusing songs about the patrols and their experiences in eluding them."[47]

Rather than being about life and death, "Run, N——, Run," for Scarborough, seems about nothing so much as her own racial privilege, delusion, and nostalgia. As Marybeth Hamilton shows, Dorothy Scarborough entered into Black folksong collecting as a romantic means by which to cast herself back into a lost South, an imaginary trans-racial idyll where white and Black knew their places. The collector's anti-modern romanticism, therefore, was inseparable from her conservative romantic racialism.[48]

Scarborough was not going to hear African American protest because her entire southern folk tableau was one of the "masquerade"—of love professed for "masters," "mistresses," and "mammies," of happy and contented "darkies," of a simple time of harmony and order. In her chapter on lullabies, she waxes about African American nursemaids, "What other nation of mothers has ever patiently and with a beautiful sacrifice put alien children ahead of its own—in outward devotion if not in actual fact?"; and, in her chapter "Work-Songs," she remarks on the "easy philosophy" of Black folk, their "tendency" to "loaf on the job when the boss is not by" and their lighter load in life with less worry about "income and inheritance taxes." The old fictions of the "Negro" and the "master" are as glaring to a reader of Scarborough's book today as is the cluelessness of her benign intent. The folklorist wrote, "If we would know the Negro, let us study his songs." But, in a final case of irony, Scarborough did not even prioritize African Americans in her base of informants. Primarily, her sources were "elderly white Southerners" who remembered for her the songs of old. "Run, N——, Run" is a striking example. Scarborough collected the song from "Dr. John A. Wyeth, of New York, who was a Southerner and knew the South of antebellum days." The doctor was a seventy-six-year-old Confederate veteran of the Civil War. On the occasion of Scarborough's visit, Wyeth took out a long-abandoned banjo and recounted learning songs from an "old darky," Uncle Billy, "who taught them to his little master." Wyeth played Scarborough "Run, N——, Run," among other songs, and grew increasingly rhapsodic about the days gone by. Eventually, he could not help jumping to his feet and dancing "some of the old breakdowns."[49]

We have looked to some degree already at the interpretive openings and closings of Howard Odum and Guy Johnson when it comes to Black songs of social critique and commentary. Odum and Johnson's folklore studies include significant numbers of lyrics of protest. On occasion, the collectors referenced these musical glimpses under the rubric "songs about the white man." By the mid-1920s, the folklorists were colleagues at the University of North Carolina at Chapel Hill. Odum had already charted considerable experience in the field of Black folksong research; Johnson was his research assistant and young co-author. Both, we might presume, were taking note of the emerging New Negro movement of the era.

In *Negro Workaday Songs* from 1926, the pair cite Harlem Renaissance luminaries Alain Locke and James Weldon Johnson in their opening pages. Author Lynn Moss Sanders in *Howard Odum's Folklore Odyssey* contends that Odum was in the process of changing his racial politics by this time through his developing work in Black folksong discovery. To an extent, a difference is clear. Odum and Johnson's second publication is more modest in tone, less assuming and judgmental, than their previous effort, *The Negro and His Songs*. At the same time, Odum biographer Wayne Brazil suggests an underlying continuity of conservativism when it came to segregation. Even by the time of *Negro Workaday Songs*, as Brazil sums up, "Odum remained unconvinced that the races had equal potential for development and, therefore, believed that there was a great need to protect the vitality of the majority group by retaining substantial separation."[50]

One of Odum and Johnson's staunchest critics in the 1920s, if only privately, was the singular Zora Neale Hurston. A trained anthropologist and folklorist, Hurston regarded the eminent pair as naïve, flawed, and presumptuous in their data and findings on rural Black folk music and culture. In a letter to her mentor Franz Boas at Columbia University, she wrote, "I have been following the works of Odum and Johnson closely and find that they could hardly be less exact. They have made six or seven songs out of one song and made one song out of six or seven. . . . Some of it would be funny," she ended, "if they were not serious scientists! Or are they?" To Alain Locke, she filed more objections: "They evidently know nothing of how folk-songs grow." And to Langston Hughes she confided, "It makes me sick to see how these cheap white folks are grabbing our stuff and ruining it. I am almost sick—my one consolation being that they never do it right and so there is still a chance for us."[51]

In *Mules and Men,* Hurston had her opportunity. Published in 1935, the book is lauded as a major collection of southern African American folklore, one in which Hurston, an African American southerner herself, melded the personal and professional in a productive insider-outsider mediation. At the outset, Hurston put on public record the kind of sentiment she had been expressing privately to her correspondents since the 1920s. She warned: "Folklore is not as easy to collect as it sounds. The best source is where there are the least outside influences and these people, being usually under-privileged, are the shyest. . . . And the Negro, in spite of his open-faced laughter, his seeming acquiescence, is particularly evasive. . . . The Negro offers a feather-bed resistance. That is, we let the probe enter, but it never comes out. It gets smothered under a lot of laughter and pleasantries."[52] For a one-time insider like Hurston, who even in her own former Florida hometown found it hard to break back into local trust, the authority of white outsiders was suspect.

Coming toward the end of the 1920s, with the benefit of all that had developed in the era, scholar Newman Ivey White perhaps thought he could do better than his white peers with *American Negro Folk Songs* in 1928. At five hundred pages, with more than eight hundred songs itemized, annotated, and cross-referenced, and with an extensive bibliography, *American Negro Folk Songs* is polished and rigorous. It also displays a different measure of self-awareness and racial sensitivity. White, for instance, has a paragraph annotation on "Run, N——, Run" followed by several stanzas reported by various correspondents. The overt "those were the days" sentimentality of Scarborough is gone, and White contextualizes the "patterolers" of the song lyrics in the relations of "discontent" under antebellum slavery. Scattered elsewhere in the book, other stanzas and fragments appear that are recognizable as part of the common stock of "songs about the white man." Some of the lyrics to "Ain't It Hard," for instance, show up in White's chapter on "Social Songs," and they are conjoined in this rendering with lines from "You Shall Be Free." In his "Songs About Animals" chapter, moreover, White exhibits sophistication in his interpretation of animal "nonsense" as in fact Black agency. He posits: "In slavery times they [animal songs] must have been especially suitable to the Negro's need, for they were a familiar channel of expression, and they were nonsense to the white man. They were not nearly so apt to get an ignorant slave into trouble as comment upon people or events. Comment upon people, unless of the flattering sort . . . was dangerous. Nonsense was the quality of antebellum Negro folk-rhymes on which most observers commented; and a very sensible nonsense it was." Later, in his chapter "Work Songs—Gang Laborers," White follows this up by acknowledging lyrical "nonsense" as a function of survival. A slave's "safest role," he writes, was "that of buffoon, since nonsense was amusing to the master, while serious thought might tread upon his sensibility."[53]

In *American Negro Folk-Songs*, White presents himself as a no-nonsense empiricist. He is more explicit than his contemporaries about his own racial standpoint, and he even includes an entire chapter on songs of "Race-Consciousness" as part of his coverage. White wants readers to know where he identifies in the heightened consciousness of the era. "It is high time," he states, that the main points of debate in the literature "be removed as far as possible from the realm of opinion and prejudice, and that an effort be made to examine the evidence judicially." On this issue, he muses:

> I am cheerfully suspicious that my own attempt will seem in some quarters to be tinged with the racial prejudice of the white man; nothing more could be expected in the state of acute race-sensitiveness that involves the discussion of anything pertaining to the Negro. I am fully aware that the white man has certain inescapable prejudices and that I am writing as a white man; but I also know that I greatly respect the Negro race for its character and accomplishments, and have had from childhood a positive affection for many individual Negroes. I shall at least examine some evidence that has hitherto been ignored or not fully considered, and shall try to reach fair conclusions.[54]

As White seeks to establish, he is a fair and impartial friend to Black Americans, and a discerning and attentive student of their music.

Still, granting the book's insights and concrete value as a song source, there are ways in which White's study hardly departs from those of his white peers. Some of the condescension of racial tradition surfaces, for example, in White's opening claim that "the Negro has always been a great singer, but the Caucasian peoples have had to be reminded of this fact again and again before they were convinced, or attached any importance to the conviction. The Negro himself was convinced last of all." Additionally, White's appreciation of lyrical "nonsense" as a form of Black resistance—though admirable in its acuity—evidently stops with the end of slavery. There is no recognition of a continuity of oppression between slavery and Jim Crow in White's handling. He writes that the "necessity for nonsense in Negro song has long since vanished" and that the "great deal of nonsense" that persists in Black folksong is about the "conservative channels of racial habit," the "long experience" in "what will please the white man," and, as well, just plain fun. Framing all of this in the book is White's original epigraph from the 1928 edition. "Sing, Sing! Darkies, Sing– / Don't You Hear De Banjo Ring, Ring, Ring? / Sing, Sing! Darkies, Sing– / Sing For De White Folks, Sing." The lines are identified simply as "Old Minstrel Song." They would seem to indicate an unstudied adherence to some of the old fictions of the Negro. Interestingly, the epigraph is removed from the 1965 reprint of the book.[55]

All scholarship is a product of its time and circumstance, of course, and must be taken on its own basis. White and his peers in early folksong scholarship can only responsibly be evaluated in the context of the era. But there were alternative voices to be heeded in this particular time of "New Negro" self-determination, intellectual assertion, and creative achievement. Some of these "alternative" voices were mixed on White's achievement. W. E. B. Du Bois, for instance, composed a review (never published) that was generally approving, if underwhelmed and somewhat guarded. Du Bois commends the book as a "work of industry and patience." Though "neither interesting or readable," he states flatly, "it is a kind of work worth doing," a book "written with poise and knowledge . . . which for a long time must remain a landmark for those who study the Negro." Du Bois, however, does not let slide White's "natural bias" in the text. As Du Bois sees it, "Mr. White apologizes for the South and this somewhat disturbs his scientific calm. He believes that the white South was interested in the religious development of the Negro and that the Negro slave was not always or even usually a child of sorrow." In the review, Du Bois credits *American Negro Folk-Songs* for its data set, we might say, but he additionally indicates the constrained parameters within which he is forced to operate as a Black reviewer of a white "expert" on Black culture.[56]

What Du Bois took as Newman White's limiting "natural bias," White touts as a point of authority in the book. Like his fellow white researchers in Black folksong, the author conveys a sense of privileged insight owing to his southern heritage. In this, White is both frankly demure and ultimately assured. He volunteers: "Every Southern white man . . . considers himself an authority on the 'Race Question.' He knows that the Negro does not say all he means or mean all he says; he is aware of a secretive strain in the Negro which attempts to keep certain things strictly within the race. He may even suspect, what is certainly the truth, that the Negro knows the white man better than the white man knows the Negro." Granting all of this, however, White ends:

> I am as confident as ever that the songs reveal the singer, if they are only read aright. From time to time throughout this volume I have indulged myself in various comments on the character of the folk Negro. He is a person invincibly likable. In his songs I find him, as I have found him elsewhere, a most naïve and unanalytical-minded person, with a sensuous joy in his religion; thoughtless, careless, unidealistic, rather fond of boasting, predominantly cheerful, but able to derive considerable pleasure from a grouch; occasionally suspicious, charitably inclined toward the white man, and capable of a gorgeously humorous view of anything, particularly himself.[57]

It is a distinct mark of Jim Crow for White to admit of all that must be hidden from his view behind the color line while at the same time insisting on his racial omniscience.

Newman White's standpoint in *American Negro Folk-Songs* echoes many of the same currents of romantic racialism as his predecessors in Black folksong research. But there is one key topic on which White professes to differ. Newman White does not subscribe to John Lomax's influential organizing thesis of Black self-pity. To accept self-pity as the core theme of African American vernacular song, White suggests in his chapter "Race-Consciousness," is to accept the notion of Black sorrow as somehow racial, a broad social condition, and one thus politically significant. This, he warns, plays into the hands of the "Negrophiles" and propagandists of the 1920s.

White allows that it "would be almost impossible . . . for any American Negro not to be race-conscious at times." But, he specifies, "race-consciousness is one thing and race-sensitiveness and racial self-pity are others." For White, the former is organic while the latter is suspect. "Many Negro writers and leaders are highly race-sensitive," he opines, and a "large number of poems have been written by Negro poets to protest against the white man's injustice." Similarly, he complains, the African American spiritual had been misappropriated by some interpreters as "racial sorrow-song—an idea good for at least one purple patch of prose sympathy in almost any treatise." White dismisses the Lomax thesis that self-pity is central to Black folksong because, for him in the intensified atmosphere of the 1920s, it risks dubious reactions. The author equates "racial self-pity" and racial protest in a convoluted formula of white denial. He discounts the idea of any real pain in contemporary Black folksong because he discounts the idea of any real pain in Black contemporary reality. "Songs about the white man"—that is, songs with lyrics of complaint, derision, and grief calling out injustice—were songs of the past (of slavery days), or songs of simple one-on-one grievance between a boss and a laborer. Or, they were songs too few in number to count for a crusade. In the atmosphere of the times, White warns, Black folk music was being over-politicized by parties interested in social foment rather than objective fact.[58]

Newman White draws a line for readers between the "more radical-minded Negro leaders" (touchy, or "sensitive" as he puts it) and the "extremely conservative folk Negro" (passive and contented, he suggests). The "radicals" hear "self-pity" in Black folksong as an indictment of American racism, White determines. African Americans are blue, in other words, because they have been wronged, and their songs of "racial self-pity" are the cries of the oppressed that name such wrongs. White sees this analysis as unfounded. It is the imposition of a small agitator-elite entirely out of touch with its own vernacular community. "Beyond question," he writes, "there are some secular folk-songs in which the Negro does indulge in self-pity, also some in which he expresses resentment of the treatment accorded him by the white race. . . . But to stop here, as has been the common practice, is to leave the story but half-told." As many would argue after him into the folk and blues revivals of the 1960s and into today, White stresses that the "very small number of such songs" in his large archive is the "matter of really primary significance." He quips, "To base a general conclusion upon them would be like concluding that all Americans in the nineteenth century were polygamists because the Mormons were."[59]

Expressive protest in Black folksong was minor, if not altogether fringe, in

Newman White's judgement. The number of songs was small, and the content misunderstood at that. First, the folklorist insists, it is "the music" and "not the words" about which the "folk Negro" cares. Second, even when the words do make an impression, they are not to be taken too seriously. Humor and hyperbole are rhetorical instruments for their own sake in Black folksong, he elaborates. "If we ignore the twinkle in a man's eye," White cautions, "it is easy to misinterpret or over-interpret the story." The "twinkle" in so much Black folk music, according to White, exposed the myth of serious protest alleged by radical thinkers.[60]

Where the collector did catalog a higher concentration of serious "songs about white man" was in his material on labor. White's chapters "Work Songs—Gang Laborers," "Rural Labor," and "General and Miscellaneous Labor" include multiple sets of lyrics protesting the seriously punishing conditions of white domination and Black exploitation so long intrinsic to US political economy. As is the case with material in Scarborough as well as in Odum and Johnson, some of these lyrics show up in Lawrence Gellert's field archive from the same basic locations and same basic time period. Nevertheless, White's summation is telling: "Of course the Negro laborer is sometimes surly; of course, he sometimes growls and is dissatisfied with his lot. But the real significance of his songs expressing race-consciousness is the fact that they show so little of this mood. Fundamentally they are striking evidence of the deep conservatism, humor, patience, and sense of present realities with which the Negro has contributed probably more than his full share to the concord of the two races in the South."[61] In this statement, White minimizes and neutralizes. The lesson of Black folklore is a lesson of racial conservatism—namely, that the Black masses, despite any "radical" provocateurs among them, are largely a happy and contented lot. Harmony between the races, White indicates, depends on the preservation of this status quo.

For Sterling Brown, this was familiar fare. In "Negro Character as Seen by White Authors" in the *Journal of Negro Education* in 1933, Brown offered a critical perspective on Black characterization in US dominant culture. "The Negro has met with as great injustice in American literature as he has in American life," he charged. "The majority of books about Negroes merely stereotype Negro character." Brown provided an itemization of the major types of ongoing white portraiture. He theorized that associations between the "Negro" and his supposed obsessions with food and women stemmed from "traditional beliefs of the Negro being a creature of his appetites," and he explained that "although pro-slavery fiction had usually (because of Victorianism) limited these to his yearnings for hog meat and greens, 'possum and yams, and for whiskey on holidays, Reconstruction fiction had stressed his lustfulness." Brown's critique resonates if we recall John Lomax's reporting in "Self-Pity in Negro Folk-Songs" that a "n—— sings about just two things—what he eats and his woman." Additionally, we might note that Newman White in *American Negro Folk-Songs* found cause to include an entire chapter on "Songs About Women."[62]

Sterling Brown saw through this collective tradition. If "a white man says that he knows the Negro," Brown asserted, "he generally means that he knows the Negro of the joke-book tradition." In the 1930s, Brown, along with Langston Hughes and Zora Neale Hurston in their respective ways, enacted a formidable challenge to the injustice of white representation. They were joined by some newcomers to the cause in the leftwing folksong revival. Lawrence Gellert counted himself among the insurgents.[63]

CHAPTER FOUR

"The Great Red Heart of the American Revolution"

LAWRENCE GELLERT, THE LOMAXES, AND THE LEFTWING FOLKSONG REVIVAL

Them n——rs is always hollerin' out in the fields, but I never paid 'em no min' enough to know what they sing about.

—A WHITE SOUTHERN INFORMANT, QUOTED IN JOHN A. AND ALAN LOMAX, *AMERICAN BALLADS AND FOLK SONGS*, 1934

Look for the complete liberation of all the Negro masses only under a Soviet America.

—LAWRENCE GELLERT, *NEW MASSES*, 1934

In the 1930s and 1940s, the white political Left discovered African American vernacular music. The rise of Lawrence Gellert and "Negro Songs of Protest" was no aberration of history. The radical Left came to folksong as part of its own ascendance in the United States from the revolutionary Third Period of the communist movement, announced in 1928, through the more broad-based era of the Popular Front, commenced officially in 1935. In the general sense, this was a product of profound shifts in the nation precipitated by the Great Depression. In more precise terms, however, the intersection can be understood as part of the genesis whereby New Deal cultural nationalism and the Popular Front policy turn of the Communist Party USA (CPUSA) coalesced in the "leftwing folksong revival."

The years surrounding the Great Depression and the New Deal were of momentous crisis and change. For the first time, the interests and struggles of working people entered into the social and political arena in broad force.

European immigrant and ethnic communities as well as communities of color moved from the margins to the center of national life during this period through the engines of an aggressive labor movement, the Democratic Party, federal public policy and institutions, and an emergent mass culture. Moreover, radical change did not stop with the end of the fabled 1930s. The war years and after witnessed unprecedented heights of working-class mobilization and dissent. With more intensity even than in the previous period of 1934, general strikes crippled a series of industrial cities throughout the nation in 1946. If, in the end, workers' self-activity in these years primarily benefited white male industrial wage earners above all others (and only for a limited time at that), it is significant nonetheless that the seeds of change had been sown. The modern civil rights and women's movements were less than a generation to come, and the 1970s would witness another surge of labor militancy. Indeed, as a striker displayed the slogan among a crowd of thousands at the beginning of a general strike in Stamford, Connecticut, on New Year's Day in 1946, "We Will Not Go Back to the Old Days."[1]

Left radicalism was at a high point in the United States in the 1930s and 1940s. Michael Denning reports in *The Cultural Front: The Laboring of American Culture in the Twentieth Century* that a 1942 poll in *Fortune* magazine "found that 25 percent of Americans favored socialism and another 35 percent had an open mind about it." George Lipsitz adds that "four separate polls conducted between 1937 and 1946 demonstrated that anywhere from 12 percent to 21 percent of the general public perceived a drift to communism as a real possibility in America" in the coming years.[2]

The Communist Left and the Folksong Revival

The leftwing folksong revival is a vital element of this history. In these regards, my research is indebted to the groundbreaking scholarship of Richard A. Reuss. Before it was published as a book in 2000, Reuss's doctoral dissertation from 1971, "American Folklore and Leftwing Politics, 1927–1957," was influential as an "underground classic." David King Dunaway writes that Reuss "set down the basic underpinnings for later research on the folk music revival of the 1930s and 1960s. In so doing," Dunaway insists, Reuss "reclaimed the subject for folklorists after distorted and bitterly anti-Communist treatment" in the postwar.[3]

Reuss's work examines the growth and development of radical attention to rural American traditional music through the rise and fall of the Old Left in the first half of the twentieth century. "In the United States," as he puts it in an oft-quoted summation, "no *a priori* stress was put on folklore materials by any political group or protest movement until the 1930s, when the left wing, spearheaded by the Communist Party, discovered intrinsic working-class values in folksongs and other folklore genres."[4] The mid-1930s and early 1940s, in particular, represented the seminal moment of activity in this modern "folksong revival," Reuss explains. For the first time, white northern urbanites turned critical attention (as distinct from the strictly commercial interest of white record producers and talent scouts starting in the 1920s) to the vernacular music of white and Black working people in the rural South. As regards leftwing politics, such a turn was "predicated on the discovery that in certain regions the folksong idiom was a convenient musical avenue of transmitting revolutionary propaganda," Reuss concludes. "Once this was recognized, the way was paved for the extension of the Left's limited *agit-prop* concern into outright aesthetic appreciation of traditional music and the further idealization of other aspects of folk culture (tales, games, dances, arts and crafts, etc.)."[5]

For many observers today, the merging of folk music and progressive politics seems a foregone conclusion, the product of natural affinity. But the original union between the American Left and rural American vernacular music was slow in coming. The advent of the Popular Front was the key ingredient in the emergence of the leftwing folksong revival. In 1935, the Communist Party softened its revolutionary hard line considerably when it announced a new program of left-liberal unity in the international fight against European fascism. Such a line change enabled a partnership between American Communism and New Deal cultural nationalism.

Before this shift in the mid-1930s, there had been some interest within the Left in agitational and solidarity singing. Songs of protest, propaganda, and persuasion had been in currency among revolutionaries and trade unionists in Europe for at least a generation by the turn of the century.[6] In the United States, the most successful early promoters after 1900 were the Socialist Party and the Industrial Workers of the World (IWW). Still, as Reuss explains, no "special attention" was devoted to folksong in these early efforts. Rather, the emphasis was as much on topical adaptations and political parodies of "standard popular, religious, and patriotic melodies" as on any traditional vernacular music. Moreover, most of these revolutionary movements (the main exception being the IWW) were geared toward an emerging industrial proletariat in the urban Northeast. In these years, such a constituency was almost entirely foreign-born. As only a small minority of the CPUSA even spoke English fluently all the way into the 1930s, the music of the Old Left early on was, quite understandably, the music of the Old World.[7]

Well into the 1930s, the "native" intellectual and artistic elite of the Communist vanguard in the United States took a dim view of American vernacular music. Party ideologues had, since the insurgent Third Period especially, been in search of thoroughly "revolutionary" artistic mediums by which to raise a thoroughly "revolutionary" working class. In 1928, Nicolai Bukharin had announced a new phase of communist history at the Sixth World Congress of the Communist International in Moscow. Certain of the imminent collapse of global capitalism, Party members in the Third Period were to abandon "gradualist" movement tactics for a new push of sectarian intensity in the cause of worldwide proletarian revolution. As such, efforts in the cultural field had taken a decidedly doctrinaire turn.

With the sponsorship of the Communist Party, the Workers Music League was established in 1931 in order to organize the many workers choruses still dominating leftwing musical activity in the urban North. The following year, the Composers Collective was formed under a League affiliate, the Pierre Degeyter Club, in New York City. Members of the Collective were committed to composing original material for just the kind of formalized group singing exemplified by the most accomplished of the radical choruses. Some of the leading figures and most promising newcomers of American music were involved, including Charles Seeger, Henry Cowell, Elie Siegmeister, Lan Adomian, Wallingford Riegger, Max Margulis, Marc Blitzstein, and, albeit more marginally, Aaron Copland. Turning their formal classical training to alternative ends, such artists sought to challenge performer and audience expectations in a direct assault against the conventions of "bourgeois" musical tradition. In terms of Marxist ideology, they subscribed to the "art is a weapon" theory of cultural politics. "Music is propaganda—always propaganda—and of the most powerful sort," declared leading emissary Charles Seeger (father of future folk icon Pete). The "special task" of the various arms of the Workers Music League, he explained, was "the development of music as a weapon in the class struggle."[8] After the example of leftwing modernist Hanns Eisler in Germany, members of the Composers Collective produced difficult, technically advanced works of jarring harmonic dissonance and acute rhythmic complexity. In the end, such efforts were almost entirely unsuccessful for the purposes of mass political organizing. At an event in 1934, one disapproving audience member captured the disjuncture between theory and practice. He complained that such esoteric and pedantic "revolutionary" music was "full of geometric bitterness," as if it had been "written for an assortment of mechanical canaries" rather than a human audience.[9]

The Popular Front enacted a major reversal. In the communist movement, the search for an appropriate "people's music" shifted from the vanguard to the vernacular. If in the early 1930s Charles Seeger expressed the prevailing negative view concerning traditional music and radical politics, he was, by the latter half of the decade, singing its praises. "Not all folk-tunes are suitable to the revolutionary movement," he told readers in *Daily Worker* in 1934. "Many of them are complacent, melancholy, defeatist—originally intended to make slaves endure their lot." Though such melodies may be "pretty," he held, they were "not the stuff for a militant proletariat to feed upon."[10] Only a year later, however, Seeger would be caught up in the groundswell coalescing around the New Deal and the Popular Front. From 1935 through the 1940s, he established a reputation as one of the most prominent of the "New Deal folklorists" that historian Benjamin Filene identifies among the emergent establishment in Washington, DC.[11] In his official roles with the Resettlement Administration and, after that, the Federal Music Project, Seeger sought to promote the simple democratic virtues of "people's music" as it currently sounded in the vernacular cultures of the United States, rather than as theorists might have thought it should sound in their own revolutionary program. Like the broader communist movement in general in the latter part of the decade, he became less concerned with propagating doctrine in the face of capitalist oppression than with building mass unity in the crush of international fascism. The old sectarianism had been left behind in the rush of progressive coalition and populist outreach. For his part, Seeger came to recall his recent past as a revolutionary composer with irony. "Everything we composed was forward-looking, progressive as hell," he reflected. Even so, it was "completely unconnected with life, just as we were in the Collective."[12]

Black Music in the Folksong Revival

Lawrence Gellert's cultural work found an eager audience and a ready institutional base in the leftwing folksong revival. Like that larger movement from which it drew currency, however, it also drew resonance from the vital push for Black self-determination that had been emergent in the United States since after World War I. In the 1920s, the New Negro Renaissance brought African American arts to the attention of white America. Issues of Black representation came to the fore in this period of race consciousness and cross-cultural contact. The economic privations of the Great Depression may have deflated some of the earnest dreams and expectations of Black artists and intellectuals, but it did not put an end to the "New Negro." Scholars have traced how some of the emergent energies that were released across lines of race and class in the 1920s continued to crescendo into the 1930s, albeit with altered pitch in the midst of changed social, political, and economic conditions. From varying perspectives, literary historians have challenged the older critical consensus on the Movement as a failure of its own undoing, an ultimately hollow marriage of Black delusion and white primitivist patronage. They emphasize continuities where predecessors saw only division, drawing out the material and symbolic affinities between Black and white, the Black arts and twentieth-century modernism, and the New Negro and the Old Left of the 1920s and 1930s.[13]

Following in the path of Richard Reuss, Robbie Lieberman confirms that folk music only started to receive widespread attention as "a great weapon for the Left" in the latter part of the 1930s. In these years, such a recognition moved apace with the radical political discovery of African American expressive culture. When it came to Black music, in particular, the Communist Party of the United States was key in politicizing as a national treasure what had formerly been regarded in dominant society as base and worthless.[14]

Alan Lomax was at the center of the leftwing folksong revival and, more specifically, the movement's attention to African American vernacular song. In 1933, the seventeen-year-old Harvard undergraduate accompanied his famous father, John, on a car tour in the first of what was to become a series of legendary field trips. Under the auspices of the Library of Congress Archive of American Folk-Song, the pair visited sharecroppers' shacks, prison farms, and other remote locations in the Black South equipped with the latest in portable recording technology. The success of the expedition would lead to similar expeditions throughout the 1930s and 1940s as well as a number of popular songbooks, including *American Ballads and Folksongs* (1934), *Negro Folk Songs as Sung by Lead Belly* (1936), *Our Singing Country* (1941), and *Folk Song: USA* (1947). Ultimately, this literature would come to define a canon of North American folksong that privileged what Alan called the "river of black African tradition flowing through Delta life" and into America's cultural bedrock.[15]

Both Lawrence Gellert and the Lomaxes worked within the cultural terrain of the leftwing folksong revival. In terms of the Lomax team, however, it was only Alan who actually sided left. Influenced by Marxism at Harvard, Alan wrote to his father at the outset of their endeavors that he hoped to make "connections between the ideas in the songs and their social implications."[16] This troubled the senior Lomax. John complained that Alan "was inclined to romanticize the conditions of the poor and rustic, and thus was disappointed that many of the blacks they had visited owned their farms and were relatively prosperous."[17] Alan, by his turn, recognized his father's leanings. Father John, "in spite of his intense sympathy for the prisoners [they recorded] and a genuine concern for black welfare," Alan reflected, "believed in the overall beneficence of the Southern system."[18]

In *Rainbow Quest: The Folk Music Revival and American Society, 1940–1970*, Ronald Cohen shows that these differences between father and son were emblematic of the poles of political orientation encompassed within American folklore collecting and scholarship over the generations. "Those searching for traditional forces and styles could have either politically conservative or radical leanings," he writes. In the former case, conservatives in the "evolutionist wing" lamented the passing of what they held as earlier, more primitive cultures. They sought out artifacts and lore that "required respect and preservation." In the latter instance, progressives took the opposing "functionalist" view of folklore. Young collectors such as Alan Lomax, Cohen summarizes, thought that "folk songs might have not only an ancient lineage but a dynamic present; they could serve practical purposes, energizing the folk to struggle against racism and oppression."[19]

Despite their political differences, John and Alan Lomax found common faith in "the uniting and rejuvenating powers of folk music," states Cohen.[20] In these regards, father and son drew on the same deep well in their mission in American folksong. Their joint collecting work in these years was founded on a shared romantic idealization of a mythic pre-industrial, pre-commercial American republic. Vernacular music represented a vital embodiment of this ideal past. It offered redemption against the vapid, homogenizing strains of mass culture and consumerism in modern twentieth-century life. The "folksongs of the Negro," as John Lomax put it, were of particular value in these respects. In "musical phrasing" and "poetic content," he wrote, the songs of rural Black singers were "most unlike those of the white race." They were "the least contaminated by white influence" and the commercial debasement of "modern Negro jazz."[21]

The Lomaxes' project in American folklore enacted romantic cultural nationalism over radical Cultural Front politics. Benjamin Filene writes that the Lomaxes' work may have been "in tune with the left wing's agenda," but their "outlook was hardly radical by 1930s standards." Compared to Gellert's "fiery"

Negro Songs of Protest from 1936, he judges, the Lomaxes' best-selling songbook from 1934, *American Ballads and Folk Songs*, appears "relatively moderate for the time." In their published output, Filene concludes, the Lomaxes "respected black culture and lamented the injustice that helped to shape it, but they did not challenge the system of segregation that produced the injustice."[22]

All collectors of similar station—whether the Lomaxes or Gellert—were, of course, subject to bias and subjectivity. In introducing their first songbook, the Lomaxes were candid about their process. "The songs in this book (we hope it will be a singing book)," they wrote, "represent the personal choice of the compilers from a large mass of material from which other legitimate and defensible choices might have been made." Academic folklorists of the day, housed primarily in university English departments, responded with disfavor to such open admissions of editorial license. The Lomaxes had veered from the prevailing literary emphasis on exhaustive accountings of song texts alone. Rather, they included musical scores in the volume, and sought to reach a popular audience of reader-singers through the "composite ballad." They explained that "numbers of the songs" in the book were "composites; that is, we have brought together what seem the best stanzas, or even lines, from widely separated sources." In other words, they elaborated, "No one person probably has ever sung entirely a number of the songs, as herein printed; but all the words given have been sung by some people." In the early days of their success, the ranks of institutional folklore took such moves by the Lomaxes as professional heresy.[23]

Still, the genteel collectors of the past were hardly scientists. They had oftentimes censored the bawdy material they had come across in their song collecting. Even the exacting Francis James Child, the commanding influence in traditional folklore studies, was not above "improving" or simply omitting lines that he deemed "tasteless." This interpretive current extended back as in-group practice. From the eighteenth-century forward, collectors selected against material they felt irrelevant, unworthy, or inappropriate.[24] In this light, we have ample reason to doubt the full representative value of any collection of folk material that has come to be touted as definitive. This is especially at issue when it comes to the contentious ground of race, class, and protest. The canon of folksong institutionalized at the Library of Congress under the care of the Lomaxes may be rich, for instance, but it is not without gaps. The work of Gellert, by the same token, reveals its own preferences and mediation. Ultimately, these parties had the power of final edit over what was documented and published from out of their fieldwork in marginalized communities.

Storied Accomplishments: Lawrence Gellert and the Lomaxes

At base, where Lawrence Gellert heard political revolution in the music of his folk informants, the Lomaxes heard cultural redemption. These distinct ideological orientations are apparent in collecting narratives from each party in their formative years in Black folksong research. In this period, white collectors discovered the perverse value of southern criminal justice. Prison farms and penitentiaries afforded a handy solution to the problem of "outside" influence on Black traditional music. In one of his first solo articles in 1934, Alan Lomax recounted how the road back in time, past the music of "canned" commercial variety, took the pair to the remote world of Black incarceration. He explained:

> We had found the educated Negro resentful of our attempt to collect his secular folk-music. We had found older Negroes afraid for religious reasons to sing for us, while the members of the younger generation were on the whole ignorant of the songs we wanted and interested only in the Blues . . . and in jazz. So it was that we decided to visit the Negro prison farms of the South. There, we thought, we should find that the Negro, away from the pressure of the churchly community, ignorant of the uplifting educational movement, having none but official contact with white men, dependent on the resources of his own group for amusement, and hearing no canned music, would have preserved and increased his heritage of secular folk-music.[25]

The prison farms of the South, the Lomaxes discovered, offered circumstances that "were practically ideal" for ballad hunters. Often the best finds were the "lifers," men who "had been confined in the penitentiary" for decades, "a few as long as fifty years." Such long-time prisoners "still sang the songs they had brought into confinement, and these songs had been entirely in the keeping of the black man."[26]

We have already looked at some of Gellert's methods as a collector of song. As Gellert recounted, these included barter, negotiation, and covert operation. But, one of the essential requirements, he stressed, was that he work outside of white supervision. In this, Gellert's reflections contrast sharply with an early collecting portrait offered by the Lomaxes. The pair introduce many of the songs transcribed in *American Ballads and Folk Songs* with informational vignettes from their field experiences. One such example is the passage that accompanies a set of lyrics that the Lomaxes group under the title "Levee Camp 'Holler.'"

Evidently, the folklorists had been on the trail of new verses to this song cycle for some time when they arrived at the Nashville State Penitentiary in 1933. A former railroad and levee worker known as Black Samson was a lucky find. A "giant of a man with an engaging smile" and a "singer of unusual quality," as John later put it, the prisoner affirmed that he was familiar with the tune. But, there was a problem. Black Samson, as the Lomaxes tell the story, had "joined the church and had turned away from the world." "Levee Camp 'Holler'" was a "devil's song," they reported, and "good church members do not dare be heard singing it." Accordingly, though their prisoner-informant "admitted" that he "knew the song and had once sung it," he was unwilling to oblige the collectors. The Lomaxes faced a dilemma. But, in the end they managed a solution. After first turning unsuccessfully to the prison chaplain, who fruitlessly assured Black Samson that "he would make it all right with the Lord," they finally enlisted the office of highest authority. "At last," they recounted, "when the warden had especially urged him to sing," Black Samson "stepped in front of our microphone." Before he commenced singing, though, when he was sure the portable recording machine had been activated, the prisoner surprised them all. "It's sho hard lines dat a poor n——r's got to sing a worl'ly song, when he's tryin' to be sancrified," he said, "but de warden's ast me, so I guess I'll have to." It was a clever statement in the impression of the collectors. Black Samson, they acknowledged, "had registered his protest before the Lord on an aluminum plate, now filed in the Library of Congress at Washington."[27]

In his autobiography, *Adventures of a Ballad Hunter*, John Lomax repeated this story with an added twist. The head warden had loaned his office to the team for the two days of their recording efforts on site, Lomax recalled. The warden had "vacated" and left the Lomaxes to their work, but on the second afternoon "came in and asked about our progress." The pair explained that Black Samson had "refused amiably but firmly to sing any of the songs" from his past working on railroad crews and levee gangs. Still, there was a particular song, "Levee Camp 'Holler,'" the prisoner knew that the Lomaxes "wanted especially," they told the warden. At that point, the official "sent a guard" for Black Samson. The "frightened Negro shuffled up," recounted John Lomax, "and took his place before the microphone."[28]

In both variants of the story, the presence of white authority (warden, chaplain, and prison guard) looms in the narrative. In one sense, this presence could be a positive inducement. Gellert had informants, for instance, who elicited a promise from the collector before they recorded that he would share their musical statements with "people that are influential" up North. Similarly, Black Samson, recounted John Lomax, repeatedly inquired after their session whether "some of dose big Washin'ton men, when dey hears my song, won't do something to help dis po' n——r?" But, these pleas were to far-off white officialdom, local authority in the South in these years was a different matter. It was a presence that Gellert, in contrast to the Lomaxes, sought adamantly to avoid in his independent fieldwork.[29]

Like the Lomaxes, and other collectors too, Gellert targeted Black prisoners on chain gangs and work details in his collecting in the South. In a formula of maximum rewards, he too conformed to the prevailing logic of greater isolation amounting to greater musical yield. But, unlike the Lomaxes, Gellert was in search of current, topical songs of protest, rather than older songs of folk heritage. If the Lomaxes were looking for tradition-bearers, Gellert was looking for tradition-busters. In his prison work, he found himself at the source, one of the very worst manifestations of naked white racial power in the South. It was a point of production, where the collector could elicit songs of protest from among the nation's most disempowered. His experience collecting in such surroundings was depicted in starkly different terms than that of the Lomaxes. In a *New Masses* article from 1932, Gellert wrote:

> A County jail in South Carolina. Obliging warden. "Sure you can visit the n——rs. Stay as long as you can stand it. Me? I never go there unless I can't help myself." No wonder. 102 in the shade outside. Yet the windows are jammed shut. And so filthy you can't see through them. Corridors strewn with filth of weeks' accumulation. Mingled heat, urine, body sweat and garbage—stench of the lion house at the zoo. Only more so. Five convicts to a cell 6x6. They're stripped naked. Stretched listlessly on tiered iron bunks. Or dirty pallets on the floor. Tongues loll out of their mouths. Like dogs panting.

It was on this trip that Gellert collected his provocative version of "Work All the Summer," mentioned in chapter 1. In the article text, he introduced readers to the embittered lyrics of the song, and contextualized such sentiment with his signature accompanying reportage. "I did stay as long as I could stand it," he concluded the passage. But, a "half hour later my visit ended in a wild rush for the wide open spaces. Just too late. I puked all over the stairs on the way out."[30]

With its characteristic agitational tone, Gellert's firsthand account of prison fieldwork reads very differently than that of the Lomax team from the same years. In *Afro-American Folksongs* in 1914, Henry Edward Krehbiel posited that the "truest, the most intimate of folk-music, is that produced by suffering." After their own intensive research, the Lomaxes, as they state in their introduction to *American Ballads and Folk Songs*, had come to agree. "The songs of the Negro prisoners in convict camps furnished confirmation of this [Krehbiel's] theory," they offered. Up to that point in their joint fieldwork in Southern penitentiaries, they commented, the two could recall only one song performed for their hearing that "reflected unrestrained abandon to joyous emotions." Still, they pondered the reasons for such a fact. "Was it the forbidding iron bars," they asked, "the stripes, the clank of occasional shackles, the cruel-looking black bullwhip four feet long, which in some places hung in plain sight inside the door of the main hall—was it such surroundings that made the songs seem sad?" No, the Lomaxes resolved, "The sadness, the melancholy, did not, it is believed, grow out of brutal treatment." On the contrary, they elaborated, "The men were well fed and their sleeping quarters looked comfortable. In most places, they worked hard, but the early 'All quiet' permitted sufficient hours of sleep. The visitors were given every freedom, and no case of cruelty was noted."[31]

In their proposed solution to this quandary of apparently sad songs under apparently comfortable conditions, the Lomaxes did reveal some latent sense of Black song-making as agency in the passage that continues below. But, they foreclosed such a reading in their concluding sentence. As is clear, they presented the case as not one primarily of harsh treatment at the hands of white domination, but rather natural Black longing and, as we see again, Black self-pity. They posited: "The melancholy in the prison songs comes doubtless from the Negro's desire, as one said, 'to git away f'om here. I jis' don' nachly like dis place.' Black Samson, huge and kindly-looking (he was a double murderer), said, 'Boss, do you think dem songs of mine will help me any up dere in Washington?' Songs that have been brought into the prison become colored with this gloomy note. The Negro makes a model prisoner, as one guard said, easy to control, but in his singing he abandons himself to a brooding hopelessness, as though freedom were beyond reach."[32] Trapped in a web of debt peonage, convict-lease imprisonment, segregation, inequality, and white racial terror, indeed, it must have seemed to many Black Southerners that freedom was quite literally beyond attainment. This was not a mood, but a social reality. The Lomaxes' proposition, then, that the "sadness, the melancholy, did not, it is believed, grow out of brutal treatment" suggests a tone-deafness unbecoming collectors who so claimed to have their ears to the ground.[33]

"Beyond the Doggerel": Lead Belly, Race, and Radicalism

In their efforts to rescue a nation astray through the promotion of its homespun vernacular traditions, the Lomaxes sought the indigenous musical expressions of an imagined, authentic American folk. Fieldwork among Black prisoners in the deep South proved essential. The Lomaxes major find on that first fateful trip in 1933, one Huddie Ledbetter from Louisiana, was just the man for the job. The soon-to-be legendary "Lead Belly" was some forty years old and a prisoner at Angola State Penitentiary. With a vast musical repertoire, the accomplished Black songster offered the chance to demonstrate, as Alan put it, "to a stream-lined, city-oriented world that America had living folk music—swamp primitive, angry, freighted with great sorrow and joy." After his release from prison, the Lomaxes promptly made arrangements with Ledbetter and took their "discovery" on a publicity tour through New York City in 1935. Introducing him to the press as, in the words of John, a "natural," with "no idea of money, law, or ethics" and "possessed of virtually no restraint," the celebrated folklorists, explains Benjamin Filene, "promoted Lead Belly" as "the living embodiment of America's folk-song tradition."[34]

John and Alan Lomaxes' popular biography, *Negro Folk Songs as Sung by Lead-belly*, appeared the following year in 1936. In surface appearance, it stands in striking contrast to Lawrence Gellert's *Negro Songs of Protest*. "A posed photograph on the frontispiece" of the book, Filene points out, "shows Lead Belly in overalls rolled to bare feet, with a handkerchief tied around his neck. Sitting on canvas sacks, he is playing guitar, with his head tilted back, eyes wide, and mouth open to show a tooth missing." In the pages that follow, and in the series of media reports that chronicled Lead Belly's rise at the time, Huddie Ledbetter was portrayed as a "slow-witted, hulking man, motivated only by a drive for sex and violence," states Filene. Just as enthusiastically as the Lomaxes touted Lead Belly as the quintessential democratic American, it appears, they put an equal emphasis on his sensational outlaw status. The collectors publicized him "as the voice of the people" and, at the same time, "focused on his convict past and depicted him as a savage, untamed animal," writes Filene.[35] In this duality, the race and class contradictions embedded in the Lomaxes' conflicted project in American cultural nationalism clearly come to light. Lead Belly, it seems, was a minstrel in two senses for the team. In both his musical and symbolic role, he was a bard and a racial "Other," a tradition bearer of oral culture and a black-face caricature of white racial imagination.

While the pair sang of his virtues and vices, some among the Left questioned the Lomaxes' treatment of Lead Belly. Gellert was one of the more vociferous critics. After ten years in the South himself, Gellert was quick to label the Lomaxes' approach as all too familiar. In an exchange of letters to the editor in *New Masses*, Gellert accosted the Lomaxes for embodying "the slave-master attitude intact." They were "good old Southern gentle folks with the good old Southern gentle folks' attitude towards 'n——rs,'" he sneered. Moreover, in their previous work, *American Ballads and Folksongs*, they failed "to get to the heart of contemporary Negro folk lore":

> Beyond the doggerel—beyond the nonsensical jingles served up for the white man's amusement, lies the heart throb of the Black Folks—the agonized voice of the mass crying out against the peonage, poverty and degradation. The savage brutality of the Law and the lynching mob. And the new attitudes toward all that exemplified by Tallapoosa, Angelo Herndon, Scottsboro boys and other vital factors in the lives of the suppressed black masses. A hundred songs current in the Black Belt freshly stamp the glorified images of members of their race who participate in the day to day struggles against their oppressors. But we catch not a glimmer of all this in the Lomax volume.[36]

Gellert was still talking about the conflict in his interviews in the 1960s. "I had a controversy with the Old Man in the press . . . about what they did to Lead Belly," he told Richard Reuss. "We on the Left, in the *New Masses*," were among the few that criticized the two, he remembered, and "Lomax [the senior] never forgave me for that." With his progressive sympathies, Alan was "different," volunteered Gellert, a "nice kid. . . . He used to come around to see what he could find out about my songs. He's sort of enterprising." Still, both men, he maintained, subjected Lead Belly to ill treatment in their touring and promotional schemes. "I knew Lead Belly very well," Gellert claimed. "He was a nice guy. . . . Boy, did they exploit him."[37]

Red, White, and Black in Leftwing Folk Discovery

If the leftwing movement generally operated at the roots of the folksong revival of the 1930s and 1940s, the specific context of emergence for Lawrence Gellert's "Negro Songs of Protest" was the communist Third Period (1928–1935) of imminent and unyielding proletarian revolution. In this era, the Communist Left discovered the revolutionary history and potential of African American working people in the Black Belt of the South. Workers of color in the majority Black counties of this cotton region comprised an "oppressed nation" in the United States, determined Party theoreticians. Accordingly, it went, they had the inherent right of collective political and economic self-determination, and this extended even to outright geographical secession if necessary. At the extreme of capitalist oppression, African Americans below the Mason-Dixon line were seen as a unique case in the revolutionary struggle for race and class justice by 1930. In the North, Communist ideologues were waging an unprecedented campaign of interracial reconciliation. There were prosecutions of "white chauvinism" within Party ranks in Harlem, for instance, and there was increased pressure placed on white organizers on the ground to breach the racial divide. The call, then, from the Party leadership was for integration and assimilation among workers and revolutionaries across lines of race and ethnicity. Class was the universal, and race was a diversion. But in the South it was a different story. There, the formal prescriptions of Communist theory validated a strategic differentiation of Black from white working-class struggle. For the first time in the history of the organized American Left, the policy line privileged revolution on behalf of Black working-class oppression over revolution on behalf of universal (read: "white") working-class oppression.[38]

Lawrence Gellert's professional ascendance in the field of Black folksong, then, did not occur in a vacuum. In the initial stages, African American vernacular performance styles and song traditions gained a favored status in the left's nascent discovery of American folk music, and Gellert's work was critical. This early preference took hold, ironically enough, even despite the more direct encounter with white radical folk aesthetics brought on by some of the Party's first organizing campaigns among what were primarily white workers in the South. In 1929, for instance, considerable Party press coverage in the North was devoted to the bitter Communist-sponsored National Textile Workers Union (NTWU) strike in Gastonia, North Carolina. A local spinner at American Mills who had come into the organizing drive, Ella May Wiggins, emerged as an emissary for the movement with her original songs fusing radical union lyrics with community-based folk culture and music traditions. When she was killed by anti-union vigilantes that year, several hundred supporters turned out for Wiggins's funeral. They sang one of her most famous songs, "The Mill Mother's Lament," as the coffin was lowered into the ground:

We leave our homes in the morning,
We kiss our children goodbye
While we slave for the bosses
Our children scream and cry.

And when we draw our money
Our grocery bills to pay,
Not a cent to spend for clothing,
Not a cent to lay away.

And on that very evening,
Our little son will say:
"I need some shoes, Mother,
And so does sister May."

How it grieves the heart of a mother,
You everyone must know,
But we can't buy for our children
Our wages are too low.

It is for our little children,
That seem to us so dear,
But for us nor them, dear workers,
The bosses do not care.

But understand, all workers,
Our union they do fear;
Let's stand together, workers,
And have a union here.[39]

Similarly, in 1931 the communist-led National Miners Union (NMU) moved into Harlan County, Kentucky, to assist local miners in their desperate strike against the coal operators of the region. The radical folksong tradition that developed out of the struggles in "Bloody Harlan" followed from Appalachia to New York City that year, with mountain singers Aunt Molly Jackson and her stepbrother, Jim Garland, performing to leftwing audiences at various meetings and events. One of Jackson's signature tunes, "I Am a Union Woman," was composed to rouse support among workers and their families in the midst of the violent Harlan County campaign. Other songs by Jackson such as "Ragged Hungry Blues" and "The Death of Harry Sims" also linked local reality and radical unionism in lyric formulations of direct address. Harry Simms, for instance, was a young Community Party organizer from Massachusetts killed by gun thugs in Harlan County in 1932. Nevertheless, these vernacular expressions of white working-class militancy did not seem to fire the imagination of the predominantly white Left headquartered in the North in a way that African American work songs and chain gang songs did almost immediately. Richard Reuss explains, for example, that the personal story of Ella May Wiggins, the union martyr, was covered extensively in the leftwing press. Though her songs are today accorded a legendary status, they were mentioned in only three of the nearly forty articles on what was depicted as her heroic life and death in Gastonia. The case gives "some indication," determines Reuss, "of the leadership's musical myopia in 1929 under Third Period ideology." Similarly, Aunt Molly Jackson was greeted with ambivalence in the early 1930s. By 1933, Jackson had been forced out of Harlan County for good. She was relocated to New York City and, as Reuss reports, attended a handful of meetings of the esteemed Composers Collective of the Workers Music League. The "Kentucky mountain woman, ballad maker, and blacklisted militant organizer . . . rose and sang some of her own strike compositions," Reuss writes, "which were set to traditional melodies and couched in the language of rural Appalachia. It was a perfect, and perfectly natural, fusion of music with social struggle, in a medium comfortable to her constituents." Unfortunately, it "went right over the Collective's collective heads," Reuss reports.[40]

In the second half of the 1930s, the rural music traditions of the white working-class South would be embraced by revivalists. But, for the time being, the rarified theoretical prescriptions of the Third Period continued to constrain the Left's southern musical discovery. In 1932, the Workers Music League published the *Red Song Book* as part of its efforts in communist movement culture. The songbook comprised "half a dozen Appalachian and other strike songs based on folk and popular tunes" of white oral culture, identifies Richard Reuss. Included in the material were Jackson's "Miners' Song," "On the Picket Line," and "Poor Miner's Farewell," as well as Ella May Wiggins's "I.L.D. Song." The book was "panned," however, summarizes Reuss. In the midst of the communist Third Period, such music was dismissed by Party critics for its "immaturity" and "arrested development."[41]

If the prevailing views on American folk music really only shifted wholesale in the latter part of the 1930s with the arrival of the Popular Front, they were pushed into motion already in the beginning of the decade when it came to Black vernacular music. Communist critics had begun to hear rural African American genres as "revolutionary" as early as 1930, in fact. In that year, just a few months before publishing Lawrence Gellert for the first time, *New Masses* ran an article entitled "Songs of the Negro Worker" by Philip Schatz. In the piece, the writer alerted readers to the fact that "Negro culture"—Black southern "workaday songs" in particular—represented "perhaps the most genuine workers' culture in America." He quoted the anguished musical plea of Black laborers and the callous response of the "white superintendent, the hardfisted taskmaster of wage-slavery," from a song familiar in the levee camps of the Deep South. The lyrics included:

> I tol' my cap'n that my feet was col'
> "God damn yo' feet, let the car wheel roll."
> Cap'n, Cap'n, old Ben won't pull.
> "God damn his soul, put the harness on the bull."
> Cap'n, Cap'n, the track is wet.
> "Knock 'er right on, black boy, till the evenin' sun do set."
> Cap'n, Cap'n, can't you tell
> The track is slick and cold as hell.

Schatz opined on the plight of the Negro, to whom "chattel slavery," he wrote, "has left a heritage of intensified exploitation" greater by "a hundred times" even than that facing the "most underpaid and spiritless white slave" of the South. The "black worker knows it" too, he added, "for the walker," an emblem of both white class rule and white racial terror, "holds life and death in the shack" right alongside of where "he keeps the time cards." The author quoted more verses:

> I don't want no,
> Want no trouble with de walker.
> I don't want no,
> Want no trouble with de walker.
> I want to go home,
> Lawd, Lawd, I wanta go home.
>
> Oh, me an' my buddy
> Jes' came here this mornin'

Wanta go home,
Lawd, Lawd, wanta go home.

I can drive it,
Drive it along as anybody.
Wanta go home,
Lawd, Lawd, wanta go home.

Desperate Black laborers, wrote Schatz, doubly oppressed by class and race, sang of this and their "other workaday woes."[42]

Writer Richard Frank followed similarly in *New Masses* in 1934. In "Negro Revolutionary Music," he contended that "a new stage in the creation of Negro music has commenced. This is the creation of Negro revolutionary folk-music." Based on his investigations, Frank determined that this dramatic step forward could be attributed to innate Black dispositions toward cultural change and creative adaptation. "Whenever the Negro has become revolutionary, he has expressed his new revolutionary spirit musically," he explained. "He has done so in two ways: first, by the singing of new revolutionary words to the music of the old spirituals and work-songs; second, by the creation of entirely new revolutionary songs." Frank offered examples of both. Sharecroppers fighting tenant evictions in rural Alabama, he reported, were singing a reformulated version of "We Shall Not Be Moved." Members of the Unemployed Council of Richmond, Virginia, as well, had added their own lyrics to the traditional song. They sang:

In spite of capitalist terror,
We shall not be moved;
In spite of capitalist terror,
We shall not be moved.
Just like a tree that planted
By the water
We shall not be moved.

As for original compositions, Frank recalled hearing "something like the following" in Norfolk, Virginia:

Oh, Hoover on the right,
And Roosevelt on the left,

Oh, Hoover on the right,
And Roosevelt on the left,
. . . .
But you ain't gonna rule no more.

For the journalist, however, a party "in the home of a Negro comrade" in Virginia left the deepest impression with respect to this new Black singing movement. "The workers were singing spirituals for amusement, and their singing was magnificent," Frank recounted. "Most of the songs were sung with the old religious words. But occasionally some comrade would inject lines of real class significance." Here, at a gathering of everyday Black working people one evening in the early 1930s in Richmond, Virginia, then, the author had discovered himself at the very center of the workers' revolt in the United States. "I thought of those who academically debated the possibility of revolution in America," he declared, "and I laughed. What did they know of it? Here was the revolution. Here it lived. Here was the great Red heart of the American Revolution itself. It throbbed in the voices of those singing workers."[43]

Just as in the case of the initial encounter between the communist Left and southern white working-class culture, researchers have examined the first encounter between Party organizers and African American vernacular cultures of resistance. From different perspectives, authors have delineated the decisive shift in Communist Party theory in the 1920s. The turn to Black self-determination in 1928 was a reconciliation in Marxist ideology of the long-stated problem of "ethnic nationalism" and "proletarian internationalism." It represented a new determination that these positions were not necessarily at cross-purposes in so far as they applied to the southern Black Belt in the United States. In his work on the subject, Robin Kelley has explored how the organized political Left, when the Communist Party gained preeminence, discovered Black peoples and culture. It was a seminal moment in which historic Black radicalism met the organized class struggle emanating from Euro-American leftwing tradition. Party organizers descended into the South only beginning in 1929, setting up a headquarters in Birmingham, Alabama. In the city, they moved to organize the vast armies of the unemployed and established a leading role in the neighborhood relief committees. In rural Tallapoosa County, Alabama, they took an aggressive step into the fierce struggles between Black sharecroppers and white southern landlords. In all cases, shows Kelley, white organizers found a vital "culture of opposition" on the ground among Black working people. Ultimately, he concludes, it was "a culture that enveloped and transformed the

Party into a movement more reflective of African-American radical traditions than anything else." In this turn, it inspired the eager admiration of revolutionary white comrades and cultural critics in a way that southern white working-class culture had not.[44]

In his article from the period, Richard Frank ends up comparing a young Black singer at the party—a "Comrade Cash, who had created a song of his own" in praise of the Communist-sponsored Unemployed Councils—in favorable terms to the "white ballad-maker of Gastonia, Ella May Wiggins." As we have seen, however, Wiggins's vernacular pursuit into organized radicalism had not achieved the same kind of critical favor so early in the 1930s. This was the case even though her original lyrics based in traditional idioms were quite often very explicit in their militant unionism, just as were Aunt Molly Jackson's. On the other hand, many of the Black work songs, field hollers, and modified spirituals cited in the articles above, and in the work of Lawrence Gellert too, were frequently quite elliptical in terms of any direct references to unionism, radical organizing, or even proposed solutions to the injustices of the world. Still, these musical items were taken as "revolutionary." Why was this the case? One key was the Third Period resolution on Black self-determination. The line change, as Robin Kelley identifies it, was a "major turning point" in 1928. It "indirectly confirmed," he states, what "many black Communists" had long held: namely, that "African Americans had their own unique revolutionary tradition." Kelley elaborates on what this shift in ideology meant. "In short," he argues, "history and culture—whether it was to celebrate traditions of black resistance or recuperate the 'folk' art of the black working class—became the vehicles through which black Communists could both 'express' and justify their collective right to self-determination." What is suggestive in Kelley's analysis is the way in which this new opening for Blacks worked in a dialectic with white discovery. For the early comers to leftwing folk revivalism, it involved an idealization of Black vernacular culture as inherently radical. It inspired the revolutionary ardor of sympathetic white comrades in ways that white working-class vernacular culture had not.[45]

What is more, much of this Black expression controverted the prevailing political and aesthetic lines emanating from communist leadership at home and abroad. While the Comintern had, for example, endorsed a policy of Black self-determination in the United States, this was a formal resolution specified only for those particular Black Belt counties of the South. On the whole, the Party's official position in the late 1920s and 1930s remained focused on interracial revolutionary coalition. Class was to supersede race, and the two major targets of communist organizing with respect to the "Negro Question" were "Negro nationalism" and "racial chauvinism." That said, Kelley has showcased verse and sentiment from out of Communist literary culture in the period that is rife with overt expressions of militant Black nationalism and in-group racial seething. In the Alabama case, communist organizers and intellectuals embraced an African American vernacular "culture of opposition" frequently characterized by themes formally proscribed by the Party's aesthetic vanguard. The "songs, rituals, religious practices, and styles of ordinary black working people," Kelley writes, "were in conflict with Communist ideology and practice." Considerable numbers of African Americans, he elaborates, "not only showed irreverence for the Party's interracialism but refused to even consider questioning their religion." Nevertheless, Kelley relates, "this level of black cultural production rarely faced the critical scrutiny of CP cultural critics." Black working peoples' cultural forms were so intoxicating in terms of a perceived inherent radicalism that they allowed for a certain latitude with respect to "folk" superstition, sentimentality, and even religious devotion and outright "race-consciousness." Whether explicitly political in content or not, whether in sync with the Party line or not, this was "art as a weapon," it seems. Party aesthetes did not dismiss Black vernacular music for counter-revolutionary "immaturity" or "arrested development."[46]

To return to our preceding primary evidence, then, Richard Frank opened his treatise on "Negro Revolutionary Music" with a pointed statement. "One of the greatest forward strides in the development of the American revolutionary movement has been the policy of the Communist Party upon the Negro question," he wrote. "In the south, the ideology of the international working-class movement is beginning to be expressed in the native Negro music." Frank's reference to the "Negro Question," the Party's landmark "Black Belt," and "native" music is crucial. It suggests the ironic turn whereby the stringent racial politics of the Third Period might have been a precipitating factor in the emergence of Popular Front folk revivalism. In other words, just as "the Comintern's thesis on self-determination in the Black Belt" actually "contributed to blacks' greater cultural freedom within the Party," as Robin Kelley points out, Third Period ideology opened the way, paradoxically, for leftwing folk music revivalism. As the Black rural and industrial laborers of the South were discovered in Marxist-Leninist interpretation as among the most oppressed and exploited of the nation's "native toiling masses," to cite Frank's words, their music was prioritized among the vanguard of indigenous revolutionary arts. After years of conflict as regards Black nationalism and its putative threat to universal working-class solidarity, in short, Black culture was redefined as revolutionary workers' culture, and of the most accomplished sort. "Many of the songs sung by white workers are Negro," claimed Frank in his article. While such music was "the expression of an oppressed people," he elaborated, "it still possesses such a virility that it has an irresistible attraction even for ruling-class whites." In the author's estimation, the infectious appeal of Black musical expression was of the highest political importance. "When the American revolutionary movement finds expression in Negro music," he wrote, "it is expressing itself in a medium capable of arousing not only the twelve or fifteen million Negroes of America, but also all the toiling masses of America who for generations in one form or another have made Negro music their own." In Frank's radical vision, this development signaled the progressive union of red, white, and Black. "In my mind's eye," he concluded, "I could see these same workers, thousands and millions strong, marching in that army of the future—the Red Army of America—marching to the singing of these same revolutionary Negro folk-songs."[47]

From the Third Period to the Popular Front: Lawrence Gellert's Rise and Fall

Before the white Left embraced white vernacular music in the folksong revival in the latter 1930s, we can trace a decisive preference for Black vernacular song tradition earlier in the decade. In the movement's ideological epicenter in the North, Lawrence Gellert was instrumental. Robin Kelley has referred to him as "probably the Party's most enthusiastic champion of black music." Similarly, communist historian Mark Solomon has identified him as "the prime collector of Negro music in the CP orbit."[48] From the field of folk revival historiography, Richard Reuss judged that in the early 1930s "relatively few urban radicals were exposed directly to black folk music. Mention of its 'new' revolutionary qualities," he concluded, "was confined principally to the discussion surrounding Lawrence Gellert's 'Negro Songs of Protest.'"[49] To that note, we can trace the considerable difference in critical reception that greeted Lawrence Gellert's as compared with the Lomaxes' first songbook publications. In contrast to the favorable reviews that met *Negro Songs of Protest* in 1936, a *New Masses* review from 1934 of the Lomaxes' *American Ballads and Folk Songs* was unreserved in its charge that "class-visioned Messrs. Lomax have become organically incapable of 'seeing'" the musical protest of the oppressed toward their oppressors. "Just as the real struggles of the American workers and farmers have never been uncovered by orthodox American historians," the piece assessed, "so the task of digging up our revolutionary folk-ballads remains a job that has scarcely been started."[50] Subsequent press comment, as well, contrasted the success of Gellert's fieldwork with the relative failure of that of the Lomaxes. In 1936, a Party musical organ, *Unison*, reported that "the recent publication of some of Lawrence Gellert's Negro Songs of Protest [*sic*] has introduced at this late date an entirely new field of folk music." Whereas the Lomaxes had, in recent years, "toured the South, and gathered what they thought to be 'representative' Negro folksongs," the notice explained, Gellert's work "has convinced" them "that the songs they collected are 'white man's songs,' sung under the surveillance of guards, foremen, and the 'bossman.' The Lomaxes have been quick to benefit from Gellert's collection," it related in the end, "and today they 'plant' Negroes in jails and on chain gangs to take down the songs sung in the absence of the guards."[51]

In 1936, the communist-sponsored Workers Music League was dissolved in favor of a reconstituted organization of less overtly partisan emphasis. The American Music League, as the new association would come to be known, was established soon afterward. It took as an explicit mission the effort to "collect, study, and popularize American folk music and its traditions."[52] One early example of this new orientation was the publication of Gellert's *Negro Songs of Protest*. Indeed, the collector's material had been a continuous presence through the shift of emphasis. In direct contrast to the prevailing leftwing ambivalence concerning white radical traditions in the South, key members of the League's intellectual center in the Composers Collective had taken an interest in Gellert's documentary fieldwork. In 1934—the same year, that is, in which he had informed readers in *Daily Worker* that "not all folk-tunes are suitable to the revolutionary movement"—Charles Seeger had been in correspondence with Lawrence Gellert. "We want to start publishing your series of researches into the negro revolutionary song in the first number of the *Music Vanguard*," he proposed.[53] Also, in 1934, another Collective member, composer Lan Adomian, made favorable reference to "Negro songs of protest," along with "work songs, railroad songs, cowboy and hill songs," in a column asking "What Songs Should Workers' Choruses Sing?" in *Daily Worker*.[54] As regards the kind of Black-oriented print culture and movement politics highlighted by Robin Kelley, the collector also received queries from Benjamin Davis Jr., editor of the *Negro Liberator* weekly based in Harlem, and letters from Louis Colman of the communist-sponsored International Labor Defense. The *Negro Liberator* was the "Official Organ of the League of Struggle for Negro Rights," a civil rights affiliate of the CPUSA. Writing on behalf of the organization in 1934, Davis asked Gellert, "How about letting us have some more of those Songs of Protest?

We've printed a number and would like to have some more on tap." Similarly, Louis Colman of the ILD wrote, "The *Daily Worker* has given me a copy of your song 'Angelo an' a Thousan' Mo.' Please send us a copy of the words with music. Have you any other songs that we could use and popularize?"[55]

Lawrence Gellert's growing body of Black songs of protest had currency in the early and mid-1930s. As we have noted previously, Mike Gold—one of the few early boosters of Ella May Wiggins, Aunt Molly Jackson, and "proletarian literature" generally in the nascent folksong revival—was the figure responsible for first publishing the work of the collector. As the story goes, Gold actually lent the genre its signature title upon Gellert's initial appearance in *New Masses* in 1930. As for less directly traceable associations, an article in music history has raised the possibility that a Gellert transcription in wide circulation, "Sistern an' Brethren," was in the background of one of the most famous of mergers between historic Black cultural politics and the organized Left of the 1930s. I have excerpted representative verses:

> Sistern an' Brethern
> Stop foolin' wit' pray
> When black face is lifted
> Lawd turnin' way
>
> We're buryin' a brother
> They kill for the crime
> Tryin' to keep
> What was his all the time.
>
> Your head tain' no apple
> For danglin' f'om a tree
> Your body no carcass
> For barbecuein' on a spree.
>
> Stand on your feet
> Club gripped 'tween your hands
> Spill their blood too
> Show 'em yours is a man's.[56]

Author Nancy Kovaleff Baker speculates that "Sistern an' Brethren" was a "probable" additional inspiration for Abel Meeropol's "Strange Fruit," made famous by Billie Holiday in 1939.[57] Whether or not such a connection is born out, Gellert clearly played a role in the genesis of the leftwing folksong revival. The collector was not only among the first in the field of Black music research, but as well a distinctive presence in the seminal union of American vernacular music and American political radicalism. To this point, Richard Reuss provides one final illustration. Following the failed attempt at including traditional music in the *Red Song Book* in 1932, the Composers Collective had retrenched. The book had been "panned," if we recall, and members for the most part retreated back to their original efforts in abstract "revolutionary" composition and promotion. But in 1935, two striking examples of American vernacular music would signal the eventual shift attendant to the rise of the Popular Front. "Sistern an' Brethren" and "I Went to Atlanta"—both Gellert transcriptions that had appeared in *New Masses*—were "among the first indigenous American 'folk' creations to appear in a communist songbook anthology," states Reuss. Alongside of the radical compositions of the avant-garde Composers Collective, they stood out in the group's *Workers Song Book No. 2* in that year. Indeed, they pointed the way at mid-decade for the intellectual vanguard of the leftwing folksong revival.[58]

The left critical response to Lawrence Gellert was more favorable than that toward the Lomaxes in the earliest stages of the folksong revival. But where Gellert was briefly a Left favorite, the Lomaxes were positioned for popular embrace. Folklorist Dorothy Scarborough, for instance, praised *American Ballads and Folk Songs* in the *New York Times* in 1934: "Here is a book to read with eager enjoyment, to keep safe from would-be borrowers, to cherish permanently." The volume encapsulated the "choice pickings of a lifetime of collecting," she wrote, and "gathered together a treasure of ballads and songs that will delight not only the folklorist but the general reader as well."[59] Left thinkers and artists in 1934, by contrast, had little interest in treasures and delights for popular consumption. In the context of Third Period aesthetics, the Lomaxes' work was too rosy with respect to an ideal American spirit, too conciliatory with respect to the perceived conflict of capital and labor, and too complacent with the status quo of white and Black in the United States. The cultural politics of the Lomaxes' work was hazy and muted, and their institutional affiliations—embodied in the client relationship with the Library of Congress most prominently—too close to the official cultural apparatus of the state and government.

All this was about to change with the advent of the Popular Front in 1935, and all these distinctions favoring Gellert would end up being the very reasons the Lomaxes' canon of American folksong would come to outshine Gellert's seemingly doctrinaire specialty in "Negro Songs of Protest."[60] This historical light helps us to clarify Gellert's different experience in the formal era of the leftwing folksong revival, as it is conventionally dated between the mid-1930s and the mid-1940s. Indeed, as communist historian Mark Solomon puts it, "As the popular front expanded, Gellert's formulaic variant on 'socialist realism' weakened." Rather, he elaborates, a "more holistic 'black and white people's culture' emerged" in the latter 1930s, "which heralded folk art as the honest articulation of the experiences of working people of all races and ethnic backgrounds."[61] If Gellert's cultural work resonated in the insurgent movement culture of the Third Period, then the Lomaxes' project found its audience in the less strident Popular Front. The Lomaxes provided a vibrant soundtrack to liberal American cultural nationalism just as the modern ideology was starting to take hold in US public consciousness. The era of progressive feeling and industrial unionism that reached its peak in the years of World War II saw the rise of "working-class Americanism," and as well the emergence of Communist Party general secretary Earl Browder's slogan "Communism is the Americanism of the twentieth century."[62] In 1936, the CPUSA backed a major party candidate, Franklin Roosevelt, for president. They accommodated a no-strike pledge during World War II, reached a peak membership of 85,000 in 1942, and dissolved as a formal political party for a year in 1944. So as the organized left went mainstream in America, so did the aesthetic and political spirit of the leftwing folksong revival. In this shift, the Lomaxes' conciliatory "American ballads and folksongs" gained in favor where Gellert's confrontational "Negro songs of protest" gained in controversy. Lawrence Gellert's rise had come and his fall was imminent. "Jesus Christ, I look back here and I did a terrific amount of chasing," Gellert reflected to his interviewer in 1969. "I wasn't important, but the stuff at that time was important. . . . And, all I got for it" in the end, he complained, "was the back of the hand."[63]

CHAPTER FIVE

Big White Fog

CONTROVERSY AND CONTAINMENT IN THE POSTWAR

In my bewilderment that late afternoon, it suddenly occurred to me that we as a people were engulfed by a pack of lies, surrounded, in fact, by one big white fog through which we could see no light anywhere.

—THEODORE WARD, PLAYWRIGHT OF *BIG WHITE FOG*

In 1938, the Negro Unit of the Federal Theatre Project in Chicago mounted the social realist play *Big White Fog,* written by African American playwright Theodore Ward. As the author recalled later in life, he was "hoboing on a westbound freight train through the Rocky Mountains" when he "sickened" at the realization expressed in the epigraph above. He composed *Big White Fog* to break through the disorienting fog of lies that clouded the judgments and divided the interests of Black and white working people. Like Lorraine Hansberry's acclaimed *A Raisin in the Sun* from twenty-one years later, *Big White Fog* is a family saga set in Black Chicago. It chronicles the competing faiths and fortunes of three generations of the Mason family starting in the 1920s and culminates in crisis for them all at the knife's edge of housing eviction in the Great Depression. In the climactic scene of the play, the rival interests in the family (Garveyite and capitalist) unite with the radicalized son's communist allies in an interracial working-class alliance. Family and community come together to resist the eviction and to defy the power structure. By seeing past the lies of race difference and capitalist success, the collective models a way through the "big white fog" of American injustice to a more perfect union.[1]

Ward's play is a fitting point of reference for the narrative of Lawrence Gellert. Theodore Ward was born in 1902, only four years after Gellert. His most celebrated work, *Big White Fog* was produced only two years after Gellert's best-known publication, *Negro Songs of Protest*, from 1936. Like Ward, Gellert also worked in the Federal Theatre Project in the latter 1930s, albeit in the "Negro Unit" in Harlem rather than in Chicago, as did Ward. I have found no record of contact between Gellert and Ward, but Gellert did know and collaborate with Langston Hughes, who was involved in the New York City revival of *Big White Fog* in 1940. Gellert also claimed to have known Richard Wright in the "Negro Group" of the Federal Writers' Project in New York City. Early on, Ward impressed Wright as an up-and-coming playwright in Chicago, and Ward, Wright, Langston Hughes, and Paul Robeson ultimately co-founded the Negro Playwrights Company. For a time, these cultural workers saw their paths converge in the movement ferment of the 1930s. But as the radicalism of the Cultural Front was attacked and eclipsed, each saw a change of course in the decades that followed. Richard Wright renounced his radicalism; Robeson, Hughes, and Ward were blacklisted. Lawrence Gellert and "Negro Songs of Protest," in turn, came under a cloud of suspicion.[2]

This chapter and the following one track Gellert into the postwar and into his relative obscurity. They look closely at the charges of fraudulence that have attached to Gellert's character and archive since his rise in the 1930s. They ask questions posed then and still today. Was Gellert an honest collector? Are his songs genuine vernacular material? Was he credible personally? Was he sincere in his politics, or was he something else—an opportunist, a dupe, a careerist? As we will see, falsehoods and misperceptions have shadowed Gellert's name since the 1930s. Even his most outspoken one-time booster, Bruce Conforth, has become a critic. In his 2013 biography of Gellert, Conforth dramatically reverses his original assessment. Where Conforth in the 1980s once touted Gellert as a pioneering collector-radical, the author now denies Gellert was a genuine radical at all. The organized American Left, Conforth indicates, used Black music and Black struggle for its own ulterior ends. Gellert's involvement is cast as similarly suspect. Conforth writes of Gellert as a "chameleon," a lost soul who womanized and lived a life of "misinformation" and "false pretenses" in a chronic need for self-invention.[3] Accordingly, Conforth judges: "Based upon existing material and interviews, it seems clear that 'Negro Songs of Protest' (as a special body of material collected by Gellert) never really existed within the folk music tradition, but were, rather, the creation of the left wing and U.S. Communist Party in order to use as propaganda, with Lawrence as either their unwitting or identity-hunting dupe."[4] Conforth is only the latest in a line of skeptics including Irwin Silber in the 1960s and blues scholar Sam Charters in the 2000s. Though Gellert's full archive of papers and field recordings are open to the sunlight of public scrutiny at Indiana University, though his associates in the African American community never expressed reservations, and though his critics have been answered by some scholarship (my own and that of folk-music historian Dick Weissman, most recently), the record on Lawrence Gellert remains murky. My research in these concluding chapters is meant to clear away the fog.[5]

Backdrop to Controversy: The Cultural Left and the Culture of Containment

In the late 1940s and 1950s, the Old Left of the folksong revival saw its movement collapse under the weight of external suppression and internal disillusionment. Even Alan Lomax—despite all his prominence and achievement—was forced into a self-imposed exile in Europe in the 1950s. If the acute failure of the progressive Henry Wallace campaign for the presidency in 1948 was any indication, the foundation for a leftwing singing movement in the United States was anything but assured. Nevertheless, the legitimacy of American folksong more generally, as a field of research and scholarship, had been secured to a relative degree.

In the Roosevelt years, folklore studies became professionalized in the United States in tandem with the currents of American cultural nationalism. The field achieved a long-overdue legitimacy and was institutionalized as a federal arts program and academic discipline. New Deal progressives and leftwing cultural workers labored to move American folksong to the center of American consciousness. In World War II, many found themselves at an opportune juncture in the nation's cultural and political mobilization against fascism. Alan Lomax, for instance, left the Archive of American Folk-Song to assume a post at the Office of War Information (OWI) in 1942. Gellert's *Negro Songs of Protest* appeared in the bibliography to the Lomaxes' second volume, *Our Singing Country*, in 1941.[6] But it would never again be referenced in a Lomax publication. Gellert's younger contemporary in Black folksong research was without doubt an outspoken and influential progressive, and the folksong revival of the 1930s and 1940s that he helped to steward was also a leftwing movement. Nevertheless, what the folksong revival gained in legitimacy, it lost in political acuity. There was a prevailing turn of emphasis from overt politics to a more muted progressive poetics in the war years and afterward.[7]

Lawrence Gellert did not relent, however, in his imperative weighing politics over aesthetics in Black music research. Years afterward, he still espoused the classic radical critique of Franklin Roosevelt and his administration's New Deal reformism. Roosevelt was seen by such detractors, ultimately, to have saved capitalism from itself by addressing only its most blatant predations. On these matters, Gellert commented to his interviewer that the fervor for revolution was "fantastic" in the 1930s. "If it hadn't been for Roosevelt, we might have done it," he argued. "Roosevelt did the greatest favor to the capitalistic system that any president has ever done. He saved it. He really saved it. He was a tremendous guy. But, his heart was in the right place, and I mean Right."[8]

At the same time, Gellert faulted the Communist Party, too, both for turning mainstream in backing Roosevelt by the late 1930s and for its earlier hard-left policy of African American "self-determination" in the Black Belt of the southern United States. In this, Gellert felt that his song material might have played a counterproductive role in reinforcing what were inflated expectations and naive Party assessments of Black revolutionary sentiment. "The Central Committee of the Communist Party, on the basis of these folksongs," he stated, "made tremendous mistakes in the South. . . . They thought the Negroes were really revolutionary and were ready to do something about it." But an independent Black movement for national liberation in the South would have led to a "slaughter," Gellert believed, considering prevailing conditions. "I think Stalin devised [the plan] for them," he said. "It was the mistake of the century. I think that was as much responsible for the downfall of the whole structure, the whole leftwing movement of the Thirties" as anything external, he indicated. Though Gellert never doubted African Americans' determination for freedom, he bemoaned the Party's misconceived prescriptions for change. "The Negro has always wanted nothing to be . . . but just an ordinary man, just like anybody else," he held. In the North and in the South, Blacks "came around the Communist Party because that's the only place they thought they'd be accepted" as "human beings and nothing else. And, the Communist Party broke its [own] neck. That was the beginning of the downfall of the Communist Party in this country." Always the iconoclast, Gellert remained a critical thinker with a philosophical commitment to socialism to the end of his life. Never a strict disciple of anything, however, he marveled at fellow radicals, his brother Hugo among them, who maintained unfailing dedication to the Party. Lawrence was an agitator, and he wanted revolution, but he was never disciplined. Frequently, he was the contrarian.[9]

The close connections between the Left and American folksong were a boon and a bust for Gellert. As the climate for folksong research shifted with the larger realignments of American politics, Gellert found himself on shaky ground. In 1937, Alan Lomax was appointed the first salaried Director of the Archive of American Folk-Song at the Library of Congress. Lomax was beginning his ascendance at the institutional center of American folksong. But Lawrence Gellert had reached a pinnacle. In that same year, he both won and promptly lost a prized grant for field research from the Rockefeller Foundation. "Gellert is not interested in folksongs; he is interested in revolution," read the report revoking the award, as the collector griped later.[10]

On the Outs: Lawrence Gellert in the Postwar

While Popular Front folklorists moved to the center of American life, Lawrence Gellert remained doggedly, and vocally, on the margins. During World War II, as Lomax promoted folk culture and singing under the auspices of the Office of War Information, Gellert was collecting songs and sentiments from disaffected Black Army soldiers. Gellert published "Jim Crow in Khaki" in *New Masses* in 1946 as well as his piece "Talk in Monroe" on the Georgia quadruple lynching from that year. In "Jim Crow in Khaki," he ended with the remarks of "a Negro top sergeant" who, Gellert said, despite all the indignities of an apartheid US military, "did his part in knocking Hitler into a cocked hat." With irony, the sergeant told Gellert, "Boy, I made believe all them Germans was just crackers from Georgia. And didn't we give 'em hell!" Such public sentiment was going to find zero tolerance as the Cold War set in by 1947 and intensified in the 1950s. In "Talk in Monroe," as we have seen in chapter 2, Gellert went undercover and let racism speak for itself in a series of short "person-on-the-street" testimonies. The piece was prefaced with an annotation that Gellert had "recently returned" from his trip to investigate the lynching "in behalf of the Civil Rights Congress [CRC]." Like *New Masses* itself, the CRC was a communist-affiliated entity that would be red-baited out of existence in the 1950s.[11]

Gellert's open associations were fuel to the fire of anticommunism, but he continued fusing his political concerns for racial justice with his collecting interests in Black music. In a letter in *New Masses* from December 1946, Gellert shared his views on the origins of jazz in Black America and praised a previous article titled "What Is Jazz?" by Marxist culture critic Sidney Finkelstein. Gellert asserted that "Finkelstein's piece . . . is about the best I've seen in print on the subject to date." He concluded, "And, I'd rather listen to Count Basie or Ted Williams than go to the Met." The reference to "Ted Williams" is likely a misnomer for jazz pianist Teddy Wilson. All three figures—Finkelstein, Basie, and "Williams" (Wilson)—would soon suffer under Cold War containment. Finkelstein, one of the prominent US communist intellectuals of the period, published his classic *Jazz: A People's Music* in 1948; he was called before the House Un-American Activities Committee (HUAC) in 1957. Basie and "Williams" (Wilson) were pressured by management in the latter 1940s to sever all progressive ties or risk black-listing. As Michael Denning writes, "The anti-Communist purge took its toll on the jazz left."[12]

Meanwhile, Gellert pressed on. His activities could hardly have been casual or uncommitted. Activists who fought for labor rights and racial redress were denounced for ulterior motives as "race-mixers" and "red" criminal conspirators in this period of conservative repression. The push for civil rights met the crush of anticommunism. Even now-revered "bipartisan" heroes like Rosa Parks and Martin Luther King Jr. were targeted as suspect. To side openly on the left in these years was to court the devil of Cold War intolerance.[13]

Gellert contributed letters and articles to *New Masses* through 1947, and when the journal dissolved into a merger with fellow Marxist quarterly *Mainstream* in 1948, he published further pieces on the left in the resulting *Masses & Mainstream.* These items drew on his travels and collecting work, present and past, and they continued to display his signature tone, acerbic and outspoken. In "Fishin'" from September 1947, Gellert marked the passing of notorious Mississippi segregationist Theodore Bilbo with ridicule. Gellert recounted three occasions of contact with Bilbo, including a fishing trip gone awry down South in the early 1930s. He joked that Bilbo was a "wind-bag" who frightened off the fish and compared the deathbed Bilbo's white handkerchief in hospital in New Orleans to a Ku Klux Klan hood. Gellert closed the piece with political analysis. "The Negro as well as the disenfranchised poor white man," Gellert opined, "knows that the rulers' choice among the dozen or so lesser fry scrambling to fill Bilbo's place in Mississippi politics will be made on the basis of the greatest alacrity and effectiveness in pursuing the traditional role. Bilboism by any other name sure smells the same."[14]

Later in 1947, the collector offered his piece "Lynchers Are Not Born." With a fictionalized reconstruction of his time spent boarding with a family in South Carolina, and how a young "Johnny" he once knew came to hate, Gellert made his point that racial violence was learned behavior, not born instinct. In 1951, as the Korean War, McCarthyism, and segregation intersected as Cold War Americanism, William L. Patterson of the dissident Civil Rights Congress issued an apt analysis. "The lyncher and the atom bomb are related," Patterson insisted.

"White supremacy at home makes for colored massacres abroad. Both reveal contempt for human life in a colored skin."[15] Gellert, who had worked with the CRC on the Monroe lynching, was drawing from the same palette fusing antiracism and pacifism. In 1951, he published an original song, "Atom Bomb Blues." Gellert recalled, "I was living with Edith Segal at the time. She wanted us to write a peace song. Actually, we wrote it together. She sent it out as a Christmas card from both of us." Segal, a longtime radical, was the founder of the Red Dancers in New York City. The composition appeared in *Sing Out!* magazine, the leading organ of the emergent postwar folk music movement.[16]

Gellert had chosen political sides in the 1940s and 1950s, and he was not shy about it. Archival items among Earl Conrad's papers give us additional insight on Gellert's renegade persona in the period. A glimpse of exchanges in 1947 between Conrad in New York and an itinerant "Larry" in Atlanta and New Orleans shows the two plotting ways to, as Conrad put it, "crack the thing open down there" with Conrad's book *Jim Crow America.* Gellert sent a January postcard to Conrad from Atlanta. He provided a "care of" local address with the note: "If you should want anything." Conrad wrote back in March, saying that perhaps a group of student-activists in Atlanta "could be got to bring a copy of the book in a delegation to Talmadge or to the head of the Klan, or something like that. If a stunt like that could be pulled and if it cracked the press it would be a great thing." Conrad closed that he hoped Gellert had "enjoyed" his advance copy and was "picking up some songs" while he was in the field down South.[17]

Gellert responded from the Hotel Lynrose in New Orleans. "I expect to be back in Atlanta in another week or two and will cook up something," he replied. "Maybe take your book to Hoiman myself . . . with a photographer to snap me being thrown out the window."[18] "Hoiman" was a reference to Herman Talmadge, son of segregationist Georgia governor Eugene Talmadge, who had died before beginning his fourth term in office; in 1947, the younger Talmadge was vying with two other Georgia politicians to assume the governorship.[19] Gellert joked that he would make sure to "feature the book title prominently so folks won't get the idea looking at the photograph that I'm being ejected because I have B.O. That would ruin my reputation." In a more serious vein, he wondered about alternatives in a subsequent note. "Maybe a photo of your book hanging on the end of that chain at the Monroe lynching site?" he wrote. Then, in a further letter from the Hotel Lynrose, he offered an update: "Mahomet couldn't go to the mountain—too expensive with a photographer. So the mountain comes to New Orleans. I'll go to the gentleman with his book, for autograph[,] and yours, just incidentally, for comment and photograph." By this point, the plot had seemed to have evolved from a publicity ambush of Herman Talmadge in Georgia to Mississippi's Theodore Bilbo, then ailing in New Orleans. In 1947, Bilbo had published his own book, *Take Your Choice: Separation or Mongrelization*, and this was presumably the item (the "his book") to which Gellert referred in the scheme. Gellert commented that he had press credentials by which to pull off the stunt. These were *New Masses* credentials "which I'll pass off for a religious publication—reformed Catholic," he kidded.[20]

The Conrad papers from Gellert include a news clipping on Bilbo's impending medical arrival in New Orleans and a concluding letter from "Larry" detailing how it all unfolded in the end. Gellert explained:

> It's a long story. But the part that should interest your publisher:–
>
> Bilbo and a 6'4" Lieutenant Colonel arrived at the Ochsner Clinic . . . at 1:55 Tuesday afternoon. Bilbo wore a Klansman like sheet (square handkerchief probably) from his nose down to his chest. He was hard to identify because he'd gained weight, the bastard pot belly and what I could see of his face was round and sunburned instead of the haggard [. . .] one I remembered. It was only when the aide . . . announced "Senator Bilbo" that things began to happen. The book [*Jim Crow America*] was handed over . . . the Senator opened the very loosely tied package and when he saw what it contained, he mumbled something . . . nothing flattering to judge from the tone of voice. Then I hastened to get the photographer who was seated near the desk reading a newspaper. . . . He too was thrown off by the mask. By the time I could exclaim, the Senator had started for the elevator. The photographer rushed after him, but was intercepted by the Lieutenant Colonel who blocked him off until the Senator had disappeared into the elevator. That picture with Bilbo in the KKKlanlike mask would have been priceless. Why in hell don't I learn to use a camera?

Thus, Gellert was unable to perfect the caper. The photograph of Bilbo with *Jim Crow America* in hand was never taken. But Gellert appeared undeterred. He ended the letter by saying he was next heading "up to Atlanta" where, perhaps, he was retuning the plot yet again to its original proposed target, Herman Talmadge.[21]

Gellert's letters about the ambush reveal an individual undaunted and even gleeful as a saboteur in unfriendly environs. Indeed, just as Earl Conrad described himself, Gellert seemed to relish the role of "white war correspondent" in the "racial fight" for social justice.[22] The letters also show an individual in motion. Gellert repeatedly prods Conrad for funds and opportunities. Gellert responds to Conrad's parting wish hoping the collector is "picking up some songs" in the March letter with a determined negative. "No I'm not gathering any more songs," Gellert answered. "I have more than I'll ever use. I offered some—50+ of it to the aluminum drive during the war and had them rejected." Gellert reported instead that he was "gathering material for a chapter on Louisiana for a book I'm projecting." In a postscript to the letter, he seems to reference the book project again. He states, "I'm looking at sugar plantations with obliging Sheriffs and other gentry with whom I spend a lot of time cursing "n——rs all to goddam for ruining the country!" and he adds, "I certainly could use a concert of Negro Songs of Protest by the People's group or any other, as a benefit after all these years!"[23] The lines resonate with Conrad's description in *Jim Crow America* that Gellert "looks like a native Southerner and 'passes' as such when he is there."[24] Additionally, they indicate that whatever the collector's feelings about any further song hunting, he was still interested in promoting the fruits of his fieldwork. Gellert ends the last letter to Conrad with what seems a pitch for a story on the Bilbo ambush: "Full story—all the stratagems and maneuvers in a whole chapter. Later."[25] At almost fifty years old, Gellert remained active. He was traveling, writing, and hustling for work. Making a living on the fly, on the move, and on the left in these years could not have been easy.

In the latter 1950s and into the 1960s, Gellert continued to publish on racial struggle and Black folklore in the leftwing press. Now settled with a permanent address at 148 Sullivan Street in Soho on the border with Greenwich Village in New York City, Gellert contributed a series of documentary vignettes from continuing travels in the South and even from the famous fountain in Washington Square Park in his own relative backyard. As the editors of *Masses and Mainstream* put it about the series, these "dialogues" were "not imaginary encounters but re-creations of conversations overheard or told to the author."[26] Additionally, Gellert published two such "dialogue" pieces in the magazine under a pseudonym, William Fay. These two items, "Folks Are Real Friendly Down Here" and "Overheard in Fayette County," were published in 1961.[27] Both related to the "Tent City" civil rights encampment in Fayette County, Tennessee, from 1960 to 1962. Local Black sharecroppers had been evicted by landowners for the simple act of registering to vote, and Gellert documented attitudes and activities on the scene. Bruce Conforth reports that this was possibly the collector's last trip to the South to capture sentiment and sounds, and that Gellert employed the pseudonym to protect his identity on such forays.[28] I first encountered Gellert's pseudonym through research into an unpublished manuscript, "Tales of One Time I'shman, Told by Southern Negroes," a collection of some seventy Black folktales lampooning the Irish in the South. The title page mock-up of the manuscript indicates "From the collection of Lawrence Gellert," but the introduction page lists "By 'William Fay'" in green ink in Gellert's recognizable handwriting.[29] Whether the pseudonym was for commercial purposes to maximize publishing opportunities or for security, or both, Conforth relates that Gellert remained under FBI investigation through these years. From the 1930s into the 1960s, Conforth writes, the Federal Bureau of Investigation kept a file on the "subversive Lawrence Gellert."[30]

Gellert's presence in the folk music press became more unstable as the 1950s wore on. A Gellert transcription under the title "Steel Got to Be Drove" appeared in *Sing Out!* in 1953. The item was prefaced by the editors with an annotation that the song was "typical of the many steel-driving chants which were sung during the period" of John Henry folklore and that the "chant printed here is from Lawrence Gellert's fine collection of chain gang and protest songs, 'Me and My Captain.'"[31] There were a few other short Gellert appearances in *Sing Out!* in the early 1950s, but then the outlet appears to have gone cold.[32]

In the 1960s, folk music impresario Israel "Izzy" Young became friendly with Gellert. Young was proprietor of the famed Folklore Center in Greenwich Village, about a ten-minute walk from Gellert's apartment. In these years, Young contributed a regular column to *Sing Out!* titled "Frets and Frails." Young registered Gellert's activities along with those of key individuals in the "folk boom" of the era. In anecdotal entries dated to 1960 that were intended as "a running commentary on the trade" for Young's columns, he recorded several interactions with Gellert in his store and on the street. Gellert told him about his conflicts with the Lomaxes over Lead Belly; about crossing paths with the Lomaxes in his southern fieldwork; and about deriving royalties from a song, "Look Over Yonder," released by artist Harry Belafonte. In 1962, Young reported in "Frets and Frails" that Gellert was "contemplating the production of an LP based on his field recordings of Negro protest in the 30's [*sic*]. This would nicely complement new protest albums being issued by the Student Nonviolent Coordinating Committee, Audio-Fidelity and Folkways Records." Young also printed in 1965 that "Mort Freeman and Elie Siegmeister are working on a project based on Larry Gellert's collection of *Negro Songs of Protest* that he made in the 1930s." In these years, Gellert was on the hunt for a record company to release his documentary recordings and a folksong repository to archive his materials.[33]

In email exchanges and a phone interview with me in 2002, Young recalled his friendship with Gellert. "Larry wore a simple black suit just about all the time," he remembered. The two would go book collecting to far-flung destinations around the city. Gellert did not own a phone and never had guests up to his apartment. This included Young, who always met Gellert outside on the sidewalk. The collector evidently talked some about his archive, but never let on that he had done so much work in the field, nor that he had so many field discs languishing at home. In his exchanges with me, Young expressed surprise at the extent of Gellert's archive. "How could he have kept it secret that he had made" hundreds of field recordings? wondered Young. "That would put him on par, easily, with the Lomaxes, for the time that he was recording!" Young continued that had he known about the scope of the collection, he "would certainly have written about it in *Sing Out!* as a lead item in my column. I would have considered it important and mindboggling."[34]

As it happened, in a summer 1963 column, Young instead referenced, without taking a position, a print dispute that would signal trouble as regards Gellert's standing vis-à-vis the Lomaxes and other peers: "Larry Gellert and Irwin Silber take great issue as to the origins of Negro songs collected by Gellert in the 20s in the current issue of 'Masses and Main-Stream [*sic*].'"[35] In the July 1963 issue of *Mainstream*, Gellert had suffered censure by one among his own in the leftwing folksong community. In February 1963, under the familiar title "Negro Songs of Protest," *Mainstream* published five song texts credited to Gellert. These were "Uncle Gabriel," "Nat Turner," "Old John Brown," "Scottsboro Boys," and "Baton Rouge." Gellert called them "milestones on freedom road" and dated them chronologically to each respective historical period ("Nat Turner," for instance, to "Virginia, 1831").[36] In response to the piece, Irwin Silber, editor of *Sing Out!* magazine[37] and a one-time Gellert enthusiast, went public in the July 1963 *Mainstream* with a profound change of stance. In "Dubious," a letter to the editor, Silber wrote:

> Frankly, as a person familiar with folk music and folklore materials for considerable time, I find it very difficult to accept the material presented by Gellert as folk songs which he really collected. Aside from the fact of documentation which would let us know where and under what circumstances, etc. the songs were collected, the fact that no one else has ever been able to collect similar songs or the same song in a different version, would tend to indicate that this material should be approached with a great deal of care. . . . I am strongly of the opinion that these songs of

> Lawrence Gellert are more likely his or someone else's original creation rather than material, which by any stretch of the imagination, could fall into the domain of folk songs.[38]

The statement of dismissal was more a renunciation than denunciation. Silber's charge of fabrication derived from a suspicion from the inside of Communist Party agitation. For much of the 1940s and 1950s, Silber was, like Gellert, active within the CPUSA. As such, he was no stranger to the internal workings of the Party, nor its devices for agitating both inside and outside its own ranks. In 1958, Silber ended his Party membership, though he retained independent radical socialist viewpoints. Ironically, as we will see, Silber's low opinion of Gellert's work, which he continued to express long afterward, bore striking similarities to some of the collector's own reservations concerning Communist Party practice. Silber explained that his skepticism was to do with the Party's tendency in those heady days to create "illusions" that radical "influence" was "greater than it really was." In that sense, he elaborated, it was "painting a picture that doesn't stand up. . . . The black masses weren't ready for revolution, no matter how much I and others wanted to believe it."[39]

Just below Silber's letter, *Mainstream* printed Gellert's reply in that same July 1963 issue. The collector responded that the "dates given" with each song "were for the actual events themselves," not for when Gellert encountered the material, as "any sixth grade school child could point out." He added that "variants and other evidence of currency of these songs more than 100 years old, are extant" in scholarship "more qualified than that which Mr. Silber parades here," and that "Negro Songs of Protest are cries reaching out to all mankind everywhere . . . seeking kinship, consolation, understanding, guidance and help." Gellert's points had merit. But, as the "sixth grade school child" retort suggests, Gellert's letter went low with vitriol more than it stayed high with kinship and understanding. Gellert called Silber a crass entrepreneur, venal and hypocritical in his feigned concern for folk purity. He ridiculed Silber for a Folkways Records release of "Rebel yells, whoops, and Hollers," and he complained that another Folkways album, produced by Silber, had used an item from his collection without permission or payment. "It all adds up," ended Gellert, "to the fact that Mr. Silber's 'scholarly' concern for Negro folk songs is like that of the Southern hound dogs for the dark meat of the chicken."[40]

Irwin Silber's letter ultimately proved the more enduring "last word." Gellert had published the "Nat Turner" transcription before, in *Daily Worker* in 1949. In that article, the collector compared opposing white and Black songs from

Virginia about the "great Negro freedom fighter." The "one current among the whites," he wrote, "is a doleful dirge, as well it might be," and the other, "the real Nat Turner Song," he stated, came "from the lips of the Negroes." It was "a robust, spirited concoction, fresh and impudent." And it had a secret buried in the wording. The ending refrain for each verse might have sounded like this: "But you can't keep the World from moverin' around / And not turn her back from the gaining ground." Gellert, however, explained that African American singers meant this: "You can't keep the World from moverin' around / And NAT TURNER back from the gaining ground."[41]

In 1949, no one disputed the claim. Gellert was still regarded as sound enough among the Cultural Left of the old folksong revival. By 1963, though, a new "folk boom" was underway with a new cultural and political orientation. Some of the same people were involved (Irwin Silber and Alan Lomax, for instance), but they had new positions of leadership and influence. Now, Gellert's material—"Nat Turner" and more—was deemed suspect, possibly fraudulent. Was it genuine Black folklore or inauthentic white propaganda? In his interviews from the 1960s, Gellert told Richard Reuss that Silber's dismissal in *Mainstream* had base origins relating to an earlier financial dispute during the Henry Wallace presidential campaign in 1948. "It had nothing to with songs," Gellert charged. "It's a personal attack. But, it didn't matter much to me. What purpose would I have for making up songs like this? If I were making up songs, I'd make up some songs I'd get some money out of it. I set myself up [for failure] with these songs," Gellert contended, since they were politically sensitive. Reuss granted, "I suppose, you get typed." Gellert stipulated, "Look, I was a revolutionary interested only in" agitation. "I got sort of on fire with the condition of the Negroes, and I really concentrated on that."[42]

Folksongs versus Songs of Protest

The details and accuracy of Gellert's allegations concerning the 1948 backstory to his conflict with Silber are unresolved. In an interview with me, Silber denied memory of any such thing, as did Pete Seeger in a separate interview.[43] What is important is the larger debate of folksongs versus songs of protest to which Gellert's material was ultimately subjected.

In the Cultural Left of the 1930s and 1940s initially, where the stress was on protest rather than folk purity, Gellert's credibility was relatively secure. In *American Folk Music and Left-Wing Politics*, Reuss explains: "For urban radicals familiar with Negro folk music principally in the contexts of minstrel buffoonery and mournful spirituals performed by soothing chorales, such militant fare was electrifying indeed. In time, some folk song scholars tried to cast doubt on the authenticity of Gellert's material because the genre was not well documented and because he included creations not strictly in oral tradition. Yet at the time of initial publication, few questioned their genuine quality. They had a considerable impact in communist music circles from the start."[44] Gellert told Reuss, "The people that were interested in the songs originally were the leftwing movement. And, that was my only outlet at that time. . . . I didn't get to know Silber and his gang until the '40s. . . . My only contact with this material was with the leftwing magazine[s], the leftwing press." Reuss specified, "Well, in other words, it was only later that your collection came under attack." Gellert affirmed, "It was never under attack until [1963] . . . Openly, it was never under attack. The first time anyone's really come out is this Silber." Again, in the interview exchange, Reuss sought to highlight the twists and turns of the chronology of acceptance and denial. "Didn't *Sing Out!* in its early days publish some of your material?" he asked, to which Gellert responded, yes, presumably in reference to the "Steel Got To Be Drove" piece from 1953. In that item, if we recall, with Silber at the helm of the journal, Gellert's "fine collection of chain gang and protest songs" was seen fit for publication as genuine and meaningful.[45]

In fact, and in ironic concert with Irwin Silber, Gellert in hindsight felt that left ideologues put too much faith in his "Negro Songs of Protest" in the original folksong movement. In his 1960s interviews, Gellert concurred that Communist thinkers "over-idealized the proletariat," as interviewer Reuss put it, in part on the basis of his songs. Party people "thought it was the beginning of the revolution in America," elaborated Gellert, when actually a song "doesn't mean . . . all it says," necessarily. "A good many of them are sort of just looking ahead" without any specific agenda. Gellert added, "And, they have an expression down there—'He's big-mouthing'—But, when the white man was around, you don't sing these songs." In these comments, Gellert indicated that the vernacular expression he documented reflected genuine feelings of alienation, but that the conditions for revolution remained far on the horizon. In life, no matter how oppressive, he asserted, it is "just a small group" that is "fighting back" while "the majority of them are just looking out of the corner of their eyes. That's the way it always is. See, it's a small group, always, that leads the way, that's battling." Revolution would come someday, but the time was not right in the 1930s, nor in the 1960s, Gellert insisted. "Communism will succeed in the world simply because it's a superior society to capitalism, and because the natural resources will only be retained with a cooperative world. . . . On that basis, I'm sure that communism is the future of the world, and eventually, the various communist parties will find a way."[46]

After World War II, culture and politics in the United States shifted from a left lean to right retrenchment. The energies for radical change were suppressed, diffused, and driven underground. Gellert felt the change. "I went off in 1941 with the Army,"[47] he said. "And then, when I came back, folk music, somehow or another, you know, flip-flopped. And, I always had trouble because the title of my songs, 'protest songs.' . . . Nobody would touch it for a while."[48]

In the interview conversation for the comments above, Reuss was joined by Izzy Young. Young asked the obvious question considering all these individuals' overlapping associations in the postwar New York folk scene: "What about Moe Asch at Folkways? Has he ever been interested, or expressed interest?" Gellert answered that "Courlander came to me several times. I was pretty friendly with Courlander." From Folkways Records' beginnings until 1960, Harold Courlander, a writer and folklore freelancer, oversaw the famous independent label's Ethnic Library series. According to Gellert, Courlander proposed, "Why don't you grab you an armful of this stuff" to take to owner Moses Asch? Gellert added that Courlander "wanted me to come around. But, this was fifteen years ago [1953]. Since then, no one has ever approached me." Gellert explained that "it was the height of the McCarthy period, and I think I frightened him a little bit because I told him, 'You know . . . the consequences of this at this time.' They're all protest. I've got nothing but protest records. I made a specialty of it." In response, Young pressed for a renewed effort. "Why don't you approach Moe now?" he asked. Gellert stated, "I would be glad to, but without Silber." As of 1958, Silber was in business with Asch at *Sing Out!* magazine and Folkways Records. Nevertheless, Young assured Gellert that Silber would have "nothing to do with it." Gellert was clearly pleased. He stated, "You tell Moe I'd be tickled to death." Despite the fact that Young pledged that he would "talk to his [Asch's] son right now," there is no indication of any follow-up. The proposal never came to fruition.[49]

Political and disciplinary conservatism coalesced as the leftwing folksong movement gave way to a folklore mainstream after World War II. It was not just that Gellert was too far and too openly on the margins politically; it was that Gellert was too untethered institutionally and too contrarian academically. Nevertheless, even in the midst of this realignment, from his first songbook in 1936 through the 1940s and into the 1950s, Gellert remained a reputable enough name in the field to warrant occasional mention in the *Journal of American Folklore*, the peer-reviewed publication of record for the discipline. *Negro Songs of Protest* was included among a list of new works by Franz Boas, Frances Densmore, Miguel Covarrubias, George Herzog, Dorothy Scarborough, and Stith Thompson, among others, in the "Some Recent Publications" list in the Book Reviews section in 1936. Gellert's book was again cited as a source in two *JAF* articles in 1943, including Russell Ames's notable "Art in Negro Folksong." In a state of the field report, "Afro-American Folklore," in 1947, Gellert's *Negro Songs of Protest* was still regarded highly enough to be included as one of the "noteworthy collections" selected in a bibliography by academic folklorist J. Mason Brewer; Gellert's text was there in the bibliography among those of more established figures, from the Lomaxes to Courlander, Odum and Johnson, Scarborough, Newman White, and Zora Neale Hurston. In 1951, Richard Dorson, a heavyweight if ever there was one in post-War academic folklore, included a citation to Gellert in a list that he compiled in the *JAF* on "Folklore in Periodical Literature." Significantly, Dorson included in this list Gellert's "Two Songs about Nat Turner," the 1949 article with the "Nat Turner" transcription that ended up coming under fire for fraudulence by Silber in 1963. Dorson in 1951, however, did not doubt the material.[50]

Silber's 1963 charge, though, appeared to signal a chill, and this came during the key decade in which folk revivalism intersected with civil rights as a popular phenomenon. Gellert's name did not reappear in the *JAF* until 1972, when folklorist D. K. Wilgus reviewed Gellert's privately released documentary album from that year. Wilgus wrote, "One recalls the skepticism that greeted Lawrence Gellert's *Negro Songs of Protest* (New York 1936). Independent collection since then has tended to validate a good deal of Gellert's material, and Gellert himself has privately issued [this] 12" LP *Collection of Lawrence Gellert Negro Songs of Protest* (Timely TI-112), which gives considerable documentation to his book." Even though Wilgus offered a partial vindication and returned Gellert's name to a *JAF* readership, he also aired the rumor of doubt that had come to settle on the archive. As we have seen, the validity of Gellert's material did not actually seem to be in question at first in the 1930s and 1940s. Even outside the political Left, references to Gellert were included in the *Journal of American Folklore* without qualification or disclaimer. But what D. K. Wilgus had tapped into in 1972 was the deeper issue of folksongs versus songs of protest that had come to stigmatize the Gellert collection. In his review of the LP, Wilgus granted, "There is no doubt that these are field recordings." He now felt, he conveyed, that folklorists could trust that Gellert had indeed done real collecting in the field and not simply used the folk idiom to pass off propaganda lyrics of his own invention. Still, the material was "questionable," Wilgus contended. One of the most strident songs, for instance—"In Atlanta, Georgia"—"may have been simply a nonce-creation by a militant black," he posited. Were these one-time songs tainted by political influence, and thus suspect for their vernacular purity? Or were they songs in common circulation and in the common spirit of genuine Black folk? Wilgus expressed the reservations of a conservative disciplinary mindset in the field. Gellert may have been a real collector. But these songs were not really folklore.[51]

In the 1960s, Gellert told interviewer Reuss that he was never openly accused of fabrication until 1963 when Silber issued his allegation. Still, Gellert related that he felt suspect in the eyes of some folklore traditionalists all along. He explained: "I was attacked when my first book came out. There were lots of the academicians at the various places. They were English professors. . . . They attacked it on the ground that it wasn't old stuff. One of them said that folklore had to go underground . . . and then emerge like water in a well. It wasn't good until it had been seasoned underground for years and years."[52] Gellert later vented in the same interview session, "Scholars are shit." When asked, though, if there were any folklorists he did like, he commented, "Herbert Halpert ran to my defense." Indeed, Halpert, an anthropologist and folklorist with credentialed tutelage under Ruth Benedict and George Herzog, published an article in *Southern Folklore Quarterly* in 1938 that applauded Gellert for valuable work. "No similar collection had ever been published before Mr. Lawrence Gellert issued" *Negro Songs of Protest* in 1936, stated Halpert. "Some old-line scholars sneered that the material was modern," but "folksongs that spring from new social conditions, such as the industrialization of the South makes inevitable, are songs we hail with enthusiasm because they show the true vitality of folklore in the South."[53]

Radical in the Woodpile

In the postwar, some of this same disciplinary "sneering" held sway. John Greenway, one of the only authors of the period who included Gellert's songs in a formal publication, became a target. Greenway published the renegade *American Folksongs of Protest* in 1953. As a doctoral student, Greenway wrote to Gellert for guidance two years before.[54] In his book, Greenway references a number of Gellert's songs texts and even titled a chapter "Negro Songs of Protest." The study was dismissed. Such work may have been fine for most "historians, and others who have no special interest in folklore," wrote leading folklore emissary Stith Thompson in a review in 1954, but it was "something else" for the trained practitioners of his emergent discipline. "Here is a book called American Folksongs which contains not a single example of what a competent folklorist would call by that name," Thompson argued. "Folk songs are songs that are traditional, that are handed down from singer to listener and that are still alive. The songs in this collection . . . are not and never were folk songs."[55]

Greenway's book did not sit well with folklore traditionalists, especially in the context of the Cold War. Oddly enough, though, Greenway himself issued a dictum in *American Folksongs of Protest* that would come to be directed at Gellert, a putative ally in the merging of folk and protest. In "The Genesis of the Protest Folksongs," a subsection of his introduction, Greenway detailed his terms. "The degree of outside influence" on a song, he specified, "can be estimated by reference to the object of protest. If it is the immediate purveyor of injustice, the Negro prisoner's captain or the miner's gun thug," for instance, he wrote, then "there has been little outside stimulation." But, he added, "if the song contains lines like 'I hate the capitalist system,'" a more abstract ideological target Greenway intimated, then "there is a radical in the woodpile."[56]

This debate over "outside" radical influence and "insider" purity troubled academic folklore greatly in the years of Cold War sensitivity. David King Dunaway explains: "A continuing issue in the debate among folklorists on the folk-protest song has been whether folksongs are themselves carriers of protest and dissent, or if these are value-neutral plaints, usurped by social reformers—particularly those associated with the communist Left—to serve specific political agendas. . . . Scholarship of the 1950s and 1960s was dominated by researchers of an anticommunist bias." Dunaway periodizes this intellectual history from the beginning of the Cold War to the early 1970s. He relates that folklorist Thelma James set the terms in a "scathing" piece "alleging abuse of folk materials by political reformers" in the *Journal of American Folklore* in 1948. Greenway countered with an alternative viewpoint that "American social protest songs must be categorized as folksongs" in his book in 1953. This thesis was rejected, as we have seen, by Stith Thompson, and, as Dunaway points out, by ballad scholar Tristram Coffin in *New York Folklore Quarterly* in 1958. In the 1960s and 1970s, anticommunist authors David Noebel and R. Serge Denisoff added their voices of rebuke. It was not until Richard Reuss's 1971 dissertation and labor lore specialist Archie Green's 1972 *Only a Miner*, concludes Dunaway, that "research on the folk-topical tradition took a turn for the neutral."[57]

The sticking point of folksongs versus songs of protest is in part what Reuss tried to tease out with Gellert in their 1960s interviews. For his research on the Left and American folk music, Reuss wanted to clear up the controversy that had come to cloud Gellert's "Negro Songs of Protest." In their conversations, Reuss stressed the question of purpose. "You wanted to use it [the act of collecting songs] for certain purposes," he volunteered. Gellert affirmed, "I'm not a folklorist—I never claimed to be a folklorist. . . . I pointed my songs in a particular way. I used it as a weapon. In that respect, I think it has as much influence on our society of the 1930s as anyone else's." Reuss added, "You were publishing this stuff not in any sense for folkloristic purposes." Gellert, in agreement, emphasized again that his goal was politics not folklore. He said he wanted to "push the Negro movement, such as it was. I think if they have any value, they'll have a great deal of value to the Negroes themselves. I should really give these to a Negro university." Sterling Brown "expressed a wish for them" at Howard University, Gellert claimed. This reality—that Gellert was operating with alternative purposes outside of the rules and mainsprings of disciplinary folklore—was key to a fair reassessment, indicated Reuss. "I've got to bring this out," he interjected. "This is a very important point."[58]

Because Gellert had no easy way to process or play his field discs in the 1960s, Reuss worked exclusively from the basis of Gellert's print archive. The interviewer set about documenting the circumstances, setting, and dates of many of Gellert's published song transcriptions. He addressed the allegations of creative license directly in multiple exchanges over the span of their interviews between 1966 and 1969. Reuss asked plainly, "Did you write any songs yourself?" Gellert stated, "No, nothing published of my own. Those were songs which I had." Reuss inquired as to any editorial input. Gellert answered, "I wouldn't touch up anything. I printed them pretty much the way I got them." Reuss followed up, "Did you take down names of informants?" Gellert replied, "No, those kinds of songs, they wouldn't want any names mentioned." What about "dates, places?" Reuss asked. Gellert commented that the "notes-with-songs" annotations in his Nancy Cunard anthology essay and in his *New Masses* article series usually included locations. These were "little stories that I got fresh," he stated. They were meant to serve, in other words, as field documentation from the point of encounter. But as Gellert also freely admitted, he was "not systemized" in his collecting. His work in the field was motivated by political urgency rather than folklore professionalism. Reuss underlined, "Again, this was not part of your purpose. This needs to be made clear."[59]

As regarded the movement culture of the 1930s and Black freedom, Reuss pushed these questions farther. He asked, "Did people like [Sterling] Brown or [Langston] Hughes ever write songs that you included in your collection?" Gellert responded, "Never. Never." Reuss then brought up "Scottsboro," a song that had come under suspicion for outside tampering or outright invention.[60] Was it a folksong of old and anonymous origin, or a song of protest, recent and topical? "I got it in the area of the Scottsboro thing, of the case itself. Somebody had written it there," Gellert remarked. "So, they [critics] said, 'How can it be a folksong if you just got it?'" But Gellert was unconcerned.[61]

Reuss continued in this line of inquiry. He wondered if any of Gellert's informants had "political consciousness." Were any of them politicized locals? In a spirit befitting his claimed indifference to folkloristic formalism, Gellert was casual in his response. "Well, you find the ones that have the most political [content] are either the very urban, the ones in the cities, or the ones in the country who have been educated by the Sharecroppers' Union," he explained. "Between those two, they were the most militant in the group [his archive]. On the isolated farms, they'd be all individual protest." By his reference to the Sharecroppers' Union (SCU), Gellert meant the famous organization that took root and took up arms in Alabama under the auspices of the Communist Party. Indeed, Gellert collected in the region during the 1930s. In his reference to "individual protest," by contrast, Gellert seemed to be denoting the kind of one-off songs, or "nonce-creations," about which D. K. Wilgus speculated in his 1972 review. Such specifics mattered, stressed Reuss. "That's what I want to get clear," he stated. "Occasionally, you would collect songs from Negroes who had been influenced say, by the Sharecroppers' Union." Gellert reiterated, "Definitely. Definitely. Don't forget I was around there quite a bit before I was cut off from it completely."[62]

As his answers make clear, Gellert was untroubled by informant distinctions such as politicized versus unpoliticized, and he did not attach such characterizations to value judgments measuring folk authenticity. "Practically every Negro down there is a revolutionist," he stressed. Life under such conditions, he insisted, almost guaranteed a culture of protest. On the issue of folksongs versus songs of protest, therefore, Gellert was ultimately defiant. "Look, I hadn't the slightest idea what folksongs were. I still don't know what folksongs are. And, I don't think anybody knows what folksongs are!" he exclaimed. "I became more aware of it because the standard folklore collectors became more aware of it and took notice of it." The "it" to which Gellert referred was that body of song that he came to call "Negro Songs of Protest" and that collectors Odum and Johnson before him had come to call "songs about the white man." Gellert's predecessors and peers in white collecting on Black music "never took notice of it before," he stated, "and at the beginning and for a long time after, it was merely tied in with the protest of the Negro people. It had nothing to do with folksongs or folklore at all." The point of Gellert's archive of "Negro Songs of Protest," then, was just that—protest. "This was the function of the songs in the Thirties. That any damn fool objects to them because they're not folksongs" is immaterial. "I didn't claim they were folksongs," he said. "I don't give a damn now whether they call it folklore or what the hell they call it."[63]

From his experiences on the ground collecting Black music from the 1920s forward, Gellert assumed an outlook that would come to be defined later in contemporary historical scholarship.[64] Black could be red and still be genuine, as we might put it; folksongs could be songs of protest, by the same logic, and still be true. This is in fact what John Greenway was getting at in *American Folksongs of Protest* in 1953. Greenway's full meaning with the "radical in the woodpile" passage is more nuanced than typically appreciated. In the remainder of the paragraph, just following the "radical in the woodpile" line, the author wrote, "But the injection of social enlightenment does not lift the singer out of the folk. . . . A textile worker can be hungry and know why without being educated. Agitators and organizers do no more than stimulate protest that has been simmering inarticulately in the singer."[65] On the same page, Greenway gives the examples of Woody Guthrie and John Handcox. The first is well known, and crossed paths with Gellert in the folk music Left of New York City; the second is less known to the general public, but is an essential example of the merger of Left organizing and an indigenous Black "culture of opposition," as Robin Kelley applied the term. Handcox emerged from a farming background in rural Arkansas. In the 1930s, he was inspired by the Socialist Party's important integrated radical union, the Southern Tenants Farmers' Union. Handcox joined and began composing organizing songs combining movement calls to action with local southern African American idiom. Handcox's songs—"Raggedy, Raggedy Are We," "There is Mean Things Happening in This Land," and "Roll the Union On," for instance—were documented by the Library of Congress in the 1930s. No one doubted their truth as expressions from the grassroots. As historian Michael Honey shows in *Sharecropper's Troubadour: John L. Handcox, the Southern Tenant Farmers Union, and the African American Song Tradition*, Handcox's life and music stand as a stirring testament to the honest dialectic of "folk" and "protest."[66]

John Greenway's "radical in the woodpile" formulation was never an absolute disqualifying metaphor. He explained: "The evidence of outside influence, frequently of persons of some education if not sophistication, upon the folksong makers has antagonized many folklorists who have had to make a decision about the authenticity of modern songs of protest. . . . Most of the composers of these songs whose identity we know have been stimulated in their protest by some orienting influence."[67] This "orienting influence" of protest, though, does not negate the music as "folk," Greenway posited in the book. A third way is possible. Greenway argued for an alternative that circumvented the impasse between old, anonymous, and a-topical ("folksong") versus contemporary, traceable, and topical ("protest song"). His book title, *American Folksongs of Protest*, after all, was a statement in and of itself to this third way. None of this rested easy with Greenway's peers in academic folklore.

Gellert's material is featured in Greenway's book, alongside that of John Handcox and Woody Guthrie. Gellert's *Negro Songs of Protest* is listed in the bibliography alongside that of the Lomaxes. Greenway adopted "Negro Songs of Protest" as a title for his second chapter. What seems clear is that Greenway did not doubt the validity of Gellert's "Negro Songs of Protest." That the culture of times under McCarthyism did not occasion a fuller and fairer hearing for Gellert in 1953 when *American Folksongs of Protest* was published is not surprising. What does seem odd, however, is that a persistent fog continues to obscure the Gellert archive to this day.

Gellert's work did start to resurface eventually. In 1970, scholar William R. Ferris, future founder of the Center for the Study of Southern Culture and chairman of the National Endowment for the Humanities, opened his article, "Racial Repertoires among Blues Performers," with coverage of Lawrence Gellert. The item was published in the journal *Ethnomusicology*. Ferris stated that the songs of protest that Gellert collected were "not intended for white ears," and he added, "We must assume an exception was made in Gellert's case because he was a sympathetic outsider."[68]

In 1973, Alan Dundes, a major figure in academic folklore, included Gellert material in a key text in African American folklore studies, the anthology *Mother Wit from the Laughing Barrel*. Dundes featured Russell Ames's "Protest and Irony in Negro Folksong" right after a piece from Alan Lomax in the book subsection "Folk Music." Ames had exchanged letters with Gellert, and he drew heavily on the collector's print archive for "Protest and Irony," which was originally published in the Marxist journal *Science & Society* in 1950. Now, in the *Mother Wit* anthology, Dundes reprinted the Ames's article for a new generation. Interestingly, the article showcased the same "Nat Turner" lyrics that had earned Silber's reprobation. Within the reprint, Dundes reproduced author Ames's original footnotes. Ames wrote, "It is precisely the lack of published parallels to many of Gellert's protest songs which has made some folksong scholars suspicious. . . . However, Gellert's songs texts . . . do seem authentic. The fact remains that it is not easy for a white man to collect Negro songs of protest in the South and also that the majority of southern gentleman and lady folksong collectors would not have been likely to have elicited them."[69]

By 1978, Gellert's name was back in the *Journal of American Folklore*. Another specialist who would become particularly known in blues scholarship, David Evans, offered a positive review of the 1973 Rounder re-release of Gellert's independently produced *Negro Songs of Protest* album from 1972. Evans acknowledged that in the liner notes Gellert "disparages academic folklorists" and "states that his main interest in these chain gang and prison songs was in their themes of social protest" rather than in purity or preservation. Still, he concluded, Gellert "must certainly be commended for his ability to collect such material under adverse conditions."[70] Folklorist Norm Cohen followed this up in a further *JAF* piece in 1986. In "Record Reviews: The American Folklife Center's Selected lists of Recordings," Cohen highlighted the second Rounder LP of Gellert field recordings, *Cap'n You're So Mean*, from 1982, and also mentioned the third installment in the Gellert album sequence, *Nobody Knows My Name*, from 1984. He held that "Gellert's field collecting in the south, which resulted in some remarkably candid protest material (the genuineness of which was at one time questioned) has been neglected too long." He stressed, "If ever an album required and deserved extensive documentation, this is it—and not because we still doubt its authenticity." Cohen was impressed with what he heard, but not with what he read, however. "The hastily written jacket notes, with many unfair or unfounded generalizations," he wrote, "should have been discarded in favor of the proper documentation that [producer] Conforth has the wherewithal to provide." The review was a vindication of sorts. But the reference to "unfair or unfounded generalizations" reflects that the air had not year fully cleared on the work of Lawrence Gellert.[71]

"Woodpile" Redux

In his recent biography of Gellert, Bruce Conforth cites John Greenway's "radical in the woodpile" metaphor in order to affirm a line of doubt on Gellert's "Negro Songs of Protest." Music that may sound homegrown, but that shows signs of social commentary and political analysis, Conforth alleges, hints at artificial outside influence. Reprinting only the first portion of Greenway's quotation, Conforth asserts in *African American Folksong and American Cultural Politics* that Gellert did indeed fabricate some of his more strident "Negro Songs of Protest." Conforth writes, "There may, in fact have been a 'radical in the woodpile' assisting in the creation of these songs and their political interpretation, and in this case, as we shall see, the radical finger will point directly to Lawrence Gellert."[72]

In 1953, Greenway noted that an outside "orienting influence" of social consciousness was not necessarily antithetical to "folk" authenticity. Greenway counseled his peers to be mindful of this "orienting influence," to scrutinize and be discerning, but to avoid outright disqualifying thinking. In the postwar, the "orienting influence" deemed suspect as far as the Gellert archive was not the collector himself so much as the Left orientation of past movement collecting itself. The conservative disciplinary strictures of academic folklore coalesced with Cold War anticommunism to the point where narrow academic theory about what did and did not count as "folk" blurred with general US patterns of what did and did not count as authentic "Americanism." Formal theory in folkloristics blurred with a general culture of "red-baiting." That was then, of course. But this is now. Bruce Conforth's evocation of the "radical in the woodpile" thesis seems a strange relic by which to resurrect doubt on the Gellert archive. Certainly, it is a far remove from Conforth's original excited embrace of Gellert as a vital alternative folklorist and radical.

How is one to take this dramatic reversal on Conforth's part? In the 1980s, when he was first researching and promoting the Gellert archive, Conforth called the discovery "more than a half-century overdue." He urged that Gellert be granted a "rightful place" in the annals of folklore alongside Cecil Sharp, Robert Winslow Gordon, and the Lomaxes. In addition to the fact of Gellert's early activity (dating back to the 1920s even) and rich substream of blues material, what was exceptional about the collector, argued Conforth, was his extensive documentation of frank and evocative Black musical protest. Gellert achieved what even his more famous peers could not, stated Conforth. "He provided us with an insider's look at the southern Black ethos," Conforth wrote, and "was able to tap into the songs that Blacks sang for themselves—to unveil their true social commentary."[73]

In Conforth's assessment today, Gellert is no longer to be valued as a radical collector of Black protest, but instead for his more traditional contribution of recognizable Black work songs, blues, and hollers, and as well his catalog of folktales and folk idioms. Conforth dismisses Gellert's "Negro Songs of Protest" as compromised by Gellert's own outside tampering. He instead champions what he identifies as a vast body of genuine non-protest material. He calls Gellert "one of the most misunderstood and overlooked folksong and folklore collectors of the 20th century."[74]

But, are "Negro Songs of Protest" really a fraud? To return to the Conforth lines that open this chapter, we should recall that the author now holds that such material "never really existed within the folk music tradition, but were, rather, the creation of the left wing and U.S. Communist Party in order to use as propaganda, with Lawrence as either their unwitting or identity-hunting dupe."[75] Are "Negro Songs of Protest" the product of white leftwing agitation rather than Black vernacular creativity? Was Gellert an opportunist simply looking for an outlet? Was he even a real radical?

I will address the issue of the songs in the next chapter. But, here, I will conclude with a summary take on Gellert's sincerity vis-à-vis the political Left and the Black freedom struggle. I submit that Gellert was a real radical with real credibility. He had real knowledge and convictions as regards the Left, Black music, and social struggle.

First, on the issue of Gellert's Left politics, we need recall what appears, on public record, as a years-long commitment to racial justice and anticapitalism. Through the 1930s and into the difficult 1940s and 1950s, Gellert published and agitated on the Left without pause. He was vociferous. Often, in his writings and activities, he seemed to relish the part of the rogue and radical against white supremacy and exploitation. As we have heard from his interviews in the 1960s, Gellert, as an older man, continued to tout the superiority of communism over capitalism through the decades of the Cold War.

Second, we should linger on an interview that Gellert provided in 1976 for an oral history project on the Work Progress Administration's various New Deal arts projects. In the latter 1930s, in the midst of his comings and goings South and North, Gellert worked in the "Negro Units" of both the Federal Theatre and Federal Writers' projects in New York City. The collector was at the Lafayette Theatre in Harlem in 1936 with John Houseman and Orson Welles for the all-Black "Voodoo" *Macbeth*, as the hit production came to be nicknamed, and his song archive was the basis for the successful Helen Tamiris dance production *How Long Brethren* in 1937. Gellert then moved on to the Writers's project, where he completed numerous written pieces ranging from "Popular Negro Idioms—North & South" and "Folk Origin of the Negro Dance" to "Negro in Theatrical Unions," "Folk Origin of the Negro Dance," "Negro in Art," and "Tales, Rhymes and Children in Harlem." Much of this material dates from 1939 and 1940.[76]

In his interview from 1976, Gellert, then seventy-eight years of age, talks for more than two hours in sharp and animated ways about his experiences. He speaks with fluency about Black arts and history, and he refers in detail to individuals of note such as Rose McClendon, Langston Hughes, Paul Robeson, Richard Wright, Arthur Schomburg, and Roi Ottley. Even more surprisingly, Gellert lingers on the memory of Zora Neale Hurston. Though Alice Walker's rediscovery article, "Looking for Zora," had come out in *Ms.* magazine in 1975, Robert Hemenway's landmark book, *Zora Neale Hurston: A Literary Biography*, was not published until 1977. Hurston had yet to be broadly recovered in public awareness. Gellert, though, enthuses. "She should have been head of the [Federal Theatre] Project," he states. "She was a dynamic human being. She could have handled anybody. She's really a fighter." As his interviewer, Lorraine Brown, an acclaimed specialist in the field, struggles to recognize the name, Gellert asserts that Hurston was "a better writer than any Negro on our entire project there. . . . her books are marvelous." In these interviews, the collector comports himself as a man invested for years in African American arts and politics. He shows a level of expertise uncommon for a person outside of academia, and of his age and station, in a time when Black Studies was still struggling for a foothold in US culture.[77]

Finally, in one specific instance at least on the point of Gellert's convictions, Conforth is mistaken in his statement of the facts. In the biography, Conforth highlights a Gellert article published in the leftwing journal *Music Vanguard* in 1935.[78] Conforth employs the article as supporting evidence for his position that Gellert was not interested in politics and only allowed the Left to use his material in order to build a name for himself. Conforth relates some of the details of the eleven-page piece by Gellert and stresses that—aside from the title "Negro Songs of Protest in America," which, he suggests, was applied by leftwing editors independent of the author's hand—Gellert himself never uses the word "protest" in the article text. Gellert was reticent to use the word, Conforth argues, and was "conspicuously avoiding" it "in his own essays." Radical editors attached the language artificially, Conforth suggests.[79]

But, the primary evidence reads otherwise. Gellert includes the word "protest" in his prose four times in the article. He also uses the words "insurrection," "revolt," and "revolutionary" to refer to Black vernacular song tradition. Gellert is hardly shy about his politics. He contextualizes antebellum spirituals in the larger tradition of social struggle in America, writing that "while some of the group were unquestionably the devotional chants of bamboozled slaves—others, any number, had hidden allegorical significance in their religious symbolism." These, he insists, "belong in the very van of our revolutionary literature. They are actually the forerunners of the present day Negro Songs of Protest." Similarly, Gellert calls out the "oligarchy" of the South and their "armed plug-uglies" who oversee a racial order, past and present, to ensure that the Negro stays "merely an element of production." Of the modern secular lyrics that he showcases, Gellert holds, "This then is the stuff of folklore. We see the Negro, belonging to a suppressed national group, after more than three hundred years of hard labor in the land, a peon and an alien still." He is emphatic:

> In these songs we find reflected the contemporary environment—on the one hand, the peonage, poverty and degradation, the savage brutality of the Law, and the lynch mob; on the other hand, the new attitude toward all that is exemplified by the battles of the Sharecroppers' Union in the deep South, and by the mighty struggles for the freedom of the Scottsboro boys, Angelo Herndon and other prisoners in the South. . . . Despite the strict censorship maintained by the Overlords, the grapevine telegraph "strews" the news of the latest developments. . . . The Black Belt is aflame with the injustices of a hostile world.

Radical composer and musicologist Charles Seeger, a Gellert associate from the Communist-affiliated Composers Collective, had solicited the piece for the journal in 1934. *Music Vanguard* was one of the short-lived "little magazines" on the Left in the period, and the article is replete with movement references au courant, including those to the Scottsboro and Angelo Herndon criminal justice campaigns of the Communist Party's International Labor Defense. And in contrast to what Conforth suggests, Gellert expressed elsewhere that his use of the word "protest" was never halting. Indeed, he said, it was *New Masses* editor Mike Gold who came up with the moniker "Negro Songs of Protest," but the word "protest" came directly from the collector himself. "When I sent him the first article," probably around 1928 or 1929, "I used the word protest in there. . . . He just turned them around and called them 'Negro Songs of Protest' in the article" and for what became the series published in *New Masses* starting in 1930.[80]

I contend that Lawrence Gellert included the word "protest" in this piece and elsewhere because, like his leftwing editors, he meant it. With a record of activist-oriented projects and publishing from the 1930s forward, the collector staked a position on the left that did not appear to waiver, even during the hazardous years of Cold War recrimination. Gellert heard something real in the music that he encountered in the vernacular culture of Black America. If Gellert was the real thing, is his archive of "Negro Songs of Protest" the real thing as well? In the next chapter, I investigate the songs to further penetrate the fog.

CHAPTER SIX

Scholarly Rigors

PROPAGANDA OR PROTEST IN THE GELLERT ARCHIVE?

To argue that Negro secular song has functioned primarily or even largely as a medium of protest would distort black music and black culture. Blacks have not spent all of their time reacting to whites and their songs are filled with comments on all aspects of life. But it would be an even greater distortion to assume that a people occupying the position that Negroes have in this society could produce a music so rich and varied with few allusions to their situation or only slight indications of their reactions to the treatment they were accorded.

—LAWRENCE W. LEVINE, *BLACK CULTURE AND BLACK CONSCIOUSNESS*, 1977

It is only in his music, which Americans are able to admire because a protective sentimentality limits their understanding of it, that the Negro in America has been able to tell his story.

—JAMES BALDWIN, "MANY THOUSANDS GONE," 1951

As we have seen, influential figures in folklore collecting, scholarship, and promotion put Lawrence Gellert to rigorous scrutiny in the postwar. By 1963, Irwin Silber in the folk music community had denounced Gellert as a charlatan with a "dubious" folk archive of songs likely made up by him or some other party. In academic folklore, the preoccupation was less on outright creation and more on the question of folksongs versus songs of protest. Where was the line, and where did the Gellert material fall in that dichotomy? In either case, doubt was cast on the value of Lawrence Gellert's "Negro Songs of Protest" as a reliable measure of African American thought and expression.

Lawrence Levine argued in his landmark *Black Culture and Black Consciousness* that a "large body of songs from the first four or five decades of this century make it unmistakably clear that Negro music has been a crucial and perhaps central vehicle for the expression of discontent and protest."[1] Gellert's predecessors and peers in white collecting on Black folksong in the first decades of the twentieth century misheard, or missed altogether, songs of protest. Odum and Johnson reported that there were "a good many songs about the white man" but did not follow up or take them seriously; John Lomax heard "self-pity" in Black vernacular music-making; Dorothy Scarborough was caught up in a romance of Southern nostalgia; and Newman White warned that "racial sorrow-song" was suspect fodder for New Negro propagandists. Lawrence Gellert heard something different when he entered the field as an amateur in the 1920s, and he advanced his commitment in the Cultural Front of the 1930s. Lawrence Levine drew, without qualification, on songs in the Gellert archive in *Black Culture and Black Consciousness* in 1977. The 1970s and 1980s saw statements of vindication from a number of figures in folklore and blues scholarship, including that of William Ferris, David Evans, Norm Cohen, and also the most serious student of Gellert research in the period, Bruce Conforth. Gellert and "Negro Songs of Protest" were on the way to restoration. Still, they remained largely a footnote.

Can of Worms and a Smoking Gun

Musician and author Dick Weissman takes stock of Gellert's standing today in a balance sheet rendering in *Which Side Are You On? An Inside History of the Folk Music Revival in America.* Weissman describes Gellert controversy as a "can of worms." Gellert documented "examples of resistance and hostility toward the prevailing white culture that were virtually inaudible and invisible to the bulk of folk song collectors" in the established canon, states Weissman, including that of the revered Lomaxes for the Library of Congress. "The very existence of his collection threatened the credibility of what other collectors had found," Weissman asserts. This is a point that was made by Richard Reuss to Bruce Conforth in the early 1980s. In correspondence between the two, Reuss warned Conforth that affirming Gellert's contribution would likely generate a backlash. "Publicizing Gellert's accomplishments will have the effect of reducing the Lomax family 'center ring' star status as pioneer collectors on Negro secular song in the United States," he wrote. "Moreover, Gellert severely attacked Alan's radical credentials in the 1930s, about which Alan is still extremely ambivalent even yet. The two hated each other passionately," Reuss summed up. The veracity of such hearsay is beyond our scope. It suggests that personal rivalries and professional territorialism are what lay behind Gellert denial. While this could be true in part or in whole, the wider issue of white denial of Black agency and protest is of far more historical relevance. In that spirit, Weissman pans out in his assessment from the base personal to the broader public concerns of race, music, and power. "The white collectors existed in a sort of patronage relationship with their informants," he offers. "It did not seem to occur to them that a Black singer would be hesitant to sing a song about a lynching to a white middle-class" listener "in a southern venue." He contends: "The bottom line is that Gellert's collection of over five hundred songs remains the largest collection of African American music prior to World War II. The over two hundred protest songs in the collection are far and away the best testimony to the fact that Black songs of protest were present in profusion in the southern United States, whether or not other folk song collectors were able to find them." Weissman concludes, "Whatever one thinks of these controversies, it is obvious that Gellert has not received proper recognition for his unique work."[2]

Weissman's *Which Side Are You On?* appeared in 2005, and seemed to signal a final reversal in the new millennium from censure to acceptance for the Gellert archive. Currently, however, there has been a resurrection of doubt, exemplified most prominently in Bruce Conforth's 2013 biography of the collector. Conforth deems the mass of the archive reliable but returns to the language of denial that questions items of overt lyrical protest in the collection: "Although the vast majority of the songs he collected is undoubtedly authentic, there are at least some that need careful scrutiny." Conforth believes Gellert coached singers, and maybe even assisted in the creation of "Negro Songs of Protest." He submits the testimony of Gellert associate Herbert Halpert as "smoking gun" evidence that, Conforth feels, seals the verdict on Gellert's tampering in the folk process. Conforth quotes Halpert's words from a letter sent in 1984: "Gellert told me they (he and the 'Negroes') would talk about working conditions, then he'd ask them if there was any song on the subject. When there was none, Gellert would say something regretful. The Negro would say, 'Boss, you want a song? Come back tomorrow and I'll have one for you.' Gellert would return the next day and the man would sing his new song for him." Conforth judges, therefore, that Gellert's "Negro Songs of Protest" did not originate in Black vernacular cultures of resistance, but rather from white leftwing agitation. He maintains: "Exactly how much Lawrence might have 'coached' his singers is not clear; however his admission that he did, coupled with Halpert's recollections and the singularity of some of his songs . . . make it impossible not to assume that he at least helped create some, if not many, of his more overt protest songs. . . . It can logically be imagined that he did so to hold onto the short-lived fame he had achieved in the 1930s." Halpert's comments, as reported by Conforth, are not to be dismissed, and the dynamic of collector and informant certainly deserves scrutiny. But whatever the inferences to be drawn from Halpert's statement, it is not a "smoking gun" of definitive meaning. Conforth relates that Halpert insisted the admission remain secret until after his death. He "never wanted to cast aspersions." Gellert, however, openly described such a methodology for gaining informant confidence in just these terms in his 1960s interviews. With "verboten" songs, some prompting and rapport was necessary, he told Reuss.[3] Additionally, in contextualizing Halpert's equivocation about this "smoking gun," we should recall that Gellert, in his 1960s interviews, counted Halpert among his only defenders in academic folklore. Halpert credited Gellert for his important fieldwork in *Southern Folklore Quarterly* in 1938. Gellert referred to "Herbie" Halpert as a friend.[4]

I will address the issue of Gellert's "coaching" subsequently, and the verifiability of "Negro Songs of Protest" is our primary focus in this chapter. But, for now, as we frame the stakes of debate, it is important to mention that doubts about Gellert's credibility, as a collector but also as a person, have reentered the public sphere in the present day. Wikipedia is not a scholarly source, but it is a common first reference for lay readers. The current entry on Lawrence Gellert has been expanded recently to include a section with the subtitle "Fabrication of Protest Songs." It also includes description of Gellert as an "inveterate fabulist," a "weak and dependent character," and a "chronic invalid" and "alcoholic" who "was manipulated" into song collecting by the radical Left. Gellert may have been an eccentric, an iconoclast, a searcher, and a wanderer. But there is no basis for these extreme judgments of personal failing, especially as they have blurred into casual dismissals as well of the Gellert archive as similarly flawed.[5]

An Inventory of Falsehoods

The Gellert archive has been subject to a litany of falsehoods and misperception.[6] A first falsehood is that the entire Gellert field archive is entirely protest. Unfortunately, this is a claim that was advanced by Gellert himself in his priority of political agitation over folklore preservation. "I never got a song that wasn't protest," he maintained in his interviews.[7] Ultimately, this assertion proved to

Gellert's own detriment when detractors registered doubt about his material. An entirely political archive of several hundred songs was too conspicuous a proposition for academic folklorists and for those suspicious of Left influence on Black vernacular expression. But as I have written consistently, and as Bruce Conforth has shown from the beginning, songs with lyrics of alienation, resentment, and resistance account for only a portion of the total Gellert collection. In the 1980s, Conforth quantified the proportion of "overt songs of protest" at nearly one half. This, he stated, compared with "less than 5 percent" in the collections of recognized predecessors and peers, including John and Alan Lomax, Howard Odum, Henry Edward Krehbiel, Dorothy Scarborough, and Robert Gordon. More recently, Conforth has shrunk that estimate of "most political" items to only about the three dozen published in Gellert's songbooks and Left print articles. These are the song texts, he now argues, that Gellert "or other left-oriented individuals" had "the most to do with creating." Conforth's current position is that "a few bad apples should not spoil the whole batch" of a "tremendous repository of actual folklore and folksong."[8]

With the advent of digitization and online electronic transfer, the possibilities for a deeper systematic inquiry into the Gellert sound archive have vastly increased. In 2015, I conducted a comprehensive review of all 505 field recordings housed at the Archives of Traditional Music (ATM). I have deposited my research index at the ATM for other researchers.[9] Beyond protest, one notable aspect of the archive also worth mentioning is the existence of many field items, particularly from Gellert's seven-inch discs from the 1920s, that parallel commercial blues from the decade. As Conforth stresses as well, these blues parallels provide another overlapping corroboration between the Gellert archive and the broader field of song of the era.[10]

Furthermore, there are fascinating variations to be found among these Gellert blues parallels, whether in the poor-quality, seven-inch discs or better-sounding, ten-inch discs. Among the Gellert ten-inch recordings, for instance, there is a powerful alternate version of a song familiar as Texas Alexander's "Penitentiary Moan Blues," released commercially in 1928. The Gellert field recording and Alexander release match up in melody and in three verses, but for one startling difference. Alexander sings:

> I wonder what's the matter with poor Annie Lee?
> Lord, the Captain whipped her, and she ain't been seen.
> Lord, the Captain whipped her, and she ain't been seen.

The lyrics derive from Black work song tradition. Gellert's informant draws on the same pool of lyricism, and/or perhaps the commercial version. However, he changes one word in the second repeated line:

> I wonder what's the matter with poor Annie Lee?
> Lord, the Captain whipped her, and she ain't been seen.
> Lord, the Captain raped her, and she ain't been seen.

And he adds:

> Wonder what's the matter with the walking boss.
> Lord, he called me this morning, and he would not talk.
> Lord, he called this morning, and he would not talk.

Both the Gellert recording and the Alexander release then end with the same verse:

> Out in the rain, in the cold
> Lord, when your captain call you, you got to go.
> Lord, when your captain call you, you got to.

This Gellert field item was released on the second Rounder compilation LP in 1982. However, the sound quality on the digitized field original offers a sharper listening experience. "Raped" is substituted for "whipped" in this song. The lyrics directly call out white sexual assault and impunity under racial oppression, and then lament, all the more tragically, the reality that the work of exploitation goes on whatever the circumstances.[11]

This Gellert field recording is distinctive but not without parallel. Most recently, in *No Mercy Here: Gender, Punishment, and the Making of Jim Crow Modernity*, Sarah Haley highlights a documentary recording in fact made by Gellert associate Herbert Halpert. On behalf of the Library of Congress Archive of American Folksong, Halpert visited the women's camp at Parchman Penitentiary in Mississippi in 1939. He recorded "Dangerous Blues" by prisoner Mattie Mae Thomas. The song moves from lines of militant self-defense to the rejection of gendered divisions of labor to the public outing of inter-racial rape at the hands of white authority. Thomas sang:

> You keep on talking 'bout the dangerous blues
> If I had me a pistol I'd be dangerous too

You may be a bully, said but I don't know
But I'll fix you so you won't gimmie no more trouble in the world I know

"She won't cook no breakfast, she won't wash no clothes.
Said that woman don't do nothing but walk that road."

My knee bone hurt me and my ankles swell
Said I may get better but I won't get well

There Mattie had a baby and he got blue eyes
Said must be the Captain, he keep on hanging around
Said it must be the Captain, keep on hanging around, keep on hanging around.[12]

The "blue eyes" reference is not uncommon as a motif of white rape in Black vernacular tradition. Folklorist Bruce Jackson documented similar lyrics almost thirty years later from Black workers in a Texas prison:

Carrie got a baby, Carrie got a baby, oh yeah.
It's got blue eyes, sir, it's got blue eyes, sir, oh yeah.
Blue eyes like the rider, whoa, blue eyes like the rider, whoa my Lord.
He was always there, sir, always there, sir, oh yeah.
Looka looka yonder, looka looka yonder, oh yeah.
I believe I spy the devil, whoa, I believe I spy the devil, whoa my Lord.
Who is that devil? Who is that devil? Oh yeah.
Captain McGaughey, Captain McGaughey, Oh yeah.
He's the devil in the bottom, whoa, he's the devil in the bottom, whoa my Lord.

On this stream of musical expression, Lawrence Levine wrote, "In their willingness to criticize the white boss openly through song, these contemporary prisoners were following a tradition established by black laborers long before." As is clear, this tradition not only spanned generations but also crossed genre designations (work songs to blues) and gender lines. I would add, moreover, that it crossed between folklore collections. The difference was not that Gellert had this exclusive protest material that others had not encountered. Rather, the difference was that he foregrounded it and labeled it songs of Black protest when others did not. The Lomaxes, too, for instance, documented lines similar to those above in 1934 in *American Ballads and Folk Songs:* "Mary got a baby, an' I know it ain' mine, / I b'lieve it is de cap'n's 'cause he goes dere all de time." The Lomaxes' treatment, however, buried the verse under a song "Tie-Tamping Chant" in their chapter "Working on the Railroad."[13]

This brings us to our second falsehood—that the Gellert archive is entirely unique and without parallel. This position was articulated by Irwin Silber in his 1963 statement that "no one else has ever been able to collect similar songs or the same song in a different version." John Greenway, in *American Folksongs of Protest,* got a little closer to the truth. "Gellert's finds have been questioned by other collectors, who have been unable to duplicate them," he wrote in 1953. "A few only are to be found in Odum and Johnson's studies, and a few more in unpublished recordings in the Library of Congress Archive of American Folk Song, but for the majority Gellert seems to have been uniquely successful as a song catcher." Greenway conveyed a more approving tone. Nevertheless, his claim as well of only a few matches proves false. Multiple parallels exist between Gellert's "Negro Songs of Protest" and songs in the writings and archives of established peers. Reuss and Gellert discussed this directly in their 1960s interviews, and Conforth and I, in our respective works, have refuted the "no parallels" allegation.[14]

Upon close review, it appears that Lawrence Gellert simply "made a specialty,"[15] as he said, of the kind of material that appears with general frequency, but without stated emphasis or further critical inquiry, in the literature of all his major peers in the early school of Black folksong scholarship in the first half of the twentieth century. In answer to the charges of his suspect singularity, then, we have ample evidence to the contrary. From the 1900s through the 1940s, there have been clear parallels between Gellert's "Negro Songs of Protest" and the work of others in the canon of white research. The evidence is too extensive for a full accounting here, but some illustration is in order.

Both Howard Odum and John Lomax documented open examples of Black lyrical protest—or "songs about the white man," as Odum and Johnson phrased it—from the beginning, even if they advanced an interpretive logic that effectively discounted the significance of such evidence. The song "Ain't It Hard To Be A N——r?" appeared in both of their founding studies from 1911 and 1917.[16] By the 1920s, lyrics from the title were included as a kind of standard in the first generation of full-length songbooks by Scarborough, Odum and Johnson, and White. And again, in 1934 and 1941, versions of the tune were printed in the Lomaxes' classic *American Ballads and Folk Songs* and *Our Singing Country.* In these latter cases from the 1920s, 1930s, and 1940s, some of the authors were frank in their acknowledgment of the song as a statement of racial commentary or complaint, and some ignored the protest element altogether. Still, none made an explicit argument endorsing the tune's clear sentiment of injustice, as would Gellert. The lyrics to "Ain't It Hard?" appear in the second installment of his article series for *New Masses* in January 1931. This overt identification of the song under the title "Negro Songs of Protest" contrasts markedly, for instance, with the Lomaxes' presentation in *American Ballads and Folk Songs.* In that classic text, "Ain't It Hard?" is included in the section on "Reels," between the spirited selections "Pick a Bale O' Cotton" and "Shortenin' Bread."[17]

In succeeding articles and in his two songbooks, Lawrence Gellert printed other songs and verses that surface—again, it is important to note, only in passing and largely without comment—in the work of his contemporaries. The lyrics to one of Gellert's most familiar items, "Told My Captain," appears alongside "Ain't It Hard?" in his same *New Masses* piece from January 1931, and it is also featured with a musical arrangement in his *"Me and My Captain"* songbook from 1939. Among the couplets to this common song, Gellert included these lines:

> Ah tol' mah Cap'n mah han' was col'
> Goddamn yo' han' let de wheelin roll
>
> Ah tol' mah Cap'n mah feet was col'
> Goddam yo' feet let de wheelin roll
>
> Cap'n, Cap'n, you mus' be blin'
> Look at yo' watch it pas' quittin' time
>
> Cap'n, Cap'n how can it be
> Whistle done blow an' you still workin' me
>
> If ah haid mah weight in lime
> I'd whip mah Cap'n till he went stone blin'
>
> Pay day come an' we all git nuthin'
> Cap'n he tryin to cheat me fo' suttin
>
> My Cap'n he so damn mean
> Ah think he come f'om New Orleans

I'm gonna spit in his coffee
An' spit in his tea
De lawd help dis n——r if he cotch me.[18]

Before the Gellert transcriptions, the song came up with identical lines in Howard Odum's *Journal of American Folk-Lore* article from 1911, again in Odum and Johnson's first joint publication, *The Negro and His Songs*, and also in the follow-up, *Negro Workaday Songs*.[19] As Gellert remembered of this representative case, the tune was "very prevalent all over" the South throughout this period of white fieldwork. "Everybody's got that in his collection," he said. "And, I collected it three or four times in three or four different places."[20]

Perhaps because of their common area of residence and operations in North Carolina (Tryon and Chapel Hill, respectively), there are numerous parallels between the archives of Gellert and collectors Odum and Johnson. Some of these lyric matches are fragmentary and merely suggestive, and some quite direct, with entire stanzas reproduced between collections. In the Odum and Johnson treatment, however, these lyrics are framed in ways distinct from that of Gellert. There is, for instance, "Shoot That Buffalo," a "delightful song" meant "just to help with work," explain Odum and Johnson. The song shares a stanza with "I Went to Atlanta" from the Gellert collection. The transcriptions are identical:

Went down to Raleigh,
Never been there befo',
White folks on the feather-bed,
N——rs on the flo'.[21]

Additionally, Odum and Johnson have the following lines as the last stanza to "Don't You Give Me No Cornbread":

Captain got a lugger
Tryin' to play bad,
I'm goin' to take it in the mornin'
If he makes me mad.[22]

Gellert had them as well among his "Negro Songs of Protest," as he also had these lyrics included in Odum and Johnson:

N——rs plant the cotton,
N——rs pick it out,
White man pockets money,
N——rs does without.[23]

Odum and Johnson presented the stanza in the song "Hump-Back Mule" in their chapter "Folk Minstrel Types."

The parallels extend beyond Odum and Johnson to the 1920s publications of Dorothy Scarborough and Newman White. As with the instances above, many of these matching lyrics appear in Gellert's earliest publications. Presumably, then, the parallels could have been clear to peers and readers who had encountered the folklore literature from just a few years before. "Stand Boys Stand," for instance, shows up in Gellert's very first *New Masses* article from 1930:

Stan' boys stan'
No use arunnin
Look up yonder hill
White trash acomin'
Is Acomin'

He got knife in one han'
Pistol in de odder
Stan' boys stan'
Brother stan' by brother
Stan' by brother

N——rs don' you run 'way
White trash acomin'
Is acomin'
Get dat whackin' stick in yo' han'
Ruckus boun' to happen
Boun' to happen[24]

In Scarborough's *On the Trail of Negro Folk-Songs* from 1925, there is an antecedent version. Though not identical, the parallels are revealing:

Stan' boys, stan',
Dah's now no use a-runnin',
        Use a-runnin'.
Look upon yondah hill
An' see ol' massa comin',
        Massa comin',
        See 'im comin'.

Bowie knife in one hand
An' pistol in de tother.
        Stan', boys, stan',
Brother stan' by brother,
        Stan' by brother.

Oberseer wid his stick,
Stick am comin' floppin',
        Floppin', floppin',
N——rs, ef you run away
Ruckus bound to happen,
        Ruckus bound to happen.[25]

Similarly, there is Gellert's transcription of "Work Ox" in his second songbook, "*Me and My Captain*," from 1939:

I ain't gonna be your old work ox no more,
I ain't gonna be your old work ox no more,
I ain't gonna be your old work ox no more,
I done my due, ain't gonna do no more.

Up early in the morning, way 'fore break of day, (3x)
Can't find no breakfast, got to hurry on my way.

Good God almighty, got it tough and hard, (3x)
The Captain I has never satisfied.

Drive you in the sunshine, cuss you in the rain, (3x)
Work you all day till you can hardly stand.

Well, I tell you people, and I tell you true. (3x)
You can never tell what your old work ox gwine do.[26]

Newman White included a comparable stanza in the "General and Miscellaneous Labor" chapter of his 1928 publication, *American Negro Folk Songs:*

I ain't a gonna work a no mo'!
I ain't a gonna work a no mo'!
Done an' work-ed 'til my hands got sore.
I ain't a gonna work a no mo'![27]

That same year, blues recording artist Alger "Texas" Alexander released "Work Ox Blues." It included the lines:

Mama, I ain't gonna be your old work ox no more,
Mama, I ain't gonna be your old work ox no more,
You done fooled around, woman, let your ox get cold.[28]

The dramatic persona in Texas Alexander's performance threatens his romantic partner whereas the anonymous singer-informant in the Gellert item threatens his white overseer. In the case of the Newman White transcription, we have only a fragment, but the lyric strain appears comparable. As is clear, these parallels range from indirect to direct in their overlap. Thus, the blanket idea that no parallels existed between the Gellert collection and contemporary bodies of song is patently untrue.

The point, ultimately, is not to rehearse a comprehensive cross-comparison. Rather, my intent is to highlight that this fact of parallel documentation holds true in cases from across the pages of folk music literature, and that this record of evidence was available from the start. Lyrics from Gellert's "Well on a Monday" from *"Me and My Captain"* are included in pieces in Odum's article from 1911; Gellert's "I Ain't Nothin' But Wages Hand" is among the selections in Odum and Johnson's *Negro Workaday Songs* as "Everybody calls me the Wages Man"; Gellert's "Lice in Jail" bears a pointed resemblance to the Lomaxes' "The Cryderville Jail" in *American Ballads and Folk Songs;* and Gellert's "Cap'n Got a Pistol" shows up in the lines to the Lomaxes' "Levee Camp 'Holler'" in the same volume. There are parallels of non-protest material as well. But it is the protest lyrics that have come under fire. The fact is that as acute a plain-spoken line as "Well, if I had my weight in lime, / I'd whip my cap'n till he wen' stone blind," cited in the above example for instance, pales not the slightest between the Gellert, Odum, and Lomax versions. The difference is what the compilers did with this primary song evidence. From Odum and Johnson, Scarborough, White, and the Lomaxes, there was little to no comment on the matter of Black protest; from Gellert, that was the entire logic and substance.[29]

On the Claim of "Coaching"

The recent allegation by Bruce Conforth that Lawrence Gellert "coached" his informants into singing "Negro Songs of Protest" into his portable machine microphone is less a falsehood than a difference of scholarly interpretation. Conforth's "smoking gun" quotation from Herbert Halpert leads into a section where the author asserts that Gellert can be "clearly heard" on his audio recordings "speaking or singing the words to a song" to informants before he formally commences a take.[30] The accusation is that Gellert was prompting and influencing, if not actually co-creating, rather than documenting. The Gellert field recording archive is now fully digitized for researcher access at Indiana University. In my own item-by-time analysis of the Gellert sound collection, I do not think such an interpretation is so clear. One certainly can hear Gellert commenting to and, sometimes, laughing with informants. But what is audible in these exchanges is Gellert saying "Start from the beginning, the way you did originally," "Try it again," "Who's got another one?" or some equivalent. Informants are very often heard telling him "That's it," "That's all I got," and "That's all there is" when they conclude.[31] What Conforth deems coaching can alternatively be heard simply as field interaction and practical methodology. Fortunately, the audio archive is available for independent scrutiny as a public holding at ATM.

It is probably only with additional review by other researchers that a consensus might emerge on the issue of "coaching" versus simple collector-and-informant exchange. A few items from the field recordings are worth spotlighting, however, for a sense of the collector's practices. These audio pieces all come from Gellert's ten-inch Presto recording discs from the 1930s. The sound is quite good for documentary recordings of the era.

On one recording of an unidentified song, an ensemble tries its best to work in harmony through a melody. After a lumbering attempt, however, the effort collapses. The informants on the recording can be heard commenting to one another and presumably to Gellert. One singer says, with apparent lightheartedness, "That ain't worth nothing." Another agrees, "No, that ain't worth nothing." Then another voice joins in, "You didn't even sing."[32] The informants seem at ease as they goof and point fingers at one another for an aborted effort.

On another item, a solo informant sings through a set of verses. At the end of the performance, a women's voice is audible with the greeting, "Good morning, Alex," followed by a faint "good morning" reply. Whatever the setting, the pleasantries indicate a warm rapport. The female voice has an English accent, raising the question of whether it is in fact Gellert collaborator Nancy Cunard, along for the trip.[33]

In the case of an additional recording, a solo informant sings lines to one of Gellert's protest items, "Well on a Monday," a song in common circulation. The aural quality on this item indicates a large enclosed space, perhaps a prisoners' quarters. Sounds in the background echo with some reverberation. There is laugher, chatter, and some whistling from others present. The informant makes it through several passages of lyrics. Upon completion, Gellert can be heard saying quietly, "All right. Thank you." The interaction sounds to be perfectly normal as a dynamic of singer delivering and folklorist documenting.[34]

On another of the digitized ten-inch recordings, the informant sings through several stanzas. He stops and says, "That's all I know there now." Gellert asks, "All right, what's the other one?" in response. And in the case of still another track from the same original field disc, the singer halts and laughs when it seems he cannot remember the next line. Gellert interjects, "Hum it. Hum it." The singer then presses on humming a melody. Again, Gellert does not appear to be directing or interfering so much as facilitating and responding.[35]

The above episodes sound natural and convivial. None of these archival items can be cited to prove anything definitively, and Gellert is long since gone as are his unnamed informants. So participant testimony is not possible. Still, a careful listening through this audio data has been valuable. In my estimation, it suggests nothing artificial, compromised, or coached about the Gellert field recordings.

Dating Gellert's Field Recordings

In addition to the open question of whether or not Gellert can be heard "coaching" informants, there has been irresolution and mistakes as regards the dating of Gellert's field recording. Numerous claims have emerged in the secondary writing on the matter since examples of Gellert's documentary material first surfaced to the general public in the 1970s and 1980s. One source of insight and error was Bruce Conforth's liner notes to the third Gellert LP compilation, *Nobody Knows My Name: Blues from South Carolina and Georgia*, from 1984. In the notes, Conforth reported that all fifteen archival selections were recorded between 1924 and 1932. But, as I have written previously, such dating is incongruous with some of the music on the album. For one, Conforth stated in the notes that the song "I Been Pickin' and Shovelin'" was recorded in Spartanburg, South Carolina, in 1926. This dating clashes with lyrics that can clearly be heard to reference the Depression-era Works Progress Administration: "I mean a W.P.A. job / I mean is a good boogin' job." In another instance, there is the item "Nobody Knows My Name." In the index to the Gellert collection at the ATM, the song is listed among the ten-inch discs recorded in the 1930s and 1940s. Conforth's album commentary, however, highlights it as one of the "album's earliest pieces . . . recorded in the surprising year of 1924!"[36]

Additional primary research on my part complicates matters further. Gellert nephews related to me that they recall their "Uncle Lou" experimenting with both wax and wire recordings in the early part of his career when they were children. Wire recordings only came into existence in the 1940s. But the mention of "wax recordings" refers to wax cylinder recordings, the oldest medium of instantaneous portable recording technology from the early twentieth century. To this point, music researcher John Cowley provides useful context. In looking into the subject, he suggests that if Gellert began making field recordings as early as 1924, he would have used an acoustic wax cylinder unit, as was common to the period. We do not have any surviving wax cylinder recordings in the Gellert collection at Indiana University, and thus listeners have heard no such recordings from the 1920s. Instead, as Cowley concludes, "Aural and other evidence indicates" that "all items" released from the Gellert archive on commercial LP, including Conforth's *Nobody Knows My Name*, were "recorded electrically, using a semiprofessional portable disc cutter" of the kind "first developed in the early 1930s."[37]

Of the three commercial compilations of Gellert's field recordings, only the 1973 Rounder issue *Negro Songs of Protest: Collected by Lawrence Gellert* was completed with Gellert's assistance. The album documentation specifies that "at least half of the songs" on the LP were "recorded in the Greenville (S.C.) county jail. Basically, all of the single voice material was collected indoors; all the group material was recorded outdoors." In his contribution to the accompanying text, Gellert explains that the discs "were made on a big Presto machine . . . made especially for the field—in the thirties." The album's Rounder producers place the full catalogue of songs on the release in the Carolinas and Georgia between 1933 and 1937. This information, involving Gellert's direct participation, is consistent with Cowley's independent judgments, and it is representative of the Gellert commercial releases as a whole. Of the material that listeners have been able to hear on compilation LP from over the years, all field recordings are from the early 1930s onward.[38]

Conforth has now corrected for his original claims from the 1980s. In his 2013 biography, Conforth acknowledges that his dates were wrong, and he offers new evidence. He traces the patent numbers of Gellert's earliest aluminum discs (bearing the brand logo "Echo") to 1923 and states that these discs "were manufactured in New York City beginning around 1924." In addition to Gellert's interview recollections, Conforth factors in the memories of Gellert intimate Alice Lightner, who recalls Gellert beginning his recordings prior to her move from Tryon to New York in 1927. Conforth concludes, therefore, that Gellert "probably began recording in late 1924 or early 1925," and he asserts that Gellert is "the first person to produce field recordings of African Americans on disc."[39]

As much as Gellert deserves credit for pioneering collecting, this appraisal may be premature. The date of patent or manufacture does not tell us exactly when Gellert acquired or used the aluminum discs in his possession, and, just as Gellert admitted of his own memories in his interviews, Alice Lightner's dates may have faltered with age by the time she related them to Conforth by letter in 1982. Additionally, Gellert himself, in another context, indicated a later start date. In a draft proposal for an unspecified party, the collector presented a resume up through his second songbook from 1939. He began, "In the past ten years, I have made what is considered the most extensive collection of the Songs of the Southern Negroes in America." By his own word, then, this conflicting dating would push back the start of Gellert's formal sound recording in the field to at least 1929.[40]

Interestingly, 1929 is the year aluminum discs came on the market as the first widely available form of electrical instantaneous recording technology.[41] Gellert first used a manual self-rigged recording system, not an electrified system, and possibly he did acquire specialty aluminum discs for his hand-wound phonograph sooner, as Conforth reports. But it is worth noting that Gellert's very first seven-inch disc in the ATM catalog is an unaccompanied informant performance with an audible verse and melody match to Tampa Red's commercial release "The Duck Yas-Yas-Yas" from 1929. Elsewhere among Gellert's seven-inch discs, an informant sings the first two verses of this same Tampa Red record, as well as another informant on a different song item sings an exact three-verse lyrical match to artist Texas Alexander's commercial release "Tell Me Woman Blues," also from 1929. Among the audible seven-inch discs there are identifiable item matches to commercial recordings dating from as early as 1923 to as late as 1930, but the preponderance of matches are to commercial releases from 1927, 1928, and 1929.[42] These extant disc recordings do not preclude the possibility of earlier discs no longer in existence or on file at ATM, and the fact of commercial music parallels from the latter 1920s does not mean that Gellert did not earlier collect verses already floating in Black oral circulation prior to commercial performances. This data only speaks to multiple elements complicating certainty. Gellert's 1936 profile reviewing *Negro Songs of Protest* in *Time* magazine, after all, suggests even another competing dating. The piece has it that the collector had been "touring the South for the past nine years."[43] This would place the beginning of Gellert's efforts in 1927. Finally, recall from chapter 1 that the episode in Tryon that Gellert always identified as his gateway into Black music discovery—the local African American "sing fest" church fundraiser—took place in 1926.

What seems clear in all this is that the listenable material that has been issued to the general public on commercial record is not from the 1920s. Gellert's best quality field recordings were processed on a Presto electrified portable disc cutter, which only became available in the early 1930s. The Presto Recording Corporation was founded in 1933 and began marketing its discs and cutters in 1934. In these years, Presto recording discs—composed of an aluminum plate coated with a cellulose nitrate-based lacquer—gained preeminence as the industry standard for instantaneous sound reproduction. They were known for their durability and improved sound quality, and it would seem only logical that such discs stood out among his collection in terms of the requisite playability for commercial release when producers were reviewing the material in the early 1970s and 1980s.[44] Again, this is not to say that Gellert was not recording in the 1920s. Rather, it is simply to identify that what has been made available to scholars and enthusiasts in the general public likely dates from the decade afterward, a period in which the collector expanded and professionalized considerably his efforts in the field. In the 1920s, Gellert was resourceful in devising his own methods of mechanical sound inscription. Still, his earliest field discs—his "soft" seven-inch aluminum recordings, as he called them—were never meant for posterity. They were simply a personal means by which to more effectively take down and review his own written lyric transcriptions in an age when folk music collecting was primarily a textual as opposed to an aural endeavor.

The issues raised here carry considerable weight for specialists in Black music and folksong research. If Lawrence Gellert's recordings, whatever the medium, were to be verifiable back to the early 1920s, such a distinction would establish him among the very first—before the venerable Lomax team even, and alongside Library of Congress Archive of American Folk Song originator Robert W. Gordon—to compile aural data (as opposed to merely written transcription) from the field on Black folksong in the southern United States. John A. and Alan Lomax began their field recording for the Library of Congress in 1933; Robert Winslow Gordon was the founding director of the Library's Archive of American Folk Song. Gordon made wax cylinder recordings of African American singers in North Carolina and Georgia in 1925 and 1926. In fact, Gordon and Gellert collected variants of the same song in North Carolina. This instance is a useful case by which to end one aspect of our discussion of parallels, dating, and methodology before moving on to the specific question of Gellert's protest archive.[45]

Robert Gordon recorded the song "Let's Go to Bury" from African American informants in 1925 in the community of Brickton, North Carolina, only thirty miles from Gellert's base, Tryon. One chorus and verse of the item should give a sense of its form and content:

> Come on, come on, let's go to buryin',
> Come on, come on, let's go to buryin',
> Come on, come on, let's go to buryin',
> Way over in the new buryin' ground.
>
> Somebody's dyin' way over yonder,
> Somebody's dyin' way over yonder,
> Somebody's dyin' way over yonder,
> Way over in the new buryin' ground.

Gellert documented versions of the same song on three field recordings, and he included a transcription, "Let's Go To De Buryin'," as the final item in *Negro Songs of Protest.* The continuities and discontinuities are worth examining. The three Gellert field recordings appear to be from three separate circumstances. The earliest recording, from among Gellert's seven-inch discs of the 1920s, is a barely audible unaccompanied solo performance. Though the surface noise and accelerated playing speed on the digitized reproduction make aural examination difficult, the song is identifiable in melody, form, and in lyric fragments as "Let's Go to Bury / Let's Go To De Buryin'." The other two field recordings are group performances from Gellert's superior ten-inch Presto discs from the 1930s. The sound quality is good. In melody, chorus, and in several of the stanzas, these items match up identically with Gordon's 1925 field recording.[46]

These parallel audio examples suggest that Gellert collected some of the same songs in some of the same areas around the same time as Gordon, one of the earliest practitioners in the field. The three sound recordings also provide an audio index for Gellert's published transcription. Chorus and verse on the Gellert audio match up with the Gellert print rendering in *Negro Songs of Protest*, but for one difference. Gellert's "Let's Got To De Buryin'" in the songbook includes a calling line not heard on either the Gordon or Gellert audio: "Cap'n kill my buddy, let's go to buryin'." The line is repeated three times, as with the other verses in Gordon and Gellert, and then it is answered with the identical refrain, "Way over in de new buryin' ground." Is this a protest verse grafted on to the spiritual? Did Gellert actually hear it sung, or did he add the lyric in himself? Bruce Conforth highlights these Gellert field recordings in his book. Detractors who cry foul of the Gellert archive might reasonably seize upon this example as evidence of fabrication. Interestingly, though, Conforth cites these Gellert field items to highlight the collector's straight folklore contribution of non-protest material; Conforth spotlights the material as genuine.[47]

A detailed inquiry into the Gellert archive, parallel folklore collections, and the contextual histories of Black vernacular cultures of opposition leads me to believe that there is no reason to doubt the likelihood of an alternate set of Black resistance lyrics. Just because we do not have an audio recording of a documentary informant singing exactly the one line printed in *Negro Songs of Protest* does not mean that lyric was not genuinely encountered by Gellert. Field recording was a costly and laborious endeavor in the first decades of the twentieth century. Not everything the collector heard could easily be captured on instantaneous recording disc. That the audio record and print record are an imperfect match is more probable than that of direct print to audio symmetry. What we do know, moreover, is that the Gellert archive includes considerable numbers of sound recordings on which we can hear informants singing lines that we read in Gellert's print transcriptions. Did Gellert feed those lines to African American singers to fool the ears of posterity? How could Gellert have expected that his independently made recordings-on-the-go would one day be compiled for commercial release and scholarly evaluation decades in the future?

The simplest explanation for discontinuities, based on the simple calculation of Black agency and creative resistance, is that African American informants shared with the collector real songs with real meaning for their community, and that the outcome of these exchanges varied depending on the nature of circumstances. Sometimes Gellert took this music down on audio disc and sometimes in shorthand. If the print and audio archives do not perfectly match up, the burden of disjuncture likely rests with the reality of the times, not the unreliability of a bad-faith dealer fabricating songs. In the case of Gordon and Gellert, to further address this issue of asymmetry, the lyrical difference (only slight, at that) between "Let's Go to Bury" and "Let's Go To De Buryin'," can reasonably be theorized on at least two grounds. First, Robert Gordon was a very different kind of collector. A folklorist interested in preserving and promoting American traditional music broadly, Gordon was searching for something different than Gellert in his fieldwork, and his informants may have understood that. Second, the factor of timing should not be discounted. Perhaps local Black community members felt more comfortable calling out injustice in the politicized culture of the 1930s when they sang for Gellert as opposed to the 1920s when they sang for Gordon. People of color, after all, were experiencing the same shaken circumstances and movement organizing in the United States as the majority society during the Great Depression. To mention a Gellert counterpart once again as a reference point, the Langston Hughes of the 1930s was not the Langston Hughes of the 1920s. The "race" poet had become a "red" poet, and he was far more outspoken and emphatic in his terms of expression.[48] Lawrence Gellert may have heard a different version of "Let's Go to Bury" than had Gordon in part because of his distinct collecting persona but also because he was collecting in new circumstances of mass suffering and resistance in the Depression.

Furthermore, we can expand this case of similarity and dissimilarity, tradition and variation, beyond the specific instance of "Let's Go to Bury" and "Let's Go To De Buryin'." A broader explanation for overlap and discontinuity between items in the Gellert collection and that of folklore peers is the vernacular music principle of "communal re-creation." As Lawrence Levine relates, this concept can be traced in scholarship to the work of folklorists Bruno Nettl and Phillips Barry in the 1950s and 1960s. Levine applies it as an essential theme in *Black Culture and Black Consciousness*, and it applies here as equally essential. Tracing this dynamic of Black music-making from antebellum spirituals to twentieth-century seculars, Levine writes that this music was a "product of an improvisational communal consciousness." Black folksongs "were not, as some observers thought," he elaborates, "totally new creations, but were forged out of many pre-existing bits of old songs mixed together with snatches of new tunes and lyrics and fit into a fairly traditional but never wholly static metrical pattern." Levine cites examples from throughout African American vernacular tradition, and in his chapter on secular music makes specific reference to lyrical protest. He references, for instance, the "White man settin' on a wall" lyrics mentioned in chapter 1 of this book. Based on a shared musical point of reference, Levine recounts, the Black workers that Howard Odum observed improvised words on the spot to send a message to the collector. As they toiled, he sat in repose "Wastin' his time, wastin' his time." Levine offers a further example "provided by the blues and jazz pianist Sam Price in relating an incident" from his childhood in the early twentieth century. As Levine reports, Price recalled: "I'll never forget the first song I ever heard to remember. A man had been lynched near my home in a town called Robinson, Texas. And at that time we were living in Waco, Texas—my mother, brother and myself. And they made a parody of this song and the words were something like this: I never have, and I never will / Pick no more cotton in Robinsonville, / Tell me how long will I have to wait, / Can I get you now or must I hesitate?" The chorus will be familiar to blues fans as "Hesitation Blues," but the preceding lines reflect the operation of communal re-creation. The Black laborers of Odum's encounter and Price's family members as well drew on a "familiar structure" and "familiar tune," as Levine summarizes, and improvised "new words that fit their surroundings and their mood."[49]

Levine asserted in *Black Culture and Black Consciousness* in 1977 that "anyone who has read large numbers of Negro songs is familiar with this process," and he added that the "phenomenon impressed all of the major collectors of black music" before and during Gellert's era. Improvisation, adaptation, recombination, and cross-fertilization between the sacred and secular, group work songs and solo blues, was an established fact of African American musical tradition. Nina Simone said, "Negro music has always crossed all those lines." Black folksong, Levine stressed, was "simultaneously the result of individual and mass creativity." "Wholly spontaneous and original song did exist, of course," he granted, "But insofar as these creations became part of the communal tradition, they took their place within the large reservoir . . . which belonged to the community at large and which its members felt was at their disposal to do with what they liked."[50]

Only through such a lens can the case of Lawrence Gellert's "Negro Songs of Protest" fairly be evaluated. The protest and non-protest content, the overlap and discontinuity, that characterizes the Gellert archive comes into clearer view in the focus of communal re-creation. And yet, this principle of folklore studies seems to have been denied in the instance of "Negro Songs of Protest," in Gellert's lifetime and again recently. In his 1960s interviews, the collector expressed frustration to Reuss about the language of a 1936 *New York Times* review. The article was approving of Gellert's newly published *Negro Songs of Protest*, and Gellert welcomed the praise. But he described as "bullshit" the reviewer's claim that Gellert had unearthed a "new genre" of Black music dealing with "the realities of Negro life." There was nothing new about such song making, he insisted.[51] What was new was the reality of white discovery of Black protest in the dominant culture. Too often in dominant consciousness, this discovery has been surfaced to consideration and then returned to denial.

The Songs: Fabrication or Vindication?

Finally, we have the particular "suspect" body of song to consider. Are "Negro Songs of Protest" real or made up by Lawrence Gellert? As indicated previously, detractors have cited a lack of original audio to back up the print transcriptions in Gellert's articles and two songbooks as evidence of his dubiousness. The collector did not circulate or deposit his field recordings until late in life in the 1960s and 1970s. But the technology to reproduce and circulate such material was not so simple a prospect before the digital revolution of our age; it was costly and thus typically required significant institutional support.

From the time of his first songbook in 1936, however, Gellert claimed his print transcriptions were honest representations, as transparent and unmediated as possible from the African American originals. In his preface to *Negro Songs of Protest*, Gellert wrote:

> The melodies here given have not been "arranged" in the usual accepted sense of the word. They have been faithfully set down with hours of painstaking labor, exactly as sung into the records, or as nearly so as conventional music notation is adaptable for notating ¼ tones, slides, curlecues [*sic*], indefinite pitches, irregular shifting rhythms, intentional striking of notes off beat by way of embellishment by the singer, and other peculiarities characteristic of genuine Negro folk music. . . . Nor are the piano accompaniments made to complete or adorn the melodies. They are merely added to supply a back-ground for those who feel they want one. . . . However, it should be understood that the melodies as given are complete in themselves and may, of course, be sung without accompaniment.[52]

His comments reflect self-awareness and a determined priority of fidelity as concerns the aural to print translation.

In the 1960s, Richard Reuss pressed this line of inquiry regarding print renderings and audio back-ups. "How many of those [in the *Negro Songs of Protest* songbook] were on record, if any?" he asked Gellert. The collector responded, "A good many of those . . . are from the aluminum records," but these records were no longer playable, he stressed, and some had gone missing in back-and-forth transactions. Gellert related that he no had skills by which to notate musical arrangements from his sound recordings. Therefore, he loaned them out to a musician—a woman suggested by his friend, dancer Martha Graham, he recalled—who "went through them once" and translated the music into a notebook that was then used by composer Elie Siegmeister for the formal book arrangements. "They are documented," Gellert insisted, but there would be no way to verify this so many years after the fact, he stated, considering the fragile state of his seven-inch discs. Reuss also asked about Gellert's second book, "*Me and My Captain*" from 1939. Gellert answered, "Every song there is documented on record." For this project, the collector explained that he "turned over" his ten-inch Presto discs (his superior-quality "steel records," as he called them) to arranger Lan Adomian. "Just the way he put them down there" in the songbook, Gellert asserted, "he got them from the records." He added, "I wasn't even with him because I went South."[53]

Are Gellert's claims accurate? How many print transcriptions in the songbooks can be sourced to a documentary sound recording in the field archive? Reuss asked the questions and noted the answers, but he did not follow up. My analysis shows that Gellert's claims can be substantiated to a significant degree. Several of the twenty-four songs in *Negro Songs of Protest* can be matched to audio in the Gellert archive. Just as Gellert recalled, there are matches to his earliest seven-inch discs. Additionally, matches can be made to his good-sounding ten-inch discs. This latter case includes "Way Down South," the item disputed as "questionable" by folklorist D. K. Wilgus in his record review from 1972. Wilgus wondered whether the song was "a nonce-creation by a militant black" from the organizing campaigns of the 1930s. But the song (alternately titled "In Atlanta, Georgia" by Gellert) appears twice in the audio archive on both a ten-inch disc recording from the 1930s and seven-inch disc recording from the 1920s. We have encountered Gellert's lyric transcription from *Negro Songs of Protest* already in chapter 1, but two verses with chorus will refresh the memory:

Way down South, upon a rock quarr'l [quarry],
White folks chase N——r like chasin' a squirr'l,
In Atlanta, Georgia,
In Atlanta, Georgia.
If you don't get lynched you sho' get pinched in Atlanta, Georgia.

Same fo' N——r ev'ry place down South
It just done happen I'm talkin' about
Atlanta, Georgia,
Atlanta, Georgia.
If you don't get lynched you sho' get pinched in Atlanta, Georgia.

On the seven-inch recording, the verses are too inaudible for confident identification. However, the chorus is clearly represented just as transcribed by Gellert. In the case of the ten-inch recording, the verses above and chorus match up with the print rendering. These two field recordings, then, by two different singers from the 1930s and 1920s, counter the Wilgus argument that this overt Black song of protest, "Way Down South," is suspect. By this recorded evidence, the song cannot be dismissed as a "nonce-creation," nor can it be marginalized as a "questionable" product of "Red" outside influence in the Depression era.[54]

As for "*Me and My Captain*," a number of songs in the text can also be matched to audio in the sound archive. Just as Gellert recalled to Reuss, these matches are to the ten-inch Presto "steel records" within the collection. By my count, ten of the twenty-four transcriptions in the book can be paired with audio items. While this is not the "every song" that Gellert insisted to Reuss could be documented, there is the possibility that some discs went missing before deposit at the Archives of Traditional Music. There is also the possibility the Gellert was misremembering by the 1960s or misstating to overcompensate for the insinuations of doubt. Still, the overlap between "*Me and My Captain*" and Gellert sound recordings is much more direct than in the instance of *Negro Songs of Protest*. The songs "Atlanta Town," "Two Hoboes," "Early in the Morning," "Look Over Yonder," "Steel Got to Be Drove," and "I Hear Danger Singing" are all well captured in high-quality audio as performed by solo or group informants. The songs "Bossman Sammy," "Work Ox," "Captain Don't You Think," "Corn Pone," and "Well on a Monday" can be paired to audio as well. However, these items are sung by Gellert himself on the matching field recordings. This does raise a question. Was the collector singing demonstration records to convey what he heard in the field to arranger Lan Adomian, or was he recording folk-sounding creations of his own making? There is no definitive means by which to answer this question. But "Two Hoboes" is included among Gellert's recordings both on a disc sung by him and on a separate disc sung by a field informant. If one is inclined by this point to trust the collector, such evidence would suggest the field recordings with his voice are demonstration records meant to preserve in audio after the fact what he could not capture quickly in the field in the moment. Gellert may have written down the words but felt he needed to voice the tune.[55]

One song in "*Me and My Captain*" deserves special attention. "Atlanta Town" is the fourth item in the book. As I have excerpted it, one can get a sense of the book transcription:

> Black man ain't got no justice in Atlanta.
> Down in Georgia where you better live right,
> Down in Atlanta.
> Down in Georgia where you better live right,
> Down in Atlanta town.
> Down in Georgia where you better live right,
> Told you better not gamble and you better not fight,
> Black man ain't got justice in Atlanta.[56]

The full transcription can be sourced in a very direct match to one of Gellert's ten-inch field recordings, "Negro Got No Justice," as it was titled for release on the 1973 Rounder LP:

> N——rs ain't got no justice in Atlanta.
> Down in Georgia where you better live right,
> Down in Atlanta.
> Down in Georgia where you better live right,
> Down in Atlanta town.
> Down in Georgia say you better live right,
> Lord, you better not gamble and you better not fight,
> N——rs ain't got justice in Atlanta.
>
> Well it's Charlie bird running from door to door,
> Down in Atlanta.

Well it's Charlie bird running from door to door,
Down in Atlanta town.
Well it's Charlie bird running from door to door,
Well he lockin' up the n——rs, let the white folks go,
N——rs ain't got no justice in Atlanta.

Well A-T-L-A-N-T-A,
That spells Atlanta.
A-T-L-A-N-T-A,
That spells Atlanta town.
Well, A-T-L-A-N-T-A,
Capital G-E-O-R and G-I-A,
N——rs ain't got no justice in Atlanta.

Well early in the morning when the ding dong ring,
Down in Atlanta.
Well early in the morning when the ding dong ring,
Lord, you go to the table,
See the same old thing,
N——rs ain't got no justice in Atlanta.

Well, yonder come my momma with a laugh and a smile,
Down in Atlanta.
Well, yonder come my momma with a laugh and a smile,
Down in Atlanta town.
Well, yonder come my momma with a laugh and a smile,
"Mr. E. Tyree, Lord, I want my child."
N——rs ain't got no justice in Atlanta.

Well a-yonder come my gal, boy, how do you know?
Down in Atlanta town.
Well yonder come my gal, boy, how do you know?
Down in Atlanta.
Come my gal, how do you know?
Lord, I know my gal by the dress she wore.
N——rs ain't got no justice in Atlanta.

Umbrella on her shoulder, pocketbook in her hand,
Down in Atlanta town.
Umbrella on her shoulder, pocketbook in her hand,
Down in Atlanta town.
Umbrella on her shoulder, pocketbook in her hand,
"Lord, Mr. E. J. Weed, Lord, I want my man."
N——rs ain't got no justice in Atlanta.[57]

The audio features a strong unaccompanied vocalist. It is certainly not the collector himself and, in fact, is an informant singer who appears more than once on recordings in the Gellert archive.

The lyrics are brash and bitter, openly defiant. They call out a capital of southern injustice under Jim Crow one emphatic letter at a time ("A-T-L-A-N-T-A"), and they call out an individual by name, "Mr. E. J. Weed." The song is emblematic of the most striking and overt items in Gellert's body of "Negro Songs of Protest." In terms of Gellert authentication, therefore, this song, like "Way Down South" in Gellert's first book, carries a weight of corroboration. It can clearly be sourced to an audio match. It sounds far more real than "questionable," to recall again Wilgus's terminology.

That said, many of the audio-to-print overlaps detailed above are not so direct. Partial lyrics and melodies are identifiable, but the cross-referencing is about pieces, and sometimes only traces, rather than wholes. No one audio item in the sound archive is a perfect match to any of the book transcriptions. It is possible, therefore, that Lawrence Gellert recorded real songs, and then embellished, adapted, or recombined by inserting agit-prop lyrics of protest where none existed on the ground. Then again, what are the limits of this kind of doubt and scrutiny? When does Gellert's word, backed with reasonable primary corroboration, start to count? When is the burden of credibility lifted?

In his 2013 study, Conforth writes that he is unimpressed with Gellert's lauded first songbook, *Negro Songs of Protest.* Conforth examines ten of the book's twenty-four songs, classifying them as either "devoid of any overt protest" or unremarkable in that they are standard in other folksong collections or in the commercial record. Curiously, though, one of those songs, "Sistren an' Brethren," deemed "devoid of any overt protest" is characterized earlier by Conforth in his book as "overt" in its protest lyricism and likely not folk. Conforth in that earlier passage casts "Sistren an' Brethren" as what D. K. Wilgus called a "nonce-creation." He writes that "the song was composed for a specific situation and Lawrence collected it from a member of the community (a preacher) who would have been well versed in using rhetoric to arouse his congregation: it might never have been sung again." Oddly as well, Conforth concludes his assessment with what he describes as the last two songs in the book, "Here I Am in Dis Low Down Jail" and "I Went to Atlanta." The former is actually entry ten in the publication, and the latter is actually entry number one. Conforth is equally unimpressed with *"Me and My Captain,"* Gellert's second songbook from 1939. He states that the "twenty-four songs included in the brief thirty-two-page book were not much different than those in *Negro Songs of Protest.*" Overall, Conforth argues, the material in these books may have born the label of "protest," but they were "at best" just arrangements of "songs that had long existed, within either the oral or the commercial tradition—songs that were less than the political dynamite for which the left tried to use them."[58]

Conforth singles out certain songs in the Gellert collection as particularly suspicious or compromised. This list of "bad apples" includes "Sistren an' Brethren" as well as "Do Lak Alabamy Boys," "Scottsboro," "Georgia Work Song," "Sharecropper," "Angelo Herndon," and "Baton Rouge." Aside from "Baton Rouge," which comes from a later period and was published by Gellert in the "dubious" *Mainstream* article from 1963, the other songs on this list all appeared in the radical press prior to or in the same year as Gellert's publication of *Negro Songs of Protest* in 1936. Space does not allow for a detailed rundown of each, but some attention is necessary. "Baton Rouge," like "Sistren an' Brethren," is dismissed by Conforth as compromised in its folk currency. The author speculates that it was likely "composed for very specific purposes and events and apparently did not enter the folk tradition." The song "Angelo Herndon" appeared in Gellert's second *Music Vanguard* article, "Four Negro Songs of Protest," in 1935. Conforth judges it "an impromptu work song rather than the kind of political commentary that would have almost certainly been generated by the actual Herndon case." Conforth, therefore, seems to be arguing the reverse of his general thrust. The song, he indicates, is not political enough to be legitimate. "Sharecropper" was published in *New Masses* in April 1936. Conforth suspects it of outright fabrication. "It seems almost certain that 'Sharecropper' was a piece composed in its entirety by Lawrence, probably using small stock phrases," he argues. "It seems possible, indeed probable, that he composed this poem, and if he did, then one must ask whether or not he had a hand in embellishing some of his previous material that had suddenly become so overtly political." Conforth's own terminology here—"poem"—is important, though. Unlike all the other documentary pieces that Gellert contributed to *New Masses*, "Sharecropper" does not appear under the moniker "Negro Songs of Protest." Instead, it is featured as one of four texts, each attributed to a creator by name, in a section in the periodical titled "Poems." There appears to be no effort to present this as anything but an original poem by Lawrence Gellert.[59]

The language above in which Conforth refers to a sudden turn to overt political lyricism relates to his suspicions of "Do Lak Alabamy Boys," printed among the lyrics in one of Gellert's installments of "Negro Songs of Protest" in *New Masses* in May 1933. Conforth writes, "The song contains at least two stanzas that appear problematic from an authorship perspective." He flags the third and the last verses as suspect:

> White folks git yo' money, craps f'om offen yo' fahm
> He take mos' ov'thin' you has, 'cept de power dats in yo' ahm
> What you gwine do n——r, wit' de power dat's in yo' ahm
> Git wipin' yo eye tear, 'till de strenff is dead an' gone
>
> Wa'cher gwine do n——r, ain' nothing lak what ah said
> Do lak Alabamy boys an' win or be foun' dead

Robin Kelley cites these same lyrics in *Hammer and Hoe* as evidence of the militant inspiration of the Communist-organized Share Croppers' Union (SCU) in Black vernacular cultures of opposition throughout Alabama. But Conforth finds the text artificial in its open language of armed confrontation. "For the first time Lawrence presented a song that includes a number of lines that cannot be traced to more traditional verses and that can clearly be called protest," he asserts.[60]

In that same May 1933 installment, Gellert included "Scottsboro." Conforth calls it "the most disturbing of them all" in Gellert's catalog of "Negro Songs of Protest." Conforth explains his position on the item, and by so doing outlines his overall philosophy of doubt:

> [Gellert] claimed to have gotten the song from Meridian, Mississippi, and that it represented the "Negro slant on the white capitalist brand of justice." Never before had he mentioned any of his songs being a critique of capitalism, and none of his songs ever had such immediate currency, so one is forced to wonder, why now? And why such a major change in focus? Also curiously, this song does not appear on any of his known field recordings. . . . If the degree of authenticity of a protest song might be tied to the degree of overtly specific lyrics one finds, then perhaps

> "Scottsboro" was not without outside influence. It is hard to imagine that such a song would not have been influenced, at least in part, either by a certain more radical element with[in]] African American culture . . . or by white organizers or even Lawrence Gellert himself.

Conforth identifies "Georgia Work Song (He-i-Heria)" from *New Masses* in May 1935 as comparably extrinsic to grassroots African American culture. A version of the song is documented in Odum and Johnson's *Negro Workaday Songs*, he acknowledges. But in Gellert's transcription, the "lyrics are extremely radical, matching nothing in any of the traditional collections. . . . How does one account for such a song? . . . Surely the song must have come from a specific militant group, or it was the creation of a particularly radical individual." That "particularly radical individual," Conforth hints, may have been Lawrence Gellert.[61]

We have already broached this allegation of asymmetry in the print-to-audio sources in the Gellert archive. Audio back-ups for each of the collector's print renderings is arguably, considering the time and circumstances, an unreasonable standard by which to assess integrity. Additionally, the "why now?" allegation seems misplaced. I submit that nothing changed in May 1933. The collector had been publishing his article series under the title "Negro Songs of Protest" since 1930. The first four installments of the series were aggregated as his essay contribution to Nancy Cunard's *Negro: An Anthology* in 1934. Cunard, the notorious Communist heiress, meant it when she included Gellert's piece in her radical masterwork, and Gellert meant it when he said he heard protest in African American folksong. Gellert did not suddenly go radical in the spring of 1933. He had been radicalizing over a period of time. He expressed this to his interviewer in the 1960s, and the print record shows this from the first in 1930. Like many in the ranks of the alienated and disenfranchised, Gellert was shaken by the crisis of the Great Depression. His inchoate racial justice outlook developing in the South in the 1920s found a new vocabulary in Left political consciousness in the 1930s.

"Belinda" is the first song text in Gellert's first *New Masses* article. It is political in its critique of the grotesque practices of antebellum breeding and sexual control, and Gellert sets it up as such:

> A plantation chant of other days. Simple and archaic. One of the very few slavery songs I came across. . . . Old Ben who sang it served slavery

> eighteen years. . . . He explained, after he finished the song in a quavery cracked voice typical of ancient Negroes, that if a fellow on a plantation saw a girl he wanted, he'd have to see her Master. He'd feel his muscles. If they were powerful and stout the Master would be pleased. Yes, he'd like to have some of his stock. Come over next Friday for an hour or so. Tell your Master I'll pay him for your time.

The verses included the following:

> Belinda she love li'll Joe
> Belinda she itch fo' li'll Joe
> Belinda she wan' jump broom with li'll Joe
> But Marse he say no
>
> Marse he raise bes' horse an' cow
> Marse he raise bes' n——r an' sow
> Marse he sho' know jes' how
> An' Belinda she cain has Joe

Also, in this first article, Gellert included "Stan' Boys Stan," with its lyrics of armed self-defense:

> N——r don' you run 'way
> White trash acomin'
> Is acomin'
> Get dat whackin' stick in yo' han'
> Ruckus boun' to happen
> Boun' to happen

Conforth reports that "an audible recording of these early songs does not exist." But there are two field recordings of "Belinda" in the Gellert archive, one on seven-inch disc from the 1920s and one on ten-inch disc from the 1930s. In my recent analysis of the digital files, in fact, I identified audio back-ups for a number of song texts featured in these early articles. At this late date, Gellert's print and audio record can perhaps never be truly authenticated to an absolute point of certainty. Nevertheless, the weight of evidence in the collector's favor suggests integrity versus fraudulence, honesty versus duplicity.[62]

A Final Case: Lawrence Gellert and the Lomaxes, Again

If we return to the case of a particular protest item of note, "Atlanta Town/ Negro Got No Justice," the balance sheet tips all the more. Historian Bruce Bastin was one of the first in blues scholarship to explore the contribution of Lawrence Gellert. In *Red River Blues* from 1986, Bastin introduces the radical folklorist in the same discussion of non-commercial fieldwork in which he covers the Lomaxes. Actually, he connects the dots of the parties' crossed paths in the South in the 1930s.

First, there is the Gellert field recording, "Mr. Tyree," one of the outstanding guitar blues in the collection. I have excerpted some of the lyrics:

> Tyree, Mr. Tyree, please get my pardon to go,
> Can get out of here, Lord, I won't return no more.
> Mr. Tyree, please get my pardon to go,
> If you let me out of Bellwood, well I won't return no more.
>
> Early this mornin' just about the break of day,
> Tyree give me pick and shovel just to pass my time away.
> Mr. Tyree, please give me my pardon to go,
> If you let me out of Bellwood, I won't return no more.
>
> Early one mornin', momma, the blues came fallin' down,
> Stayed with me, baby, and stayed with me all night long.
> Mr. Tyree, please give me my pardon to go,
> Well, if you let me out of Bellwood, I won't return no more.

As Gellert recounted, "Tyree" meant "tyrant" to his African American informants. Bastin adds another layer of meaning. "Tyree," he states, "was a little-loved Atlanta prison guard" at the Bellwood institution just outside of the city. To his interviewer in the 1960s, Gellert explained that he collected the song from a Georgia chain gang in the early 1930s, but he was unable to volunteer anything further. Bastin fills in the detail. John and Alan Lomax, it turns out, visited the same Bellwood in December 1934. From a group of convicts (names unidentified), they recorded a song titled "I Promised Mr. Tyree." The tune is different and the lyrics do not appear to be protest, but the direct address from these prisoners to a "Tyree" is the same. Gellert and the Lomaxes were traveling the same roads.[63]

Then there is the case of "Atlanta Town/Negro Got No Justice." On December 15, 1934, John Lomax recorded at the state prison farm in Milledgeville, Georgia. He documented a song that was catalogued as "We Don't Get No Justice in Atlanta." The "no justice" refrain should remind readers of Gellert's "Atlanta Town/Negro Got No Justice":

> Oh, we don't get no justice here in Atlanta,
> Oh, we don't get no justice here in Atlanta,
> For if you say the law ain't right.
>
> In the jail you'll spend the night.
>
> We don't get no justice here in Atlanta.
> Oh, if you say the judge ain't right,
>
> In the jail you'll spend the night.
>
> We don't get no justice here in Atlanta,
> Oh, we don't get no justice here in Atlanta,
> If you say the judge ain't right,
>
> In the gang you'll stay all night.
>
> You don't get no justice here in Atlanta.[64]

Not only do the two items appear comparable in lyric, but, as I have discovered, the unaccompanied solo voice on both field recordings may in fact be the same singer-informant. The tenor and delivery sound very similar. Factoring all of the contextual and aural evidence, therefore, my reasoned judgment is that in this instance, when John Lomax recorded a "Negro Song of Protest" of his own akin to the material in the Gellert archive, he and Gellert not only overlapped at the same place around the same time, but that each made field recordings of the same unnamed prisoner.

The voice of this informant sounds to be the same on several of Gellert's field recordings, among them some of his most striking protest offerings, including "How Long, Brethren?" which opened this book. Gellert, I believe, documented the informant multiple times. The possibility that a Lomax recorded him too may signal a fascinating point of intersection considering their reputed status as feuding camps, but the prospect is logical. When a good singer with a valuable repertoire was located in a closed environment such as a prison, multiple recordings makes sense. That two different collectors, on separate visits but in the same period, documented the same man and a similar song is reasonable. Moreover, I have identified additional field recordings from this same Lomax trip to Milledgeville that sound very much like performances captured in the Gellert archive. For instance, the Lomax recording of "Oh Lawdy Me, Oh Lawdy My," credited simply to "group of Negro convicts," bear enormous similarity in voice, melody, and lyrics to Gellert ten-inch field recordings from the early 1930s.[65] Neither collector took down informant names for these items, and Gellert, moreover, did not even leave us the identifiers of place and date. So, again, this interpretation cannot be conclusive. My theory is that Lawrence Gellert and the Lomaxes not only worked in parallel in their southern collecting but that, in at least once instance in Georgia, they recorded some of the same singers and same songs.

Specialists Ronald Cohen and John Szwed, in their respective studies of Alan Lomax, provide additional context. In *Alan Lomax: Selected Writings 1934–1997*, Cohen reprints the younger Lomax's early article "'Sinful' Songs of the Southern Negro," published in 1934. In a statement that attests to the dynamic of communal re-creation, Lomax reported, "Our singers classed all these songs, to distinguish them from recorded music and from written-out songs in general, as 'made-up' songs. So it was that when we visited the Smithers Plantation in the Trinity River bottoms near Huntsville, Texas." Alan and John Lomax on this early trip found the Black workers reticent during the day about singing such "made-up songs" when summoned by the "plantation manager." Instead, they recorded at night in a school house on the property. The workers present called up Blue, one of the plantation's tenant farmers, and goaded him. "White man ain' gwine hurt you. What you scai'd of?" they prodded. After some negotiation, Blue sang. Lomax recounts the scene in his article: "And with his eye cocked at the manager, amid the giggling of the women that rose into a roar of nervous merriment, Blue sang of the tribulations of the Negro renter in the South, living and working under a system which is sometimes not far different from the peonage of Old Mexico." Lomax's transcription reads:

> Po' farmer, po' farmer, po' farmer,
> Dey git all de farmer make.
> His clothes is full of patches,
> His hat is full of holes,

Stoopin' down pickin' cotton
F'om off de bottom boll.
Po' farmer, po' farmer, po' farmer,
Dey git all de farmer make.
At de commissary,
His money in deir bags,
His po' li'l wife an' chillun
Sit at home in rags.
Po' farmer, po' farmer, po' farmer,
Dey git all de farmer make.

John Szwed reports the same story of Blue and "Po' Farmer" in *Alan Lomax: The Man Who Recorded the World*, and he unpacks the dynamics even more significantly in terms of both Black protest and white discovery. The Lomaxes had initially asked for the song "Stagolee," a common folk item "about a legendary badman, a figure whose celebrated feats he [Alan] suspected were sung by black men as an allegory to express dissatisfaction with their own lives in America," Szwed explains. Still, even masked with allegory, such a song was risky. Szwed writes, "Protest, even in poetic form, was out of the question in the South, and could lead to beatings, or worse." No one stepped forward to sing it. Then, Blue was pushed forward and sang "Po' Farmer." Szwed contextualizes the "giggling" and "nervous merriment" as anxious laughter in a setting thick with the weight of racialized power and repercussion.[66]

John Szwed stresses that the emergent Alan Lomax saw this as a pivotal moment. Young Alan recognized "his calling to be more than just a folk song collector. He was also to be a messenger for the masses," Szwed elaborates. Alan recalled: "That experience totally changed my life. I saw what I had to do. My job was to try and get as much of these views, these feelings, this unheard majority onto the center of the stage."[67]

In these passages on Blue, "Po' Farmer," and Lomax, John Szwed mentions Lawrence Gellert too. His coverage shows an overlap between the Lomaxes and Gellert that seemed to have been written out of common awareness in the folk music community at some point after World War II and before the folksong revival of the 1960s. Such episodes as above show that the Lomaxes and Lawrence Gellert did encounter similar Black songs of protest, that Alan was especially inspired by such music, and that Alan saw his role as more than simply to document. Lomax, like Gellert, had a social mission in folksong collecting. Alan and Gellert were, perhaps, not that different in their experiences and motivations in the field after all. As Szwed reports, Alan and Gellert were still cohabiting the same movement culture a few years after the transformative "Po' Farmer" encounter in 1939. Szwed states that "Alan was planning cabarets for TAC [Theatre Arts Committee], scouting through Harlem with Lawrence Gellert in search of black singers, and doing lecture-performances at Café Society." Lomax was in the Cultural Front of New York City and had "joined the widening circle of performers and playwrights who saw the arts as a key to political change."[68]

As Szwed shows, the continuity between Lomax and Gellert remained into the 1940s. He writes: "Alan knew that when Lawrence Gellert published texts of black songs of protest, some folklorists and political activists accused him of having fabricated them—the proletariat could not be that class-conscious, they argued. Even years later, when Gellert's recordings were made public, there were still doubts about their authenticity." Szwed relates this understanding about Gellert to Lomax's ongoing motivations in trying to "bridge the gap" between Black protest and white discovery in America. Lomax felt he had achieved his key breakthrough, finally, in 1947, when legendary blues singer and pianist Memphis Slim confided that "blues is kind of a revenge. You wanta say something, you wanta, you know, signifyin' like. That's the blues . . . we fellas," he elaborated, "we had a hard time in life and like that," and there were "things we couldn't say or do. So, we sing it." Slim, along with fellow bluesmen Big Bill Broonzy and Sonny Boy Williamson, had been assembled by Lomax in New York for a documentary recording session on "what the blues are all about," as Lomax had prompted. The dialogue that ensued was unique in its candor. For Lomax, it was a key milestone in a decades-long course of investigation. He reminisced near the end of his life that "it was a source of deep satisfaction to me that at last I, a white Southerner, could penetrate the Southern façade and learn something about what life was like on the other side of the Jim Crow line." Szwed highlights the significance of this milestone in his biography of Lomax, and Gellert appears in the background. To protect his informants, Lomax fictionalized the "blues is kind of a revenge" documentary session as "I Got the Blues" in the progressive periodical *Common Ground* in 1948. In that same period, Gellert was publishing in *New Masses*. Both collectors were on the Left and had a special interest in "Negro Songs of Protest." But only one would be renounced and forgotten by revivalist peers in the years to come.[69]

EPILOGUE

Freedom Songs, Sixties Revivalism, and the Tragedy of White Denial

> The literary scholars, who seldom went into the field and collected their song in the homes, have failed generally to perceive the undercurrent of tragedy and protest that underlay the songs they footnoted and published. . . . Our own tradition contains many great folk songs with a powerful statement of social protest.
>
> —ALAN LOMAX, *HARD HITTING SONGS FOR HARD-HIT PEOPLE*

In 1967, Irwin Silber finally achieved the release of a text more than twenty-five years overdue, *Hard Hitting Songs for Hard-Hit People*, a songbook compiled through the work of Alan Lomax, Woody Guthrie, and Pete Seeger. Silber explained in his "Publisher's Foreword" that the songbook was a collaborative product of these key figures of the 1930s folksong revival. The manuscript was completed, he wrote, and "then came Pearl Harbor and World War II and the whole project was shelved." The leftwing folksong movement collapsed after the war, and the manuscript was "broken down," with chapters separated from one another and pages "simply walked off with" in the haste and disarray of a movement scattered and under siege.[1]

But civil rights, Vietnam, and resurgent social dissent in the 1960s meant that the time was right again for everyday songs of struggle of, by, and for American working people. *Hard Hitting Songs* featured Depression-era blues and country by commercial artists as well as folk figures Lead Belly, John Handcox, Ella May Wiggins, Aunt Molly Jackson, Sara Ogan Gunning, and Woody Guthrie. Alan Lomax affirmed the value of the material in his Compiler's Postscript:

> Since for most scholars folk song study has provided an escape from humdrum scholarship, they have too often presented their findings as simply entertaining and amusing . . . as a quaintly phrased view of a bygone time or as a fantasy escape from life. This is the reason, it seems to me, that academic critics have generally refused to accept the validity of the more pointed songs of protest that Woody and I put together in this volume. . . . As a song editor, I believed that this collection was a testament to an unknown America, the folk poets who had become politically active and still kept their gift for song-making.[2]

Much of the outlook and content of *Hard Hitting Songs* was in harmony with the outlook and work of Lawrence Gellert. Gellert's "Negro Songs of Protest" were "hard hitting songs for hard-hit people," to borrow the phrase. Nevertheless, the return of *Hard Hitting Songs* from out of the ashes of postwar anticommunism, and the return of folksong revivalism in the 1960s as a mass popular phenomenon, did not spell a sustained rediscovery of Lawrence Gellert and "Negro Songs of Protest." Gellert's work was of interest to a few but not again in the spotlight as were the contributions of Silber, Lomax, Seeger, and Guthrie.

The blues revival of the 1960s issued from out of the "folk boom" of this era. Folk revivalists embraced the early rural acoustic blues as a roots music alternative to commercial rock and pop. Samuel Charters was the American dean of blues revival scholarship. His book, *The Country Blues* from 1959, is widely credited for launching the blues revival out of the broader folk movement in the United States. Charters was a pioneer in the 1960s, but to Gellert he was a latecomer. Sam Charters only discovered Gellert and "Negro Songs of Protest" in 2004.

In his 2004 career anthology, *Walking a Blues Road*, Charters includes "The Blues' Angry Voice" as the most recent piece, written in that same year. Meant to introduce the blues reading public to the curious Gellert and his obscure archive, the essay is ultimately mixed in its appraisal. Charters opens: "I am aware that for many years I was only one of many people who sought in the blues some explicit protest against the rigid system of apartheid that controlled the lives of African Americans, not only in the South, but in the North as well. . . . I kept listening for overt hints in everything I recorded or heard that would express this angry consciousness, but I could never say that I had found something that made the open statement of protest I hoped to find."[3] Then, Charters recounts, he came across something new. "I wasn't expecting a collection titled *Negro Songs of Protest.* My wife Ann noticed it," he writes, in the "crowded pages of the Swann Gallery catalog, a New York City auction house that has a once-yearly sale." The original copy that the couple secured had evidently come from First Lady Eleanor Roosevelt's personal library and was signed by Gellert. "No one had ever collected such a range of African American material from the rural South which expresses so openly these feelings of black anger," Charters determined of the song texts inside. "So, as I held the collection and carefully turned its pages, I found myself asking, 'Can I trust it?' 'What can I say about the songs?'"[4]

In the essay, Charters details how he subjected the Gellert volume to a careful examination. The publisher of the songbook, the "American Music League," was "one of several fronts," Charters says he knew, "which had as their ultimate source the American Communist Party." Gellert, he identified, was "a young New York Greenwich Village Communist with a Hungarian background." The songs, Charters concludes, were intriguing but fraught. Some "have more of the feel of a political meeting than they do of a backroad cabin," and some display a "more literary style," he judges, that "suggests that even if Gellert had collected them from a black singer, the singer could have had some contact with the Party organization, or with the labor organizers who were struggling for union recognition in southern factories." In these suspect instances, it is the notion of contact that seems to give Charters pause. Hints of self-conscious artistry or overt political agitation, for him, run counter to genuine "folk process" and authentic indigenous folklore. Still, some of the Gellert verses ring true, Charters relates. When consulted, for instance, a colleague in musicology at the University of Connecticut immediately responded with excitement to "Went to Atlanta," the first item in the book:

> I went to Atlanta, never been dere a-fo'.
> White folks eat de apple, N——r wait fo' co'.
> Catch dat Suth'n, grab dat train,
> Won't come back no mo'.
>
> I went to Charleston, never been dere a-fo'.
> White folks sleep on feather bed, N——r on de flo'.
> Catch dat Suth'n, grab dat train,
> Won't come back no mo'.
>
> I went to Raleigh, never been dere a-fo'.
> White folks wear de fancy suit, N——r over-o'.

Catch dat Suth'n, grab dat train,
Won't come back no mo'.

I went to Heaven, never been dere a-fo'.
White folks sit in Lawd's place, chase N——r down below.
Catch dat Suth'n, grab dat train,
Won't come back no mo'.[5]

"That was a song we used to sing when I was growing up in Savannah," said Dr. Robert Stephens to Charters. "It's just the way we sang it!"[6]

In sum, Charters considers the songbook a "fascinating though troubling volume" that perhaps answers some questions "but raises almost as many more." What is possible, Charters volunteers, is "that there could have been another layer of black song that constituted the angry cry we have been searching for. We were just never given the chance to hear it." Early on, had his generation of revivalists known about the Gellert collection, Charters speculates, it "would certainly have had an effect on our attitudes."[7]

This extension of Gellert's interest into the realm of blues is significant because blues music remains a vital realm of mass appreciation, particularly with a white popular audience. For many celebrants and purveyors today, blues is the quintessential Black roots music, the source at heart of all modern African American offshoots, and the blues, "Blackness," and "folkness" are synonymous. But if protest is absented from the blues, then a historic cultural form, originated under American Jim Crow, is limited to pathos and partying. Black agency is buried, and the depth and reach of racial injustice is clouded in a "big white fog."[8]

In the early 1960s, at the ground level of blues revival research and writing, Charters and his English counterpart, Paul Oliver, established a historiographic convention that became nearly axiomatic in the literature. "There is little social protest in the blues," runs Charters oft-quoted assertion from his 1963 study, *The Poetry of the Blues.* Sometimes, there is "complaint"—individualized, fragmentary, and ultimately, therefore, not political, he suggests—but "there is little open protest at the social conditions under which a Negro in the United States is forced to live." In England, Paul Oliver affirmed this foundational tenet. In part, he attributed the limited number of protest items that had come to light to "black acceptance" of historic stereotypes of racial inferiority. "As surely as southern Whites intended them to 'keep their place,'" wrote Oliver, "the majority of Blacks were prepared to accept it." Some thirty years later, as the compact disc generation was discovering the music in the 1990s, specialist Pete Welding informed new listeners that blues is "a lyric song form that, as any student of the music knows well, primarily has concerned itself with interpersonal relationships. Most blues have been in one way or another love songs."[9]

To be sure, Sam Charters's and Paul Oliver's respective contributions inspiring and advancing the blues revival should not be reduced to a single point of contention on the question of blues protest. Over the course of the 1960s and 1970s, moving apace with developments in the Black freedom struggle in the United States and globally, both scholars complicated their viewpoints in sensitive and sophisticated ways. Oliver, for instance, began to theorize that surface lyrics of sexual travail channeled deeper meanings of racial antagonism, and was, by the 1970s, equating blues spirit with Black nationalism and racial power.[10] Sam Charters, as well, could hardly be called narrow, politically or culturally. In the 1975 reprint of *The Country Blues*, he reflected self-critically on the biases and romanticism of the original edition, and contextualized his entire mission in blues research as an earnest effort in racial justice. Additionally, in a different role in the rock music world, Charters was the longtime producer of Country Joe and the Fish, arguably the most experimental and politically radical of all the Bay Area psychedelic bands. After the Kent State shootings in 1970, Charters's opposition to the US war in Vietnam was such that he left the country, moving in protest with his family to Sweden.[11]

Despite these ardent liberal political attitudes, in their scholarly texts Oliver and Charters were founding influences in a revival consensus that consigned the idea of expressive protest in the blues to the margins of scholarly consideration. The "common-sense" of dominant interpretation was, and widely remains, that the blues are apolitical by origin and nature. As Charters himself frankly admits in his 2004 Gellert piece, he wanted to find protest in the blues, and it would have suited his politics, but it just wasn't there.[12]

But how had Sam Charters missed Gellert's work all those years? The cover of Charters's *Walking a Blues Road* features a 1964 photograph of Charters posing fraternally with several bluesmen and proprietor Israel "Izzy" Young on the doorstep of Young's legendary Folklore Center in New York City. By 1964, Lawrence Gellert was a Greenwich Village denizen. Young and Gellert were friendly, and Young mentioned "Larry" periodically in his *Sing Out!* magazine column. How did Gellert and Charters not cross paths? Why was the founder of blues revival scholarship in America only coming to the Gellert archive in 2004? Was there a conspiracy of silence? Was this a product of base professional territorialism? Was it personal? Was it just poor research skills? As we have seen, the story is not so simple.

One of the likely issues was that blues studies—a field, we might think, well positioned already to take the lead in Gellert investigation—had yet to fully turn inward to identify its own biases, presuppositions, and politics. In "Reconstructing the Blues: Reflections on the 1960s Blues Revival," ethnomusicologist Jeff Todd Titon advanced the way for the "reflexive" investigation of revivalist authorities and audiences. "The governing metaphor at the time for what we were doing was 'discovery' and 'rediscovery,'" he wrote in 1993, "as if what we were doing was finding something that was unknown or had been lost. But the notion of discovery is complex," he insisted, "as anyone knows who has thought about the gradeschool 'fact' that Columbus discovered America. Our discoveries," Titon concluded, "like those of the European explorers, were mixtures of invention and interpretation, and in a way instead of finding our object, blues, we constituted it."[13]

Titon's "Reconstructing the Blues" is a crucial intervention. Foundational blues historians like Sam Charters and Paul Oliver were not sloppy scholars, and they certainly were not political conservatives opposed to Black equality. But they were members of a distinct interpretive community. Along these lines, specialist Paul Garon took stock in 1996. He stated:

> Blues research during the revival years was carried on, in the minds of the field workers, in an atmosphere of cordiality and cooperation. Yet 98% of these field workers were white. Perhaps it was pride that made it impossible for them to admit to themselves that their black compatriots were holding something back and held deep secrets that were still beyond sharing with whites. For modern researchers to ignore the possibility of protest in blues also allowed them to think of blues as a music of accommodation, a more comfortable thought than the notion that it might be a music of resistance and they might be working with singers who considered them the enemy![14]

The romance of blues discovery, then, could blind revivalists to the musical realities of racial domination and resistance in America. This tradition of white myopia traces back to the roots of Black music discovery. If we recall, George Fredrickson contextualized white romantic racialism as a liberal worldview originally of antebellum abolitionism. Well-intentioned as a sympathetic outlook, this conflicted racial doctrine, nevertheless, amounted to an expression of power where left and right of the political spectrum were incidental to the common denominator of white privilege. "Benevolent reformers," wrote Fredrickson in *The Black Image in the White Mind*, "tended to see the Negro more as a symbol than as a person, more as a vehicle for romantic social criticism than as a human being with the normal range of virtues and vices."[15]

In *A Nation of Outsiders*, historian Grace Hale unpacks the "romance of the outsider" as it relates to these dominant cultural dynamics of race, and class, emergent since the 1950s. As she points out, the cultural rebellion of a white middle-class boomer strata in the postwar could roil the waters of the status quo, but also keep those waters smooth and untroubled. Hale writes of white dominant cultural rebellion as unstable. It could be turned and tamed, sliding from "oppositional politics" to a mechanism by which "a particular political and social order maintains its hegemony." If rock 'n' roll was about "learning to love the outsiders" in the 1950s, she contends, folk came in as the new vehicle when first-generation rock appeared played out by the 1960s. In the new confluence of sixties music revivalism and sixties civil rights activism, "Blackness," "folkness," and righteousness were conjoined anew in the mindset of dominant culture rebels. This had great potential. Hale argues, "In the mid-1960s, it looked like shared feelings of alienation from American society might serve as the basis for a new politics." White middle-class discontents identified with "hard hitting" songs and people—the historically oppressed and marginalized in American life—because they felt "hard hit" themselves culturally and spiritually. The idea that the enfranchised would reimagine themselves as the alienated was "unprecedented," even "uncanny," states Hale. For a period, the "romance of the outsider" held the promise to "hold back the conflicts between being black and being white, between being poor and being middle-class, between loving and using the folk." Racial and class romanticizing could impel an alienated "insider" to genuine "outsider" engagement and social activism, but it could also stop short, ending simply at play, image, and consumption.[16]

Grace Hale has written elsewhere of the blues and blues romanticism specifically in this equation, and a healthy reflexivity has begun to complicate and interrogate blues studies itself.[17] But the shift has been slow, as has a larger collective retreat from white privilege, romance, and denial in US society. In 2014, blues authority and radio host Steve Cushing released *Pioneers of the Blues Revival*. Featuring extended interviews with seventeen of the major blues researchers associated with the 1960s revival, the book is the most recent in the "meta" turn in blues scholarship. Cushing is an unabashed admirer who believes that "the blues revival served as a second front in the 1960s civil rights movement." I agree, and disagree, with this weighted notion of blues revivalism as political activism, and Cushing's contributor Barry Lee Pearson is himself usefully ambivalent in the book's own introduction. Pearson questions to what extent the white pioneers of blues research "reinvented" the music "in their own image," and whether "this may not be viewed as such a benign project." To put it another way, Jeff Todd Titon has asked, "Revivalism is peculiar politics; is it reactionary or revolutionary?"[18]

The cross-currents of music revivalism and white romantic racialism conditioned the discovery and denial of Lawrence Gellert and "Negro Songs of Protest." The debate and doubt to which Gellert's material had been subjected was sidestepped as irrelevant by Silber and company in *Hard Hitting Songs for Hard-Hit People.* Was the music in the volume folk songs or songs of protest? Were the items sung once or genuinely a part of communal circulation? In the imperative of music of, by, and for everyday working people, such questions were beside the point, as Silber, Lomax et al. indicated in *Hard Hitting Songs.* Gellert had operated with just this mentality in collecting "Negro Songs of Protest." Still, he was dismissed. This is doubly ironic, as we have seen, since Gellert overlapped in the same social and political circles in New York City in the 1960s as the prominent figures of the postwar revival. As chroniclers Stephen Petrus and Ronald Cohen have detailed it in *Folk City: New York and the American Folk Music Revival,* the metropolis during these years was an epicenter of folk music-making and folk-inspired political activism.[19] Yet, even in this milieu, Gellert was a relative absence, a shadow in plain sight.

Sociologist Stanley Cohen has dissected denial as knowing and not-knowing. Cohen explains, "Denial is always partial: some information is always registered. This paradox or doubleness—knowing and not-knowing—is the heart of the concept." As Cohen explicated it, denial functions as "an unconscious defense mechanism. Uncomfortable truths are too threatening to 'know,' so they are unconsciously banished to some inaccessible zone of the mind." This would seem a paradox indeed to apply to white progressive peers of Gellert in the folksong revival who were fellow racial justice advocates and Black vernacular music enthusiasts. But the long tradition of romantic racialism in Black music connoisseurship and collecting could cut its way through dominant culture perspectives independent of political affiliation. For those racial conservatives who preceded Gellert, for instance, the fact of Black protest was "too threatening" a racial insight "to know," and for those racial progressives who presided over the postwar revival, the reality of Gellert's renegade ways and archive was, perhaps, "too threatening" to disciplinary practice and reputations. Revivalist academics and activists seemed primed to "know" and "not-know" about "Negro Songs of Protest."[20]

Inspired by a canon of African American commentators going back to the nineteenth century, David R. Roediger has cast "whiteness" in and of itself as a form of denial in *Black on White: Black Writers on What It Means to Be White.* Roediger's most visible field of association, critical whiteness studies, takes "whiteness" as a problem in the American past and present, and one problem for so many people of color has been that white authorities—even those who self-identified as allies—did not fully see Black insight, Black agency, Black knowing. White racial denial, in sum, has meant that many white Americans cannot see that many Black Americans can see through the "big white fog." Stanley Cohen warns that denial, whatever the context, is "a presence that evaporates, the nearer you get to defining it." The positive to the negative of denial, he argues, is "acknowledgment." In the context of Lawrence Gellert, music revivalism, and Black songs of protest, acknowledgment has been hard in coming. Gellert was not immune to the denials of whiteness or the romances of race and revolution, but he did argue for and ably document the fact of African American vernacular protest. The archive should not be denied.[21]

If we step back from the internecine battles of academia, politics, and personality, we can see that there was, very clearly, a language at hand in this era for what to call the vernacular music in the Gellert collection: "freedom songs." This body of music developed from out of a common-stock of everyday currency. Civil rights activists appropriated and adapted old and new songs for new struggles toward Black freedom in the 1960s. They did not hesitate, and they did not discriminate. Sacred or secular, folk and sometimes even pop: if the music moved people, then activists moved to employ the music. In studies of the freedom songs, participants and scholars reflect on this singing movement as unique, deliberate, and strategic. The freedom song canon ("We Shall Overcome," most famously) was forged in real time in a short period in the late 1950s and 1960s. It had not steeped organically and anonymously for years before rising to the surface; it was self-conscious and fine-tuned to political effect. Songs might catch on and be sung many times, or emerge only fleetingly as "nonce-creations." Despite these violations of folklore standards by traditional academic definition, this music was, and remains, celebrated as authentic and legitimate, not artificial and tainted by propaganda.[22]

Gellert's work was both continuous and discontinuous with the singing movement of civil rights. With shared roots in an African American vernacular culture of opposition, but a suspect recent history in the Cultural Front of Old Left communism in the 1930s, "Negro Songs of Protest" were ripe for rediscovery and doomed to a third-rail status in the 1960s. Ultimately, the archive was not revived as part of the group-song activism of the freedom song era. Gellert's music had in fact been adapted in the 1930s to some group singing in the radical choruses of the Cultural Front, but this was group-singing decidedly on the Left with pronounced anti-capitalist messaging. Certainly the changing dynamics of movement singing were a factor by the 1960s, as was the importance of Black church leadership in the freedom song movement, but it was also the taint of communism that kept "Negro Songs of Protest" from the movement culture of civil rights, and as well from the revivalist culture of first-generation blues scholarship.[23]

Gellert, however, identified the material in his documentary archive as part of freedom song tradition, past and present. In his notes to the initial Rounder release of his field recordings in 1973, he wrote, "These 'negro songs of protest' recorded in the 1930s articulate the roots of what has developed into the black revolutionary movement." Even more pointedly, in a different document from the time, he stated, "And so it happens that today the bulk of the song material is merely rewrites from old folk songs. . . . Some 'spirituals'—some from the songs of protest out of the 1930s. On every University campus where Negroes attend, 'Freedom songs' are being carefully composed by students . . . some of whom are actually participating in the Crusade."[24]

This book is premised on the fact of Black resistance and a theory of white denial. In the end, as we appraise it all in context and relief, we can say that Lawrence Gellert collected "made-up" songs of the variety specified by Alan Lomax early in his career in Black folksong. However, Gellert did not make up the songs himself. "Negro Songs of Protest" were subject to the multiple tragedies of white denial. Even among their own in the movement community after World War II, they could not find a sound hearing. As music and history, they deserve one today.

NOTES

INTRODUCTION: HIDDEN IN PLAIN SIGHT

1. Lawrence Gellert, interview by Richard A. Reuss, March 28, 1968, Archives of Traditional Music, Indiana University, Bloomington. See note 22 below for a fuller description of this material henceforth denoted as "Gellert interviews, ATM."

2. Lawrence Gellert Papers, Bancroft Library, University of California, Berkeley.

3. Langston Hughes to Gellert, February 1932; Hughes to Gellert, June 11, 1933; and Hughes to Gellert, February 22, 1934, Lawrence Gellert Papers, Bancroft Library, University of California, Berkeley. The Russian edition of NSP is *Negrityanskie Pesni Protesta*, trans. G. M. Shneerson (Moscow: Gosudarstvennoe Izdateil'stvo "Iskusstvo," 1938); there was also a German publication, *Protestlieder des Amerikanischen Negroproletariats,* trans. G. M. Shneerson and Ernst Busch (Berlin: Verlag Lied der Ziet, 1949).

4. Gellert interviews, ATM; Gellert interview by Lorraine Brown, October 22, 1976, Works Progress Administration Oral Histories Collection, #C0153, Special Collections Research Center, George Mason University, Fairfax, Virginia.

5. "Songs of Protest," *Time,* June 15, 1936, 51.

6. Gellert, *Negro Songs of Protest* (New York: American Music League, 1936), 16–17.

7. Leroy Carr, *Sloppy Drunk,* Catfish KATCD 108, 1998, CD.

8. William Francis Allen, Charles Pickard Ware, and Lucy McKim Garrison, *Slave Songs of the United States* (1867; New York: Peter Smith, 1951), 93.

9. Throughout this study, I use the term "Negro Songs of Protest" both to refer to the body of Black freedom song that Gellert documented and in reference to the titles for his many writings on the subject. Context and formatting (italics versus quotation marks, for instance) should make the distinction clear.

10. "Songs of Protest," *Time,* June 15, 1936, 51.

11. Interested readers should consult Bruce Conforth's biography, *African American Folksong and American Cultural Politics: The Lawrence Gellert Story* (Lanham, MD: Scarecrow Press, 2013).

12. Stanley Cohen, *States of Denial: Knowing about Atrocities and Suffering* (Malden, MA: Polity Press, 2001), 4–5; Michelle Alexander, *The New Jim Crow: Mass Incarceration in the Age of Colorblindness* (2010; New York: The New Press, 2012), 182.

13. George M. Fredrickson, *The Black Image in the White Mind: The Debate on Afro-American Character and Destiny, 1817–1914* (New York: Harper and Row, 1971), 1, 71–72, 107, 97–98, 114–15.

14. Fredrickson, 125.

15. Gellert interviews, ATM.

16. Grace Elizabeth Hale, *A Nation of Outsiders: How the White Middle Class Fell in Love with Rebellion in Postwar America* (New York: Oxford University Press, 2011), 10.

17. Neil V. Rosenberg, ed., *Transforming Tradition: Folk Music Revivals Examined* (Urbana: University of Illinois Press, 1993), xii, 2, 18.

18. Robert Cantwell, *When We Were Good: The Folk Revival* (Cambridge, MA: Harvard University Press, 1996), 21–22.

19. Gellert interviews, ATM.

20. Irwin Silber, "Dubious," letter to the editor, *Mainstream* (July 1963): 61.

21. John Greenway, *American Folksongs of Protest* (Philadelphia: University of Pennsylvania Press, 1953); Russell Ames, *The Story of American Folk Song* (New York: Grosset and Dunlap, 1955). Both authors consulted Gellert at the outset of their projects. John Greenway to

Gellert, January 21, 1951, and Russell Ames to Gellert, April 21, 1955, Gellert Manuscripts, Manuscripts Department, Lilly Library, Indiana University, Bloomington.

22. Totaling nearly nine hours, Reuss's oral interviews with Gellert between 1966 and 1969 constitute the only primary source evidence of such extent on the collector. "United States, 1966, 1968, 1969," interviews of Lawrence Gellert by Richard A. Reuss, Israel Goodman Young, and Margot Mayo (on six sound tape reels, analog, 3 ¾ ips, 2 track, mono).

23. Reuss, "American Folklore and Left-Wing Politics, 1927–1957" (PhD diss., Indiana University, 1971), and Reuss with JoAnne C. Reuss, *American Folk Music and Left-Wing Politics, 1927–1957* (Lanham, MD: Scarecrow Press, 2000).

24. Bruce Michael Harrah-Conforth, "Laughing Just to Keep from Crying: Afro-American Folksong and the Field Recordings of Lawrence Gellert" (master's thesis, Indiana University, 1984).

25. *Negro Songs of Protest: Collected by Lawrence Gellert,* 33 rpm, Rounder 4004, 1973; *Cap'n You're So Mean: Negro Songs of Protest, Volume 2,* 33 rpm, Rounder 4013, 1982; and *Nobody Knows My Name: Blues from South Carolina and Georgia,* 33 rpm, Heritage HT 304, 1984. In 1972, Gellert issued a private release by appropriating the defunct Timely label. This album—*Collection of Lawrence Gellert: Negro Songs of Protest,* TI-112—was repackaged with his oversight for commercial distribution as Rounder 4004. Blues hobbyist Stefan Wirz provides a useful online discography for all this at https://www.wirz.de/music/gellert.htm.

26. Paul Garon, *Blues and the Poetic Spirit* (1975; San Francisco: City Lights, 2001), 200.

27. See Steven Garabedian, "Reds, Whites, and the Blues: Lawrence Gellert, 'Negro Songs of Protest,' and the Left-Wing Folk-Song Revival of the 1930s and 1940s," *American Quarterly* 57 (March 2005): 179–206.

28. William R. Ferris Jr., "Racial Repertoires among Blues Performers," *Ethnomusicology* 14, no. 3 (September 1970): 439–49; Bruce Bastin, *Red River Blues* (Urbana: University of Illinois Press, 1986), 64–67; Paul Oliver, *Blues Fell This Morning: Meaning in the Blues* (1960; New York: Cambridge University Press, 1990); Steven C. Tracy, *Langston Hughes and the Blues* (Urbana: University of Illinois Press, 1988), and Steven Tracy, ed., *Write Me A Few of Your Lines: A Blues Reader* (Amherst: University of Massachusetts Press, 1999); Charles K. Wolfe and Kip Lornell, *The Life and Legend of Leadbelly* (New York: Da Capo Press, 1992); Paul Garon, *Blues and the Poetic Spirit* (1975; San Francisco: City Lights, 2001); John H. Cowley, "Don't Leave Me Here: Non-Commercial Blues: The Field Trips, 1924–1960," in *Nothing But the Blues: The Music and the Musicians,* ed. Lawrence Cohn (New York: Abbeville Press, 1993), 267–69; Guido van Rijn, *Roosevelt's Blues*; Elijah Wald, *Josh White: Society Blues* (Amherst: University of Massachusetts Press, 2000); Adam Gussow, *Seems Like Murder Here: Southern Violence and the Blues Tradition* (Chicago: University of Chicago Press, 2002); R. A. Lawson, *Jim Crow's Counterculture: The Blues and Black Southerners, 1890–1945* (Baton Rouge: Louisiana State University Press, 2010); and Roger House, *Blue Smoke: The Recorded Journey of Big Bill Broonzy* (Baton Rouge: Louisiana State University Press, 2010).

29. Reuss with Reuss, *American Folk Music and Left-Wing Politics;* Robbie Lieberman, *"My Song Is My Weapon": People's Songs, American Communism, and the Politics of Culture, 1930–1950* (Urbana: University of Illinois Press, 1989); Cantwell, *When We Were Good*; Ronald D. Cohen, *Rainbow Quest: The Folk Music Revival and American Society, 1940–1970* (Amherst: University of Massachusetts Press, 2002); Cohen, "Agnes 'Sis' Cunningham and Labor Songs in the Depression South," in *Radicalism in the South since Reconstruction,* ed. Chris Green, Rachel Rubin, and James Smethurst (New York: Palgrave Macmillan, 2006), 83–96; Dick Weissman, *Which Side Are You On?: An Inside History of the Folk Music Revival in America* (New York: Continuum, 2005); David King Dunaway and Molly Beer, *Singing Out: An Oral History of America's Folk Music Revivals* (New York: Oxford University Press, 2010); and John Szwed, *Alan Lomax: The Man Who Recorded the World* (New York: Viking, 2010). In a more contentious vein, R. Serge Denisoff, a contemporary of Reuss, mentioned

Gellert in his *Great Day Coming: Folk Music and the American Left* (Urbana: University of Illinois Press, 1971).

30. Mark Naison, *Communists in Harlem during the Depression* (1983; Urbana: University of Illinois Press, 2005); Robin D. G. Kelley, *Hammer and Hoe: Alabama Communists during the Great Depression* (Chapel Hill: University of North Carolina Press, 1990); James Edward Smethurst, *The New Red Negro: The Literary Left and African American Poetry, 1930–1946* (New York: Oxford University Press, 1999); Mark Solomon, *The Cry Was Unity: Communists and African Americans, 1917–1936* (Jackson: University Press of Mississippi, 1998); David R. Roediger, *Working toward Whiteness: How America's Immigrants Became White* (New York: Basic Books, 2005); Scott Reynolds Nelson, *Steel Drivin' Man: John Henry, The Untold Story of An American Legend* (New York: Oxford University Press, 2006); Grace Elizabeth Hale, *A Nation of Outsiders: How the White Middle Class Fell in Love with Rebellion in Postwar America* (New York: Oxford University Press, 2011); Grace Elizabeth Hale, "Hear Me Talking to You: The Blues and the Romance of Rebellion," in *Beyond Blackface: African Americans and the Creation of American Popular Culture, 1890–1930,* ed. W. Fitzhugh Brundage (Chapel Hill: University of North Carolina Press, 2011), 239–58; and Mechal Sobel, *Painting a Hidden Life: The Art of Bill Traylor* (Baton Rouge: Louisiana State University Press, 2009).

31. Lawrence W. Levine, *Black Culture and Black Consciousness: Afro-American Folk Thought from Slavery to Freedom* (New York: Oxford University Press, 1977); Kelley, *Hammer and Hoe;* and, Michael Denning, *The Cultural Front: The Laboring of American Culture in the Twentieth Century* (New York: Verso, 1996).

32. As of December 2017, Bruce Conforth has deposited his Gellert research materials at the University of North Carolina. See Bruce M. Conforth Collection on Lawrence Gellert #20552, Southern Folklife Collection, The Wilson Library, University of North Carolina at Chapel Hill. This collection is access- and use-restricted. Duplication or publishing of collection materials requires the personal permission of Conforth. In August 2019, the author denied my permission request.

33. Jerry Schmetterer, "80-Yr.-Olds Are Sought By Cops, Kin," *Daily News,* November 4, 1979, 84.

34. Donald Gellert, phone interview by author, September 7, 2002; James Gellert, phone interview by author, September 10, 2002; and David Margolis, interview by author, March 10, 2003, New York City. For Conforth's account, see *African American Folksong,* 227–30. On the Patz case, see Michael Wilson, "Even After Patz Verdict, a Sense of Emptiness Lingers Over Old Soho," *New York Times,* February 16, 2017, A23, and James C. McKinley Jr., "Pedro Hernandez Gets 25 Years to Life in Murder of Etan Patz," *New York Times,* April 19, 2017, A21. Gellert left a "last note." Though it does not necessarily indicate suicide, it reflects a frightened and disordered state. See Tamiment Library, NYU, Hugo Gellert Papers, TAM 150, Box 2 of 2, Folder 6, "Gellert, Jim," 1979.

CHAPTER ONE: THE ROADS TO PERDITION

1. See Louis Gordon, *Nancy Cunard: Heiress, Muse, Political Idealist* (New York: Columbia University Press, 2007); "She is Pet of London," *Washington Post,* June 28, 1915, 10; "Heiress Nancy Cunard, Negro Rights Champion," *Washington Post,* March 18, 1965, B4; and "Miss Cunard Denied Entrance to U.S.," *Christian Science Monitor,* July 24, 1941, 19.

2. Nancy Cunard, ed., *Negro: An Anthology* (1934; New York: Frederick Ungar Publishing Co., 1970), xxxi; "Cunard Anthology on Negro is Issued," *New York Times,* February 17, 1934, 13.

3. Gordon, 169–70, 200; Lawrence Gellert interviews, Archives of Traditional Music, Indiana University Bloomington.

4. Cunard, ed., *Negro,* 259.

5. Cunard, ed., *Negro,* 233–34.

6. Lawrence Gellert, "Remembering Nancy Cunard," in *Nancy Cunard: Brave Poet, Indomitable Rebel, 1896–1965,* ed. Hugh Ford (Philadelphia: Chilton Book Company, 1968), 143.

7. Lorenzo Thomas, "Authenticity and Elevation: Sterling Brown's Theory of the Blues," *African American Review* 31 (Autumn 1997): 410. On Brown, see John Edgar Tidwell and Steven C. Tracy, eds., *After Winter: The Art and Life of Sterling A. Brown* (New York: Oxford University Press, 2009), and David L. Smith, ed., "A Symposium on the Life and Work of Sterling Brown," *Callaloo* 21, no. 4 (Autumn 1998): 1038–74.

8. The year before Gellert published *Negro Songs of Protest,* for instance, Zora Neale Hurston published *Mules and Men* (1935), which conveyed the language and rhythm of African American locals in her hometown of Eatonville, Florida, in southern Black dialect. As the long-delayed publication of Hurston's *Barracoon: The Story of the Last "Black Cargo"* makes clear, Hurston was committed to dialect transcription as a "way to produce a written text that maintains the orality of the spoken word" (xxii). Gellert made the same argument. *Barracoon* was completed in 1931, but remained unpublished until 2018. See Hurston, *Barracoon* (New York: Amistad, 2018).

9. Lawrence Gellert, *Negro Songs of Protest* (New York: American Music League, 1936), 24–25. Several of the verses in "Pickin' Off De Cotton" are audible among the earliest of Gellert's seven-inch aluminum field discs from the 1920s. For a digitized version, see 7–2172 Side B1. Portions of "Way Down South" are available in digital reproduction from among both Gellert's early 7-inch and later higher-quality 10-inch discs, suggesting that he encountered the song in multiple instances over time and place. See 7–2266 Side B1 and 10–17855 Side B1 (also released on *Negro Songs of Protest: Collected by Lawrence Gellert,* 33 rpm, Rounder 4004, 1973). Gellert field recordings, "United States, North and South Carolina, Georgia, African Americans, 1920s—1940s," Archives of Traditional Music, Indiana University, Bloomington.

10. "Songs of Protest," *Time,* June 15, 1936, 51; H. Howard Taubman, "Negro Folksongs: New Genre Dealing with Everyday Life Produced, Particularly in South," *New York Times,* July 5, 1936, X5; Arthur B. Spingarn, "Books by Negro Authors in 1936," *The Crisis,* 44, no. 2 (February 1937): 48; "Songs of Protest—A Review," Hall Johnson, *Opportunity: Journal of Negro Life,* 14, no. 8 (August 1936): 241, 244, 243.

11. Max Margulies, "Negro Voices Rise in Protest," *Daily Worker,* June 17, 1936, 7; Lan Adomian, "Black Skin Coverin' Po' Workin' Man," *New Masses* (June 23, 1936): 27.

12. From oldest to youngest, the children were Hugo (b. 1892), Theodor (b. 1893), Ernest (b. 1895), Otto (b. 1896), Lawrence (b. 1898), and Celie/"Billie" (b. 1900). Adolph Greenbaum, "Petition for Naturalization," filed May 20, 1909, Department of Commerce and Labor, Naturalization Service, United States of America. Thanks to James Wechsler for sharing this valuable document. Additional family information from Gellert interviews, ATM; James M. Wechsler, "Retaining the Accent: Hugo Gellert and the Hungarian Cultural-Political Nexus," *Hungarian Studies Review* 31, nos. 1–2 (2004): 77–78; Bruce M. Conforth, *African American Folksong and American Cultural Politics: The Lawrence Gellert Story* (Lanham, MD: Scarecrow Press, 2013), 11–12, 14, 27–28; Penny Gellert Freeman, email message to author, February 8 and 10, 2005; Donald Gellert, phone interview by author, September 7, 2002; James Gellert, phone interview by author, September 10, 2002; and Billie Gellert to Hugo and Livia Gellert, April 25, 1949, Box 1, Folder 39, Series 2: Correspondence, 1949. Hugo Gellert Papers, 1916–1986, Archives of American Art, Smithsonian Institution.

13. Gellert interviews, ATM; Conforth, *African American Folksong,* 28–32.

14. Gellert interviews, ATM; Gellert, liner notes, *Negro Songs of Protest: Collected by Lawrence Gellert,* 33 rpm, Rounder 4004, 1973.

15. "Mr. Larry Goelett," *Polk County News,* September 17, 1925, 4; "Larry Goelett," *Polk County News,* October 29, 1925, 1; "Celebrate Two Birthdays on Lucky Thirteenth," *Polk County News,* March 19, 1935, 1; Larry Goelett, "Snakes of Polk County Not Particularly Dangerous nor Overly Numerous," *Polk County News,* May 21, 1925, 12; Larry Goelet, "Captain E. H. Tomlinson Veteran of Two Campaigns Typical of Old Frontier," *Polk County News,* June 4, 1925, 1; and, "Mr. Lawrence Goulette of New York," *Tryon Daily*

Bulletin, March 26, 1929. Additionally, Gellert shows up in the following society notices: September 17, 1925, 4; October 29, 1925, 1; March 19, 1925, 1; February 18, 1926, 10; March 25, 1926, 1; April 8, 1926, 2; April 15, 1926, 1; April 22, 1926, 1; April 29, 1926, 9; May 6, 1926, 1, 3; May 20, 1926, 5; June 10, 1926, 4; and, June 17, 1926, 10.

16. Gellert interviews, ATM; Conforth, *African American Folksong,* 35, 33.

17. "There Is Always a First Time," *Polk County News,* September 10, 1925, 8; *Polk County News,* September 17, 1925, 8; *Polk County News,* October 1, 1925, 8.

18. "Mr. Lawrence Goellet Leaving for White Plains, N.Y.," *Polk County News,* June 17, 1926, 10; "Mr. Lawrence Goulette of New York Is Visiting Mr. Dwight Smith," *Tryon Daily Bulletin,* March 26, 1929. Another notice in the paper also mentions that "Larry Goellet" worked "years ago on the staff of a Metropolitan daily," *Polk County News,* April 29, 1926, 6.

19. W. C. Handy to Lawrence Gellert, October 24, 1932, Lawrence Gellert Papers, Bancroft Library, University of California, Berkeley; Fitzgerald reference in Tony Buttitta, *After the Good Gay Times* (New York: Viking Press, 1974), 163.

20. *Polk County News,* June 4, 1925, 1, and *Asheville Citizen-Times,* January 5, 1938, 8; Conforth, *African American Folksong,* 35.

21. Michael J. McCue, phone interview by author, March 24, 2003; "Tryon Now Widely Known for Its Art and Music Colony," *Asheville Citizen-Times,* December 11, 1921, 27; "Spring Season Ends at Tryon: Is Reported Very Successful; Many Interesting Features," *Asheville Citizen-Times,* April 29, 1928, 27. See also McCue, *Tryon Artists, 1892–1942: The First Fifty Years* (Columbus, NC: Condar, 2001); Anna Pack Conner and Ronald Mosseller, *Tryon: An Artist's and Writer's Sketchbook* (Chapel Hill, NC: Tryon Publishing Company, 2001); Richard H. Palner, *Polk County, North Carolina History* (Dallas: Taylor Publishing Company, 1983); Jeffrey A. Byrd, ed., *A Sense of Heritage: A Pictorial History of the Thermal Belt Area* (Dallas: Taylor Publishing Company, 1991). The "good books, good music" quotation comes from correspondence between Gellert and the founding staff of Rounder Records, as they were preparing the album notes to Rounder 4004. Lawrence Gellert to Bill Nowlin, March 22, 1973. My thanks to Bill Nowlin for sharing these files.

22. Gellert interviews, ATM; Donald Gellert, phone interview by author, September 7, 2002. Drama Fortnightly was established in winter 1922, the same period when Gellert likely arrived in town. On the group's history, see Elia W. Peattie, "An Interesting Experiment in Community Dramatics," *Social Progress: A Magazine for the New Day* (April 1923): 124–25; Byrd, ed., *A Sense of Heritage,* 126–27; and Palner, *Polk County, North Carolina History,* 88. Gellert appears in multiple notices as a performer. The following *Polk County News* items mention Gellert's name alongside those of Drama Fortnightly friends that he notes in his interviews: February 4, 1926, 1; February 18, 1926, 10; April 8, 1926, 1; May 6, 1926, 1; June 3, 1926, 10; and November 11, 1926.

23. Gellert interviews, ATM.

24. Gellert interviews, ATM.

25. Gellert interviews, ATM.

26. Conforth, liner notes, *Cap'n, You're So Mean: Negro Songs of Protest, Volume Two,* 33 rpm, Rounder 4013, 1982.

27. "Big White Folks" was common terminology, used perhaps most strikingly, for instance, by Paul Robeson in his autobiography. In *Here I Stand,* published in 1958, Robeson asserts, "At the outset, let me make one thing very clear: I care nothing—less than nothing—about what the lords of the land, the Big White Folks, think of me and my ideas" (4). White anti-racist activist and folklorist Stetson Kennedy, who cuts an interesting likeness to Gellert in his projects to infiltrate the white South to expose its evils, furthers explains the general line of address in mocking guidebook-speak in *Jim Crow Guide to the U.S.A.,* published in 1959. Kennedy writes, "When you as a nonwhite have occasion in segregated territory to address a white man whose name is unknown to you, you are expected to call him 'Bossman,' 'Captain,' or some other title of respect. The plural form, to be used in addressing more than one white, is 'white-folks'" (213).

28. Gellert interviews, ATM; Gellert refers to the importance of his influential friend "Bill" Weigel in another interview as well. See Gellert interview by Lorraine Brown, October 22, 1976. Works Progress Administration Oral Histories Collection, #C0153, Special Collections Research Center, George Mason University.
29. Gellert interviews, ATM; Gellert field recordings, ATM. In correspondence to the Archives of Traditional Music concerning deposit of his materials, Gellert repeated that he "began operations in the early 1920s" with a "hand-wind table phonograph" and aluminum discs. Gellert to Frank Gillis, September 30, 1969. Gellert Mss., Correspondence, Folder 1, Lilly Library, Indiana University, Bloomington.
30. Conforth, *African American Folksong,* 45–46.
31. Gellert interviews, ATM.
32. Gellert interviews, ATM.
33. Gellert interviews, ATM. Information on the Episcopal Church of the Holy Cross and its Parish House (built in 1923) in Tryon, North Carolina, comes from Mosseller and Conner, *Tryon: An Artist's and Writer's Sketchbook,* 77–79, and the Church's current Secretary, phone interview by author, March 31, 2003.
34. *Polk County News,* April 8, 1926, 2.
35. *Polk County News,* April 15, 1926, 1.
36. *Polk County News,* April 22, 1926, 1. Readers may note that these newspaper items show three different spellings of Gellert's surname in a span of just two weeks. These discrepancies in such a short span raise the possibility that haphazard newspaper copyediting rather than strictly Gellert's self-invention may account for some of the name variations in Tryon.
37. Gellert interviews, ATM.
38. Gellert interviews, ATM.
39. Lawrence Gellert, "Negro Songs of Protest," *New Masses* (May 1932): 22.
40. Gellert, *Negro Songs of Protest,* 18–19. Field recordings 7–2194, Side A1 and 10–17815, Side B1, Archives of Traditional Music, Indiana University, Bloomington.
41. The Mississippi Sheiks, "Sitting on Top of the World," 78 rpm, Okeh 8784, 1930.
42. Brown makes specific reference to Gellert in his discussion of verboten songs. Sterling A. Brown, "Negro Folk Expression: Spirituals, Seculars, Ballads and Work Songs," *Phylon* 14 (1953): 58–59. As far as I can determine, the first application of the term "verboten" to Gellert's material actually dates back to Samuel Chavkin, "Folk Songs of the South: Lawrence Gellert Famed Collector of Negro Songs of Protest, Working on Negro Opera," *Daily Worker,* January 17, 1938, 7.
43. I have borrowed the concept here from Robin D. G. Kelley. See *Hammer and Hoe: Alabama Communists during the Great Depression* (Chapel Hill: University of North Carolina Press, 1990).
44. Gellert interviews, ATM.
45. Lawrence Levine identifies the "white homeowner" as in fact collector Howard Odum. See *Black Culture and Black Consciousness: Afro-American Folk Thought from Slavery to Freedom* (New York: Oxford University Press, 1977), 205.
46. Howard W. Odum and Guy B. Johnson, *The Negro and His Songs: A Study of Typical Negro Songs in the South* (Chapel Hill: University of North Carolina Press), 2–3.
47. Levine, *Black Culture and Black Consciousness,* 476.
48. Benjamin Filene, *Romancing the Folk: Public Memory and American Roots Music* (Chapel Hill: University of North Carolina Press, 2000), 31; Marybeth Hamilton, *In Search of the Blues: Black Voices, White Visions* (London: Jonathan Cape, 2007), 33; John A. Lomax, "Self-Pity in Negro Folk-Songs," *The Nation,* August 9, 1917, 141; and, Jerrold Hirsch, "Modernity, Nostalgia, and Southern Folklore Studies: The Case of John Lomax," *Journal of American Folklore* 105 (Spring 1992): 188.
49. James C. Scott, *Domination and the Arts of Resistance: Hidden Transcripts* (New Haven: Yale University Press, 1990), 183; Robin D. G. Kelley, *Race Rebels: Culture, Politics, and the Black Working Class* (New York: Free Press, 1996), 8; and Kelley, *Hammer and Hoe,* 53, 87, 107.

CHAPTER TWO: FREE RADICAL

1. Lawrence Gellert, preface to *Negro Songs of Protest* (New York: American Music League, 1936), n.p.
2. Gellert, sleeve notes, *Negro Songs of Protest: Collected by Lawrence Gellert*, 33 rpm, Rounder 4004, 1973.
3. Gellert interviews, Archives of Traditional Music (ATM), Indiana University, Bloomington. Alice Lightner became better known as the author Alice Lightner Hopf. According to Gellert, she fictionalized their relationship in Tryon in the book-length narrative poem *The Pillar and the Flame* (New York: Harold Vinal, 1928).
4. Gellert interviews, ATM. Alan C. Graves, "The Presto History Page," http://www.prestohistory.com/Presto.htm, accessed June 28, 2018.
5. Along with Gellert, Weigel was a member of the local theater troupe, Drama Fortnightly. For a period in the 1930s, he was a contributor to the *Tryon Daily Bulletin*. From his travels abroad in Germany and South Africa, he penned letters of observation and humor for publication at home. W. B. Weigel, "Our German Letter," *Tryon Daily Bulletin*, August 31, 1936, and September 12, 1936.
6. Gellert, notes, *Negro Songs of Protest*, Rounder 4004; Gellert interviews, ATM.
7. Gellert interviews, ATM; A. L. White to Lawrence Gellert, February 20, 1935, Folder 1, papers included with "United States, North and South Carolina, Georgia, Afro-Americans, 1920–1940," ATM.
8. Gellert interviews, ATM; Gellert, notes, *Negro Songs of Protest*, 33 rpm, Rounder 4004.
9. Michael J. McCue, phone interview by author, March 24, 2003. Also, see McCue, *Tryon Artists, 1892–1942: The First Fifty Years* (Columbus, NC: Condar, 2001).
10. Nina Simone with Stephen Cleary, *I Put a Spell on You: The Autobiography of Nina Simone* (New York: Da Capo Press, 1991), 4–5; Randy Kennedy, "Saving Nina Simone's Birthplace as an Act of Art and Politics," *New York Times*, March 2, 2017, https://www.nytimes.com/2017/03/02/arts/design/nina-simone-house-birthplace.html, accessed June 27, 2018.
11. Nadine Cohodas, *Princess Noire: The Tumultuous Reign of Nina Simone* (New York: Pantheon Books, 2010), 9, 25–28, 100.
12. Cohodas, 10–11, 26; Anna Pack Conner and Ronald Mosseller, *Tryon: An Artist's and Writer's Sketchbook* (Chapel Hill, NC: Tryon Publishing Company, 2001), 77–79; and Gina Malone, "Tryon, NC, Church Has Rich History," GoUpstate.com, http://www.goupstate.com/lifestyle/20131118/tryon-nc-church-has-rich-history, accessed June 27, 2018.
13. Cohodas, 36, 47, 37–38.
14. Gellert interviews, ATM.
15. Gellert interviews, ATM.
16. Gellert interviews, ATM; Steven Patrick Garabedian, "Reds, Whites, and the Blues: Blues Music, White Scholarship, and American Cultural Politics" (PhD diss., University of Minnesota, 2004); and Bruce M. Conforth, *African American Folksong and American Cultural Politics: The Lawrence Gellert Story* (Lanham, MD: Scarecrow Press, 2013).
17. Gellert interviews, ATM.
18. Gellert interviews, ATM.
19. Gellert, preface to *Negro Songs of Protest*, n.p.
20. Gellert, notes, *Negro Songs of Protest*, 33 rpm, Rounder 4004.
21. "Georgia Mob of 20 Men Massacres 2 Negroes, Wives; One was Ex-GI," *New York Times*, July 27, 1946, 1, 32; "Unmasked Band Massacres 2 Negroes, Wives in Georgia," *Washington Post*, July 27, 1946, 1–2; "$10,000 Is Offered for Lynchers; Georgia Policy Inquiry Thwarted," *New York Times*, July 28, 1946, 1, 12; "More FBI Men to Georgia," *New York Times*, August 1, 1946, 14.
22. Earl Conrad, *Jim Crow America* (New York: Duell, Sloan and Pearce, 1947), 224–26; "La. Joins Dixie Lynch" and "Arnall Finds Ga. Lynchings 'Hot Potato,'" *Chicago Defender* August 24, 1946, 1; Gellert interviews, ATM; Conforth, 178–79.

23. Gellert, "Talk in Monroe," *New Masses* (September 3, 1946): 21, 20. A year later, Gellert followed up in *New Masses* with a story on lynching and the children of the South, "Lynchers Are Not Born." The piece is a series of documentary vignettes about "Johnny," a boy who grows from tolerance to bigotry in a household Gellert purports to have known in South Carolina. *New Masses,* December 9, 1947, 11–12.
24. John L. Spivak, *Georgia Nigger* (New York: Brewer, Warren and Putnam, 1932). Excerpts from *Georgia Nigger* and a Spivak piece, "Flashes from Georgia Chain Gangs," appear in *Negro: An Anthology* (1934; New York: Negro Universities Press, 1969), 210–22; the newspaper story is reprinted in the same work. For cases of other white individuals who similarly subverted the racial order, see Jorge Arévalo Mateus, "Beluthahatchee Blues: An Interview with Stetson Kennedy," in *Radicalism in the South since Reconstruction,* ed. Chris Green, Rachel Rubin, and James Smethurst (New York: Palgrave Macmillan, 2006), 211–26; Edward C.L. Adams, *Tales of the Congaree* (Chapel Hill: University of North Carolina Press, 1987). Stetson Kennedy's books from the period include *Southern Exposure* from 1946 and *The Klan Unmasked* from 1954.
25. Conrad, *Jim Crow America,* ix.
26. Harold Spivacke to Gellert, October 27, 1942, and Spivacke to Gellert, November 28, 1942, ATM. Also see Conforth 175–177.
27. Gellert, "Jim Crow in Khaki," *New Masses* (March 19, 1946): 12.
28. Gellert, notes, *Negro Songs of Protest,* Rounder 4004.
29. Gellert interviews, ATM.
30. Gellert interviews, ATM.
31. Hugo Gellert dedicated his book *Karl Marx' 'Capital' in Lithographs* to Ernest (New York: Ray Long and Richard Smith, 1934). Lawrence mentions the case frequently in his 1960s interviews. Ernest Gellert's original drafts and letters of appeal to military authorities from prison are housed among the Hugo Gellert Papers, Archives of American Art, Smithsonian Institution, Washington, DC. For secondary scholarship, see James Wechsler, "From World War I to the Popular Front: The Art and Activism of Hugo Gellert," *Journal of Decorative and Propaganda Arts* 24 (2002): 204–5, and Wechsler, "The Art and Activism of Hugo Gellert: Embracing the Specter of Communism" (PhD diss., City University of New York, 2003).
32. Gellert interviews, ATM; Gellert, notes, *Negro Songs of Protest,* Rounder 4004.
33. Gellert interviews, ATM.
34. Mark Naison, *Communists in Harlem during the Great Depression* (New York: Grove Press, 1983); Mark Solomon, *The Cry Was Unity: Communists and African Americans, 1917–1936* (Jackson: University of Mississippi Press, 1998); James Edward Smethurst, *The New Red Negro: The Literary Left and African American Poetry, 1930—1946* (New York: Oxford University Press, 1999); William J. Maxwell, *New Negro, Old Left: African-American Writing and Communism Between the Wars* (New York: Columbia University Press, 1999). Also see Cedric J. Robinson, *Black Marxism: The Making of the Black Radical Tradition* (1983; Chapel Hill: University of North Carolina Press, 2000); and Robin D. G. Kelley, *Freedom Dreams: The Black Radical Imagination* (Boston: Beacon Press, 2002).
35. Gellert interviews, ATM.
36. Gellert interviews, ATM.
37. Series 1"Biographical Material," Box 1, Folder 4: "Lawrence Gellert Collected Folksong Lyrics and Notes, circa 1930–1939." Hugo Gellert papers, 1916–1986. Archives of American Art, Smithsonian Institution.
38. Gellert interviews, ATM. Gellert's article series under the title "Negro Songs of Protest" appeared in *New Masses* (November 1930): 10–11; (January 1931): 16–17; (April 1931): 6–8; (May 1932): 22; and (May 1933): 15–16.
39. Gellert interviews, ATM.
40. For leftwing press coverage on Lawrence Gellert, see Max Margulies, "Negro Voices Rise in Protest," *Daily Worker,* June 17, 1936, 7; "'Negro Protest Songs' Created Out of the

Living Fabric of South," *Daily Worker,* May 2, 1937, 10; Samuel Chavkin, "Folk Songs of the South: Lawrence Gellert, Famed Collector of Negro Songs of Protest, Working on Negro Opera," *Daily Worker,* January 17, 1938, 7; "False Theory of Negro Spirituals Hit by Noted Music Expert," *People's World,* October 31, 1939, 5. Mainstream news coverage, national and regional, on Gellert's career includes H. Howard Taubman, "Negro Folksongs: New Genre Dealing with Everyday Life Produced, Particularly in South," *New York Times,* July 5, 1936, X5; "Sadness Prevails: In Federal Theater Office Where Once Joy Reigned," *Cincinnati Enquirer,* August 1, 1937, 56–57; "Lawrence Gellert Plans Negro Opera: Receives Gift from Rockefeller Foundation to Aid Him in Research Work," *New York Times,* December 30, 1937, 13; "Composer Receives Grant from Rockefeller Funds," *Rocky Mount Telegram,* December 30, 1937, 1; "WPA Composer Honored," *Brooklyn Daily Eagle,* December 31, 1937, 6; "Former N.C. Newsman Gets Folk Opera Grant," *Statesville Daily Record,* December 31, 1937, 1; "Former Tryon Man Will Do Research Work," *Asheville Citizen-Times,* January 5, 1938, 8; "Songs of Protest Become WPA Dances," *Brooklyn Daily Eagle,* January 16, 1938, 35; "Male Glee Club to Sing in Union June 14," *Franklin County Tribune,* June 10, 1938, 4; "Negro Folksongs Stadium Feature," *New York Times,* July 6, 1938, 21. Coverage in the Black press includes "A.N.P. Correspondent Writes For Soviet Books," *Pittsburgh Courier,* December 3, 1932, 10; "Presents Negro Protest Songs," *New York Age,* June 27, 1936, 7; "Harlem to See Big Drama," *Chicago Defender,* January 8, 1938, 19; "WPA To Present Ballet in Harlem," *New York Age,* January 8, 1938, 9; "Lawrence Gellert Plans Negro Opera," *Pittsburgh Courier,* January 8, 1938, 20; "'How Long Brethren' Opens at Lafayette on January 18," *New York Age,* January 15, 1938, 9; "Musical May Hit Broadway," *Pittsburgh Courier,* March 30, 1946, 19. For secondary scholarship on the *How Long Brethren* dance production, see Susan Manning, "Black Voices, White Bodies: The Performance of Race and Gender in *How Long Brethren,*" *American Quarterly* 50 (1998): 24–46.

41. W. C. Handy to Lawrence Gellert, October 24, 1932, and January 3, 1933, Lawrence Gellert Papers, Bancroft Library, University of California, Berkeley. Abbe Niles was Handy's collaborator on the book *Blues: An Anthology,* published in 1926.

42. Gellert interviews, ATM. In his June 25, 1969, interview session, Gellert, it should be noted, placed the story in Greenville, South Carolina, rather than Marietta, Georgia. Readers may note that Marietta was the site of the infamous Leo Frank lynching in 1915.

43. Margulies, "Negro Voices Rise In Protest," *Daily Worker,* June 17, 1936, 7. Similar stories concerning the early efforts to render Gellert's material "more palatable to the conforming standard of what a Negro song should be rather than what it is" are repeated in Chavkin, "Folk Songs of the South," *Daily Worker,* January 17, 1938, 7.

CHAPTER THREE: "SONGS ABOUT THE WHITE MAN"

1. See George M. Fredrickson, *The Black Image in the White Mind: The Debate on African-American Character and Destiny, 1817–1914* (1971; Middletown, CT: Wesleyan University Press, 1987); Steven P. Garabedian, "The Blues Image in the White Mind: Blues Historiography and White Romantic Racialism," *Popular Music and Society* 37, no. 4 (2014): 476–94.

2. Patrick B. Mullen, *The Man Who Adores the Negro: Race and American Folklore* (Urbana: University of Illinois Press, 2008), 11.

3. Nolan Porterfield, *Last Cavalier: The Life and Times of John A. Lomax, 1867–1948* (Urbana: University of Illinois Press, 1996).

4. Howard W. Odum and Guy B. Johnson, *Negro Workaday Songs* (Chapel Hill: University of North Carolina Press, 1926), 115.

5. Guy B. Johnson, "Double Meaning in the Popular Negro Blues," *Journal of Abnormal and Social Psychology* 22, no. 1 (April-June 1927): 12–20. Quotes from reprint in Steven C. Tracy, ed., *Write Me a Few of Your Lines: A Blues Reader* (Amherst: University of Massachusetts Press, 1999), 172, 178.

6. Sterling A. Brown, "Negro Folk Expression: Spirituals, Seculars, Ballads and Work Songs," *Phylon 14* (1953): 58–59.

7. David Evans, *Big Road Blues: Tradition and Creativity in the Folk Blues* (New York: Da Capo Press, 1982), 87, 38.
8. Stephanie Dunson, "Black Misrepresentation in Nineteenth-Century Sheet Music Illustration," in *Beyond Blackface: African Americans and the Creation of American Popular Culture, 1890–1930,* ed. W. Fitzhugh Brundage (Chapel Hill: University of North Carolina Press, 2011), 45.
9. John A. Lomax, "Self-Pity in Negro Folk-Songs," *The Nation,* August 9, 1917, 142.
10. Eric Lott, *Love and Theft: Blackface Minstrelsy and the American Working Class* (New York: Oxford University Press, 1993), 36; Cedric J. Robinson, *Black Marxism: The Making of the Black Radical Tradition* (1983; Chapel Hill: University of North Carolina Press, 2000), 3–4, 185–99, and esp. chap. 4. See also Lee D. Baker, *From Savage to Negro: Anthropology and the Construction of Race, 1896–1954* (Berkeley: University of California Press, 1998); Rosemary Lévy Zumwalt, *American Folklore Scholarship: A Dialogue of Dissent* (Bloomington: Indiana University Press, 1988); Simon J. Bronner, *American Folklore Studies: An Intellectual History* (Lawrence: University Press of Kansas, 1986); Mullen, *The Man Who Adores the Negro*; Ibram X. Kendi, *Stamped from the Beginning: The Definitive History of Racist Ideas in America* (New York: Nation Books, 2016); Audrey Smedley and Brian D. Smedley, *Race in North America: Origin and Evolution of a Worldview,* 4th ed. (New York: Routledge, 2018).
11. Dray, *At the Hands of Persons Unknown* (New York: Random House, 2002), viii. See also Equal Justice Initiative, "Lynching in America: Confronting the Legacy of Racial Terror," 3th ed. (2017).
12. Lomax, "Self-Pity," 141.
13. I use this wording—"fiction"—deliberately, as in "true fictions" and the "partiality" of truth, in reference to the reflexive turn in modern anthropology. Specifically, see James Clifford and George E. Marcus, eds., *Writing Culture: The Poetics and Politics of Ethnography* (Berkeley: University of California Press, 1986). In the same spirit, Mullen contextualizes folklore studies in the "hegemonic discourse" of race in *The Man Who Adores the Negro,* 5–6.
14. Lomax, "Self-Pity," 142.
15. Lomax, "Self-Pity," 141, 143.
16. Howard W. Odum, "Folk-Song and Folk-Poetry as Found in the Secular Songs of the Southern Negroes," *Journal of American Folk-Lore* 24, no. 93 (July–September 1911): 284–85.
17. Odum (July–September): 284–85; Lomax, "Self-Pity," 143–44.
18. Odum (July–September): 266.
19. Odum (July–September): 266–67.
20. Odum (July–September): 267.
21. Scarborough, *On the Trail of Negro Folk-Songs,* 227–28; Odum and Johnson, *The Negro and His Songs,* 254–55; Newman Ivey White, *American Negro Folk Songs* (Hatboro, PA: Folklore Associates, Inc., 1965), 203, 385. In 1934 and 1941, versions of the tune were printed in John A. and Alan Lomaxes' *American Ballads and Folk Songs,* 233, and *Our Singing Country,* 282. In 1931, Gellert included it in "Negro Songs of Protest," *New Masses* (January 1931): 16.
22. Odum (July–September): 267–68.
23. Odum (July–September): 266–67.
24. Lomax, "Self-Pity," 144–45.
25. Lomax, "Self-Pity," 144.
26. Lomax, "Self-Pity," 144.
27. Benjamin Filene, *Romancing the Folk: Public Memory and American Roots Music* (Chapel Hill: University of North Carolina Press, 2000), 31.
28. Howard W. Odum, *Social and Mental Traits of the Negro* (New York: Columbia University Press, 1910), 286. The publication was originally his dissertation in sociology for Columbia University.
29. Jerrold Hirsch, "Modernity, Nostalgia, and Southern Folklore Studies: The Case

of John Lomax," *Journal of American Folklore* 105 (Spring 1992): 185, 189–90. For Hirsch's fuller treatment of folklore and cultural nationalism, see his *Portrait of America: A Cultural History of the Federal Writers' Project* (Chapel Hill: University of North Carolina Press, 2003). See also Lomax's autobiography, *Adventures of a Ballad Hunter* (New York: Macmillan, 1947), and Porterfield, *Last Cavalier.*

30. Fredrickson, *The Black Image,* 61, 64.
31. Hirsch, "Modernity," 189–90.
32. Fredrickson, *The Black Image,* 107; Hirsch, "Modernity," 192.
33. Hirsch, 188.
34. Hirsch, 184–86.
35. W. E. B. Du Bois, *Black Reconstruction in America: An Essay Toward a History of the Part Which Black Folk Played in the Attempt to Reconstruct Democracy in America, 1860–1880* (1935; Cleveland: Meridian Books, 1962), 726.
36. Hirsch, 184.
37. Lawrence W. Levine, "The Concept of the New Negro and the Realities of Black Culture," in *The Unpredictable Past: Explorations in American Cultural History* (New York: Oxford University Press, 1993), 88; and Levine, *Black Culture and Black Consciousness: Afro-American Folk Thought from Slavery to Freedom* (New York: Oxford University Press, 1977), 240.
38. Levine, "The Concept of the New Negro," 97; and Levine, *Black Culture and Black Consciousness,* 244.
39. Henry Edward Krehbiel, *Afro-American Folksongs: A Study in Racial and National Music* (New York: G. Schirmer, 1914), 23, vii–viii, 141–43, 17.
40. See Bruce Jackson, foreword to *American Negro Folksongs,* by Newman Ivey White (1928; Hatboro, PA: Folklore Associates, 1965), vi–vii; and Odum and Johnson, *Negro Workaday Songs,* 267.
41. Marybeth Hamilton, *In Search of the Blues: Black Voices, White Visions* (London: Jonathan Cape, 2007), 50, 46–47, 45.
42. Dorothy Scarborough, *On the Trail of Negro Folk-Songs* (Cambridge, MA: Harvard University Press, 1925), 6–7.
43. Hamilton, 50; and Scarborough, 72–73, 165, 180, 232.
44. Scarborough, 225–27.
45. William Francis Allen, Charles Pickard Ware, and Lucy McKim Garrison, *Slave Songs of the United States* (1867; New York: Peter Smith, 1951), 89; and Newman Ivey White, *American Negro Folk-Songs* (1928; Hatboro, PA: Folklore Associates, 1965), 168–69.
46. Scarborough, 12, 24–25.
47. Brown, "Negro Folk Expression," *Phylon* 14 (1953): 51; Levine, *Black Culture,* 14; and Scarborough, 23.
48. Hamilton, 66.
49. Hamilton, 61, 53, 40–44; and Scarborough, 159, 236, 230–32, 96, 23.
50. Odum and Johnson, *Negro Workaday Songs,* 1, 15; Lynn Moss Sanders, *Howard W. Odum's Folklore Odyssey* (Athens: University of Georgia Press, 2003); and Wayne D. Brazil, *Howard W. Odum: The Building Years, 1884–1930* (New York: Garland Publishing, 1988), 500–503.
51. Carla Kaplan, ed., *Zora Neale Hurston: A Life in Letters* (New York: Anchor Books, 2003), 151, 119, 172. Also see Valerie Boyd, *Wrapped in Rainbows: The Life of Zora Neale Hurston* (New York: Scribner, 2003).
52. Zora Neale Hurston, *Mules and Men* (1935; New York: Harper Perennial, 1990), 2–3.
53. White, *American Negro Folksongs,* 168–70, 202–3, 224, 251.
54. White, 19.
55. White, 3, 224–25. The book was originally published by Harvard University Press. The epigraph appears three pages in as part of the original front matter (n.p).
56. W. E. B. Du Bois, "Review of American Negro Folk Songs, 1928," W. E. B. Du Bois

Papers (MS 312). Special Collections and University Archives, University of Massachusetts Amherst Libraries.
57. White, 29–30.
58. White, 376–77.
59. White, 377.
60. White, 377.
61. White, 378.
62. Sterling A. Brown, "Negro Character as Seen by White Authors," *Callaloo* (February–May 1982): 56, 80.
63. Brown, 87.

CHAPTER FOUR: "THE GREAT RED HEART OF THE AMERICAN REVOLUTION"

1. George Lipsitz, *Rainbow at Midnight: Labor and Culture in the 1940s* (Urbana: University of Illinois Press, 1994), 20, 120. Also see Lizabeth Cohen, *Making a New Deal: Industrial Workers in Chicago, 1919–1939* (New York: Cambridge University Press, 1990); Michael Denning, *The Cultural Front: The Laboring of American Culture in the Twentieth Century* (New York: Verso, 1996); C.L.R. James, *American Civilization,* ed. Anna Grimshaw and Keith Hart (Cambridge, MA: Blackwell, 1993); Lary May, *The Big Tomorrow: Hollywood and the Politics of the American Way* (Chicago: University of Chicago Press, 2000); and Warren I. Susman, *Culture as History: The Transformation of American Society in the Twentieth Century* (New York: Pantheon Books, 1984).
2. Denning, *The Cultural Front,* 4; Lipsitz, *Rainbow at Midnight,* 168.
3. "Underground classic" quote from Judith McCulloh, "A Tribute to Dick Reuss," in *Songs about Work: Essays in Occupational Culture for Richard Reuss,* ed. Archie Green (Bloomington: Folklore Institute, Indiana University, 1993), 3; David King Dunaway, "Staking the Territory: Dick Reuss and the U.S. Protest-Political Song Tradition," in *Songs about Work,* 5. Reuss's dissertation is "American Folklore and Leftwing Politics, 1927–1957" (PhD diss., Indiana University, 1971); the book is Reuss with JoAnne C. Reuss, *American Folk Music and Left-Wing Politics, 1927–1957* (Lanham, MD: Scarecrow Press, 2000).
4. Richard A. Reuss, "The Roots of American Leftwing Interest in Folksong," *Labor History* 12 (1971): 259.
5. Reuss, "American Folklore and Leftwing Politics," 15.
6. Reuss dates such activity as far back as the Paris Commune of 1871, the early English songbook *Chants of Labor* published in 1888, and the "tradition" of "workers' choruses" that was already "firmly established in Europe, then America, by the close of the nineteenth century." Reuss, "American Folklore," 19–20.
7. Reuss, "American Folklore," 19–21; R. Serge Denisoff, *Great Day Coming: Folk Music and the American Left* (Urbana: University of Illinois Press, 1971), 9.
8. Quoted in Reuss, "American Folklore," 57–58. The statements originally appeared in *Daily Worker* on January 2, 1934, and June 26, 1934. Seeger penned both under his regular pseudonym, Carl Sands.
9. Quoted in Reuss, "American Folklore," 89. "Proletarian literature" advocate Mike Gold reported the remarks in his regular column in *Daily Worker* in 1934.
10. Quoted in Reuss, "American Folklore," 63.
11. Benjamin Filene, *Romancing the Folk: Public Memory and American Roots Music* (Chapel Hill: University of North Carolina, 2000), chap. 4, *passim.*
12. Quoted in Filene, *Romancing the Folk,* 69. See also Reuss and Denisoff, along with Robbie Lieberman, *"My Song Is My Weapon": People's Songs, American Communism, and the Politics of Culture, 1930–1950* (Urbana: University of Illinois Press, 1989); Ronald D. Cohen, *Rainbow Quest: The Folk Music Revival and American Society, 1940–1970* (Amherst: University of Massachusetts Press, 2002); Cohen, "Agnes 'Sis' Cunningham and Labor Songs in the Depression South," in *Radicalism in the South since Reconstruction,* ed. Chris Green, Rachel

Rubin, and James Smethurst, 83–96 (New York: Palgrave Macmillan, 2006); and Peter Gough, *Sounds of the New Deal: The Federal Music Project in the West* (Urbana: University of Illinois Press, 2015). The definitive musical document is Cohen and Dave Samuelson's ten-CD box set with accompanying scholarly text, *Songs for Political Action: Folk Music, Topical Songs, and the American Left, 1926–1953,* compact disc, Bear Family Records, BCD 15720 JL, 1996.

13. For classic and contemporary scholarship on the period, see Nathan Irvin Huggins, *Harlem Renaissance* (New York: Oxford University Press, 1971); Harold Cruse, *The Crisis of the Negro Intellectual* (1967; New York: Quill, 1984); David Levering Lewis, *When Harlem Was in Vogue* (New York: Knopf, 1981); George Hutchinson, *The Harlem Renaissance in Black and White* (Cambridge, MA: Belknap Press of Harvard University Press, 1995); William J. Maxwell, *New Negro, Old Left: African-American Writing and Communism between the Wars* (New York: Columbia University Press, 1999); Bill V. Mullen, *Popular Fronts: Chicago and African-American Cultural Politics, 1935–46* (Urbana: University of Illinois Press, 1999); James Smethurst, *The African American Roots of Modernism: From Reconstruction to the Harlem Renaissance* (Chapel Hill: University of North Carolina Press, 2011); Samuel A. Floyd Jr., *Black Music in the Harlem Renaissance: A Collection of Essays* (Knoxville: University of Tennessee Press, 1993); and Paul Allen Anderson, *Deep River: Music and Memory in Harlem Renaissance Thought* (Durham, NC: Duke University Press, 2001).

14. Robbie Lieberman, *"My Song Is My Weapon,"* 39, 110.

15. Alan Lomax, *The Land Where the Blues Began* (New York: Dell Publishing, 1993), xviii. John and Alan Lomaxes' major joint publications were *American Ballads and Folk Songs* (New York: Macmillan, 1934), *Negro Folk Songs as Sung by Lead Belly* (New York: Macmillan, 1936), *Our Singing Country: A Second Volume of American Ballads and Folk Songs* (New York: Macmillan, 1941), and *Folk Song U.S.A.* (New York: Duell, Sloan and Pearce, 1947). For a detailed account of the Lomaxes' joint fieldwork and publishing, see Nolan Porterfield, *Last Cavalier: The Life and Times of John A. Lomax, 1867–1948* (Urbana: University of Illinois Press, 1996).

16. Robert Cantwell, *When We Were Good: The Folk Revival* (Cambridge, MA: Harvard University Press, 1996), 76.

17. Porterfield, *Last Cavalier,* 298.

18. Cohen, *Rainbow Quest,* 13.

19. Cohen, 13, 19.

20. Cohen, 9.

21. Porterfield, *Last Cavalier,* 298; and Filene, "'Our Singing Country,'" 602–24, and *Romancing the Folk.*

22. Benjamin Filene, "'Our Singing Country': John and Alan Lomax, Leadbelly, and the Construction of an American Past," *American Quarterly* 43 (December 1991): 607–9.

23. Lomax and Lomax, *American Ballads and Folk Songs,* xxxv, xxviii–xxix. My understanding here of the Lomaxes' initial reception was enriched by Irwin Silber and others at the Alan Lomax Tribute Conference, April 11, 2003, Graduate Center, City University of New York.

24. Filene, *Romancing the Folk,* 15, 11–12.

25. Alan Lomax, "'Sinful' Songs of the Southern Negro," originally published in *Southwest Review* (Winter 1934): 105–31; quoted here from a reprint in *Alan Lomax: Selected Writings, 1934–1997,* ed. Ronald D. Cohen (New York: Routledge, 2003), 21–22.

26. *American Ballads and Folk Songs,* xxx.

27. Lomax and Lomax, 49; John A. Lomax, *Adventures of a Ballad Hunter* (New York: Macmillan, 1947), 150.

28. Lomax, *Adventures of a Ballad Hunter,* 149–50.

29. Loman, 149–50.

30. Gellert, "Negro Songs of Protest," *New Masses* (May 1932): 22.

31. Henry Edward Krehbiel, *Afro-American Folksongs: A Study in Racial and National Music*

(New York: G. Schirmer, 1914), 4; Lomax and Lomax, *American Ballads and Folk Songs*, xxxii.

32. Lomax and Lomax, xxxii.

33. These passages from *American Ballads and Folk Songs* are likely the comments of John rather than Alan Lomax. As biographer Porterfield details, the senior Lomax took charge of the writing and overall framing of the pair's first songbook. Alan, on the other hand, was more clearly in charge by the time of their second major volume in 1941. Indeed, the order of their names is reversed in the introductory essays to the two successive publications, and the prevailing tone of *Our Singing Country: A Second Volume of American Ballads and Folk Songs* shows Alan's growing prominence. See Porterfield, *Last Cavalier;* Alan Lomax, *The Land Where the Blues Began,* 286; and John Szwed, *Alan Lomax: The Man Who Recorded the World* (New York: Viking, 2010).

34. Filene, "'Our Singing Country,'" 609, 610, 603.

35. Filene, "'Our Singing Country,'" 610.

36. Gellert, letter to the editor, *New Masses* (December 11, 1934): 22; Gellert, letter to the editor, *New Masses* (November 20, 1934): 19. Porterfield covers the early controversy over Lead Belly as well; see *Last Cavalier,* 359–60. Significantly, he includes mention that Lew Ney, one of the parties involved in the dispute, stressed in the exchange of letters to the editor that "son Alan," as Porterfield relates it, "had been arrested a few years earlier for making Communist speeches at Harvard." The point, he states, was "aimed at establishing Lomaxian credentials with the *New Masses* audience."

37. Gellert interview, Archives of Traditional Music (ATM), Indiana University, Bloomington. Gellert said that he met Lead Belly in New York City, after the singer had broken with the Lomaxes and was staying temporarily with English professor and folklore scholar Mary Elizabeth Barnicle.

38. Robin D. G. Kelley, *Hammer and Hoe: Alabama Communists during the Great Depression* (Chapel Hill: University of North Carolina Press, 1990); Mark Naison, *Communists in Harlem during the Great Depression* (New York: Grove Press, 1983); and Mark Solomon, *The Cry Was Unity: Communists and African Americans, 1917–36* (Jackson: University Press of Mississippi, 1998). For additional background, see Nathaniel Mills, *Ragged Revolutionaries: The Lumpenproletariat and African American Marxism in Depression-Era Literature* (Amherst: University of Massachusetts Press, 2017); Harry Haywood, *Black Bolshevik: Autobiography of an Afro-American Communist* (Chicago: Liberator Press, 1978); Scott McLemee, ed., *C.L.R. James on the 'Negro Question'* (Jackson: University Press of Mississippi, 1996); Harold Cruse, *The Crisis of the Negro Intellectual: A Historical Analysis of the Failure of Black Leadership* (New York: Quill, 1984); Philip S. Foner and James S. Allen, eds., *American Communism and Black Americans: A Documentary History, 1919–1929* (Philadelphia: Temple University Press, 1987); Richard Iton, *Solidarity Blues: Race, Culture, and the American Left* (Chapel Hill: University of North Carolina Press, 2000); Maxwell, *New Negro, Old Left;* Smethurst, *The New Red Negro;* Jonathan Scott, *Socialist Joy in the Writing of Langston Hughes* (Columbia: University of Missouri Press, 2006); and Michael K. Honey, *Sharecropper's Troubadour: John L. Handcox, the Southern Tenant Farmers' Union, and the African American Song Tradition* (New York: Palgrave Macmillan, 2013).

39. Quoted in John Greenway, *American Folksongs of Protest* (Philadelphia: University of Pennsylvania Press, 1953), 251–52. For more on Wiggins's story, see Greenway, 244–52, and Reuss and Reuss, *American Folk Music,* 83–87.

40. Reuss and Reuss, *American Folk Music,* 86, 53. Some of this "musical myopia" identified by Reuss in the Third Period may additionally have been conditioned by gender and sexuality. In the movement culture of the time, "manliness" (so-called) and violence as much as "Blackness" was a point of revolutionary romanticism. As Robin Kelley has noted, white and Black communists could bond over "resistance as a masculine rite of passage" in this context where the "language of masculinity . . . dominated representations of grass-roots organizing and Party propaganda." In other words, the white south-

ern vernacular music of Wiggins or Jackson may not have been taken seriously initially by Party critics, not just because it was "white" but because it was "female." See Kelley, "'Afric's Sons with Banner Red': African American Communist and the Politics of Culture, 1919–1934," in *Race Rebels: Culture, Politics, and the Black Working Class* (New York: Free Press, 1996), 103–58.

41. Kelley, "Afric's Sons with Banner Red,'" 52, 83–93.

42. Philip Schatz, "Songs of the Negro Worker," *New Masses* (May 1930): 6.

43. Richard Frank, "Negro Revolutionary Music," *New Masses* (May 15, 1934): 29–30.

44. Naison, *Communists in Harlem;* Solomon, *The Cry Was Unity;* and Robinson, *Black Marxism.* The "ethnic nationalism" and "proletarian internationalism" reference comes from Kelley, "'Afric's Sons with Banner Red'" and "'This Ain't Ethiopia, But It'll Do': African Americans and the Spanish Civil War," in *Race Rebels;* for the Alabama material, see Kelley, *Hammer and Hoe,* 99.

45. Frank, "Negro Revolutionary Music," 30; Kelley, "'Afric's Sons with Banner Red,'" in *Race Rebels,* 109.

46. Kelley, "'Afric's Sons with Banner Red,'" 103–4, 115; Kelley, *Hammer and Hoe,* 105–8.

47. Frank, "Negro Revolutionary Music," 29–30; Kelley, "'Afric's Sons with Banner Red,'" 121.

48. Kelley, "'Afric's Sons with Banner Red,'" 117; Solomon, *The Cry Was Unity,* 278.

49. Reuss and Reuss, *American Folk Music,* 95.

50. Alan Calmer, review of *American Ballads and Folk Songs,* by John A. and Alan Lomax, *New Masses* (November 6, 1934): 23–24.

51. "Negro Songs of Protest," *Unison: Organ of the American Music League* (May 1936): 4. The story was repeated in Margulies, "Negro Voices Rise In Protest," *Daily Worker,* June 17, 1936, 7. Lawrence Gellert made the claim in his interviews that the young Alan Lomax "used to come around to find out how I got my songs," but that "he got no information" from me. When their association soured, Alan expressed a different attitude altogether, according to Gellert. "Once or twice," he said, "he made some snide remarks about [me] ghosting Negro songs [of protest]." Gellert interview, ATM.

52. *Unison,* 1, quoted in Reuss, "The Roots of American Leftwing Interest," 277.

53. Charles Seeger to Gellert, December 24, 1934. Gellert Manuscripts, Manuscripts Department, Lilly Library, University of Indiana, Bloomington. The effort did come to pass, as Gellert's "Negro Songs of Protest" were published in both numbers of the short-lived *Music Vanguard* (March-April 1935 and Summer 1935).

54. Lan Adomian, "What Songs Should Workers' Choruses Sing?" *Daily Worker,* February 7, 1934, 5, quoted in Reuss and Reuss, *American Folk Music,* 66.

55. Benjamin Davis Jr., to Gellert, November 27, 1934; also Davis Jr. to Gellert, December 6, 1934; Colman to Gellert, September 24, 1934; Colman to Gellert, October 6, 1934. Gellert Manuscripts, Lilly Library.

56. Gellert, "Negro Songs of Protest," *New Masses* (January 1931): 17. The transcription also appeared in Cunard, ed., *Negro: An Anthology* (1934; New York: Frederick Ungar Publishing Co., 1970), 231. It is the second item in Gellert's *Negro Songs of Protest* (1936), 10–11. The song alternated in print between "Sistern an' Brethren" and "Sistren an' Brethren."

57. Meeropol credited his direct inspiration to the infamous Lawrence Beitler photo of the double-lynching of Thomas Shipp and Abram Smith in Marion, Indiana, in 1930. Nancy Kovaleff Baker, "Abel Meeropol (a.k.a. Lewis Allen): Political Commentator and Social Conscience," *American Music* 20 (Spring 2002): 46. My thanks to Izzy Young for bringing this article to my attention.

58. Reuss and Reuss, *American Folk Music,* 97, 52.

59. Dorothy Scarborough, "American Ballads and Folksongs: The Lomax Collection Brings Together Chanteys, Spirituals, Mountain 'Lonesomes' and Desperado Ballads," *New York Times,* November 11, 1934, BR2.

60. The Lomaxes' joint publications continued to receive a warm reception by popular

critics throughout the 1930s. By the late 1940s, they were being hailed as "the outstanding authorities on indigenous American music." See R. Emmet Kennedy, "The 'King of the Twelve-String Guitar Players,'" review of *Negro Folk Songs as Sung by Lead Belly,* by John A. and Alan Lomax, *New York Times,* December 27, 1936, BR7; Horace Reynolds, "More Ballads and Folksongs Collected by the Lomaxes," review of *Our Singing Country: A Second Volume of American Ballads and Folk Songs,* by John A. and Alan Lomax, *New York Times,* December 28, 1941, BR4; and William G. Tyrrell, "Folk-Song Anthologies," review of *Folk Song: U.S.A.,* by John A. and Alan Lomax, *New York Times,* May 16, 1948, BR10. The "outstanding authorities" quotation comes from this latter citation. When John Lomax's autobiography was released in 1947, reviewer Horace Reynolds described the senior collector as "America's foremost ballad hunter"; see Reynolds, "Collecting Our Living Folksong," review of *Adventures of a Ballad Hunter,* by John A. Lomax, *New York Times,* March 2, 1947, 191. When John Lomax died in 1948, his obituary noted that "if anybody ever did, he really heard America singing"; see "J.A. Lomax, Collected Our Folk Songs, 80," *New York Times,* January 27, 1948, 26.
61. Solomon, *The Cry Was Unity,* 278.
62. Gary Gerstle, "The Working Class Goes to War," in *The War in American Culture: Society and Consciousness During World War II,* ed. Lewis A. Erenberg and Susan E. Hirsch (Chicago: University of Chicago Press, 1996), 105–27, and Gerstle, *Working-Class Americanism: The Politics of Labor in a Textile City, 1914–1960* (New York: Cambridge University Press, 1989).
63. Gellert interview, ATM.

CHAPTER FIVE: BIG WHITE FOG

1. Attenborough, "My Search," Guardian; Theodore Ward, *Big White Fog* (1937; London: Nick Hern Books, 2008); and Rena Fraden, "The Cloudy History of *Big White Fog*: The Federal Theatre Project, 1938," *American Studies* 29, no. 1 (1988): 5–27. Epigraph from Michael Attenborough, "My Search for the Lost Voice of Black America," *Guardian,* May 9, 2007, https://www.theguardian.com/stage/2007/may/10/theatre3.
2. Hughes and Ward, along with Pete Seeger and Alan Lomax, for that matter, were listed among the 151 names of purported American subversives cataloged in *Red Channels* in 1950. Paul Robeson had already come under the fire of anticommunism before 1950 and suffered continued persecution through the 1950s. See William J. Maxwell, *New Negro, Old Left: African-American Writing and Communism between the Wars* (New York: Columbia University Press, 1999) and *F.B. Eyes: How J. Edgar Hoover's Ghostreaders Framed African American Literature* (Princeton, NJ: Princeton University Press, 2015); Bill V. Mullen, *Popular Fronts: Chicago and African-American Cultural Politics, 1935–1946* (Urbana: University of Illinois Press, 2015); Robbie Lieberman and Clarence Lang, eds., *Anticommunism and the African American Freedom Movement: "Another Side of the Story"* (New York: Palgrave Macmillan, 2009); Robert Justin Goldstein, ed., *Little "Red Scares": Anti-Communism and Political Repression in the United States, 1921–1946* (New York: Routledge, 2016); Penny M. Von Eschen, *Race against Empire: Black Americans and Anticolonialism, 1937–1957* (Ithaca, NY: Cornell University Press, 1997); and Michael Denning, *The Cultural Front: The Laboring of American Culture in the Twentieth Century* (New York: Verso, 1996).
3. Bruce M. Conforth, *African American Folksong and American Cultural Politics: The Lawrence Gellert Story* (Lanham, MD: Scarecrow Press, 2013), xvi, xii, 71–72, 15, 30, 39, 53, 231–34.
4. Conforth, 159.
5. See also Garabedian, "Reds, Whites, and the Blues: Lawrence Gellert, 'Negro Songs of Protest,' and the Left-Wing Folk-Song Revival of the 1930s and 1940s," *American Quarterly* 57, no. 1 (March 2005): 179–206, and "Forgotten Manuscripts: Lawrence Gellert, *Negro Songs of Protest*," *African American Review* 49, no. 4 (Winter 2016): 297–311; and Dick Weissman, *Which Side Are You On?: An Inside History of the Folk Music Revival in America* (New York: Continuum, 2005).

6. John A. Lomax and Alan Lomax, *Our Singing Country: A Second Volume of American Ballads and Folk Songs* (New York: Macmillan, 1941), 407.
7. Benjamin Filene, *Romancing the Folk: Public Memory and American Roots Music* (Chapel Hill: University of North Carolina Press, 2000). Also see John Szwed, *Alan Lomax: The Man Who Recorded the World* (New York: Viking, 2010), and Jerrold Hirsch, *Portrait of America: A Cultural History of the Federal Writers' Project* (Chapel Hill: University of North Carolina Press, 2003).
8. Lawrence Gellert Interviews, Archives of Traditional Music (ATM), Indiana University, Bloomington.
9. Gellert interview, ATM; Donald Gellert, phone interview by author, September 7, 2002.
10. Gellert interview, ATM.
11. Gellert, "Jim Crow in Khaki," *New Masses* (March 19, 1946): 13; Gellert, "Talk in Monroe," *New Masses* (September 3, 1946): 20; and see Gerald Horne, *Communist Front?: The Civil Rights Congress, 1946–1956* (Rutherford, NJ: Farleigh Dickinson University Press, 1987).
12. Gellert, "Origins of Jazz," letter to the editor ("Mail Call"), *New Masses* (December 31, 1946): 22; Sidney Finkelstein, "What Is Jazz?" *New Masses* (November 5, 1946): 12–15; and Michael Denning, *The Cultural Front*, 425, 335. See also Aaron J. Leonard, *The Folk Singers and the Bureau: The FBI, the Folk Artists, and the Suppression of the Communist Party, USA, 1939–1956* (London: Repeater Books, 2020).
13. See Mary L. Dudziak, *Cold War Civil Rights: Race and the Image of American Democracy* (Princeton, NJ: Princeton University Press, 2000); Jeff Woods, *Black Struggle, Red Scare: Segregation and Anti-Communism in the South, 1948–1968* (Baton Rouge: Louisiana State University Press, 2004); and Jeanne Theoharis, *A More Beautiful and Terrible History: The Uses and Misuses of Civil Rights History* (Boston: Beacon Press, 2018), 87, 176–79, 182, 185.
14. Gellert, "Fishin,'" *New Masses* (September 23, 1947): 21; and, Gellert, "Lynchers Are Not Born," *New Masses* (December 9, 1947): 11–12. Theodore G. Bilbo, US senator and twice governor of Mississippi, was an unabashed white supremacist and Ku Klux Klan member. Lawrence Gellert was not the only one to celebrate his passing. In 1947, African American blues artist Andrew Tibbs released the sarcastic "Bilbo Is Dead" on Aristocrat Records, the precursor label to Phil and Leonard's Chess Records in Chicago. The record was banned in southern markets. Francis Davis, *The History of the Blues* (New York: Hyperion, 1995), 178; and Nadine Cohodas, *Spinning Blues into Gold: The Chess Brothers and the Legendary Chess Records* (New York: St. Martin's Press, 2000), 38–39.
15. Kimberley L. Phillips, *War! What Is It Good For? Black Freedom Struggles and the U.S. Military from World War II to Iraq* (Chapel Hill: University of North Carolina Press, 2012), 10.
16. Gellert interview, ATM; and Ronald D. Cohen and Rachel Clare Donaldson, *Roots of the Revival: American and British Folk Music in the 1950s* (Urbana: University of Illinois, 2014), 160.
17. Lawrence Gellert to Earl Conrad, January 1947, and Earl Conrad to Lawrence Gellert, March 1, 1947. Earl Conrad Collection, Cayuga Community College, Auburn, New York.
18. Gellert to Conrad, n.d. (Saturday), 1947, Earl Conrad Collection.
19. Harold Paulk Henderson, *The Politics of Change in Georgia: A Political Biography of Ellis Arnall* (Athens: University of Georgia Press, 1991), 182.
20. Gellert note to Conrad, n.d., 1947, and Gellert to Conrad, n.d., 1947, Earl Conrad Collection.
21. Gellert clipping to Conrad, "Bilbo Will Return Here for Check," and Gellert to Conrad, n.d. (Wednesday noon), 1947, Earl Conrad Collection.
22. If we recall, the language was Earl Conrad's in *Jim Crow America* (New York: Duell, Sloan and Pearce, 1947), ix.

23. Gellert to Conrad, n.d. (Saturday), 1947, Earl Conrad Collection.
24. Conrad, *Jim Crow America*, 224–25.
25. Gellert to Conrad, n.d. (Saturday), 1947, Earl Conrad Collection.
26. See Gellert, "My Cotton Comes First," *Masses and Mainstream* (July 1956): 18–27; "Greenwich Village Southern Style," *Mainstream* (December 1959): 37–42; "Spilin' Jipsons," *Mainstream* (October 1959): 23–35; "Make Way for the Negro Child," *Mainstream* (April 1959): 12–19; and "Negro Songs of Protest," *Mainstream* (February 1963): 19–23. As late as 1972, one of Gellert's "Negro Songs of Protest" was published in the radical press. See "Things Is Changed Blues," *American Dialog: A Cultural Quarterly* (Summer 1972): 11. The editorial comment about the "dialogues" comes from "My Cotton Comes First" (July 1956): 18.
27. William Fay, "Folks Are Real Friendly Down Here," *Mainstream* (February 1961): 25–28, and "Overheard in Fayette County," *Mainstream* (September 1961): 58–60.
28. Conforth, *African American Folksong and American Cultural Politics*, 211–12.
29. "Tales of One Time I'shman, Told by Southern Negroes," Lawrence Gellert Scrapbook, #4442, Southern Historical Collection, Wilson Library, University of North Carolina at Chapel Hill.
30. Conforth, 155–57, 175, 199, 203. When I made a Freedom of Information Act request in the early 2000s, I was notified that no files on Gellert existed. Clearly, this was inaccurate. Recently, historian Aaron Leonard confirmed that a New York file covering 1947 to 1964 with subject "Lawrence Gellert" does exist at the FBI and is being processed for release. Aaron Leonard, email message to author, October 17, 2019.
31. Gellert, "Steel Got to Be Drove," *Sing Out!* (February 1953): 3. On fact and fiction in the legend of John Henry, with mention of Gellert as well, see Scott Reynolds Nelson, *Steel Drivin' Man: John Henry, The Untold Story of an American Legend* (New York: Oxford University Press, 2006).
32. Gellert, "Atom Bomb Blues," *Sing Out!* (March 1951): 9; letter to the editor, *Sing Out!* (May 1952): 14; "Steel Got to Be Drove," *Sing Out!* (February 1953): 3; and "Look Over Yonder," *Sing Out!* (May 1953): 11.
33. "Young's Anecdotes" from 1960, Izzy Young to author, 2002; and Young, "Frets and Frails," *Sing Out!* (December-January 1962): 65, and (July 1965): 75. This material is now published in Scott Barretta, ed., *The Conscience of the Folk Revival: The Writings of Israel "Izzy" Young* (Lanham, MD: Scarecrow Press, 2013). The Belafonte album was the Grammy-winning *Swing Dat Hammer* released by RCA Victor in 1960. Letters in the Gellert collection at the ATM that show Gellert searching for a way to release his field recordings and deposit his materials span the 1960s and 1970s. These include Gellert to Elie Siegmeister, December 4, 1962; Gellert to Maynard Solomon (Vanguard Record Co.), April 18, 1965; Rae Korson (Archive of American Folk Song, Library of Congress) to Gellert, November 30, 1965; Gellert to John Hammond (Columbia Records), October 14, 1967; Folk-Legacy Records to Gellert, January 31, 1969; Gellert to Frank Gillis (ATM), September 30, 1969; Gillis to Gellert, October 14, 1969; Gellert to Gillis, January 20, 1971; Gillis to Gellert, January 27, 1971; Klaus Kuhnke (Archiv für Populäre Musik, Germany) to Gellert, December 17, 1978.
34. Izzy Young, phone interview by author, July 18, 2002; and Young, email correspondence with author, July 19, 2002.
35. Young, "Frets and Frails," *Sing Out!* (Summer 1963): 61.
36. Gellert, "Negro Songs of Protest," *Mainstream* (February 1963): 19–24.
37. Irwin Silber was editor of *Sing Out!* from its founding in 1950 until 1967.
38. Irwin Silber, "Dubious," letter to the editor, *Mainstream* (July 1963): 61.
39. Irwin Silber, email to author, January 3, 2001, and Silber, interview by author, June 13, 2002.
40. Gellert, "Reply," letter to the editor, *Mainstream* (July 1963): 62–64. The LPs to which Gellert alluded were *Songs of the Civil War*, Folkways Records FW05717, 1960, and *Hoote-*

nanny Tonight!, Folkways Records FW02511, 1959. Both were indeed produced by Silber, and the latter did include "Told My Captain," credited to the "Lawrence Gellert collection."
41. Gellert, "Two Songs about Nat Turner, Great Negro Freedom Fighter," *Daily Worker*, June 12, 1949, 8.
42. Gellert interviews, ATM.
43. Irwin Silber, interview by author, June 13, 2002; Pete Seeger, phone interview by author, June 28, 2002.
44. Reuss with JoAnne C. Reuss, *American Folk Music and Left-Wing Politics, 1927–1957* (Lanham, MD: Scarecrow Press, 2000), 97.
45. Gellert interviews, ATM.
46. Gellert interviews, ATM.
47. Gellert clarifies in a different interview that he was in the "entertainment unit" during the war. His interviewer, Lorraine Brown, specifies that he means the "Special Services" unit of the Army. Gellert, interview by Lorraine Brown, October 22, 1976. Works Progress Administration oral histories collection, Collection #C0153, Special Collections and Archives, George Mason University, Fairfax, Virginia.
48. Gellert interviews, ATM.
49. Gellert interviews, ATM. On Asch, Folkways Records, Courlander, and Silber, see Peter D. Goldsmith, *Making People's Music: Moe Asch and Folkways Records* (Washington, DC: Smithsonian Institution Press, 1998).
50. "Some Recent Publications," *Journal of American Folklore* 49, no. 193 (July–September, 1936): 280; Catharine Ann McCollum and Kenneth Wiggins Porter, "Winter Evenings in Iowa, 1873–1880," *Journal of American Folklore* 56, no. 220 (April–June 1943): 102; Russell Ames, "Art in Negro Folksong," *Journal of American Folklore* 56, no. 222 (October–December 1943): 253; J. Mason Brewer, "Afro-American Folklore," *Journal of American Folklore* 60, no. 238 (October–December, 1947): 381; and Richard M. Dorson, "Folklore in Periodical Literature," *Journal of American Folklore* 64, no. 251 (January–March, 1951): 136.
51. D. K. Wilgus, "From the Record Review Editor: Afro-American Tradition," *Journal of American Folklore* 85, no. 335 (January–March 1972): 105–6.
52. Gellert interviews, ATM.
53. Gellert interviews, ATM; Herbert Halpert, "Federal Theatre and Folksong," *Southern Folklore Quarterly* (June 1938): 82–83.
54. John Greenway to Gellert, January 21, 1951, ATM. Folklorist Russell Ames also contacted Gellert by letter, and he included Gellert songs texts in *The Story of American Folk Song* in 1955. Ames to Gellert, April 21, 1955, ATM.
55. Stith Thompson, review of *American Folksongs of Protest*, by John Greenway, *American Historical Review* 59, no. 2 (January 1954): 454.
56. John Greenway, *American Folksongs of Protest* (Philadelphia: University of Pennsylvania Press, 1953), 12. Indeed, as Greenway knew, there was a song "I Hate the Capitalist System," composed in the 1930s by Sara Ogan Gunning from the Kentucky mining region.
57. David King Duñaway, "Review: Folk-Topical Recordings and American Left-Wing Politics," *Journal of American Folklore*, 110, no. 438 (Autumn 1997): 418–19.
58. Gellert interviews, ATM.
59. Gellert interviews, ATM.
60. The song, also printed at times in Gellert publications under the title "Scottsboro Boys," was among those dismissed as fraudulent by Silber in his "Dubious" letter in 1963. As we will see in the next chapter, authors Sam Charters and Bruce Conforth have registered continuing suspicion of the item in the present day.
61. Gellert interviews, ATM.
62. Gellert interviews, ATM.
63. Gellert interviews, ATM.
64. See for instance Robin D. G. Kelley's *Hammer and Hoe: Alabama Communists during the*

Great Depression (Chapel Hill: University of North Carolina Press, 1990) or Cedric Robinson's *Black Marxism: The Making of the Black Radical Tradition* (Chapel Hill: University of North Carolina Press, 1983).
65. Greenway, 12.
66. Michael K. Honey, *Sharecropper's Troubadour: John L. Handcox, the Southern Tenant Farmers' Union, and the African American Song Tradition* (New York: Palgrave Macmillan, 2013).
67. Greenway, 11.
68. William R. Ferris, Jr., "Racial Repertoires among Blues Performers," *Ethnomusicology* 14, no. 3 (September 1970): 440.
69. Alan Dundes, ed., *Mother Wit from the Laughing Barrel: Readings in the Interpretation of Afro-American Folklore* (1973; Jackson: University Press of Mississippi, 1990), 489.
70. Evans, "Afro-American Music: Early Commercial and Field Recordings," *Journal of American Folklore* 91, no. 360 (April–June 1978): 737.
71. Norm Cohen, "The American Folklife Center's Selected Lists of Recordings," *Journal of American Folklore* 99, no. 391 (January–March 1986): 107.
72. Conforth, *African American Folksong,* 141.
73. Conforth, liner notes, *Cap'n You're So Mean: Negro Songs of Protest, Volume 2,* 33 rpm, Rounder 4013, 1982.
74. Conforth, *African American Folksong,* 1.
75. Conforth, 159.
76. Gellert discusses his FTP interactions with Houseman and Welles, and as well the Tamiris production, in Gellert interviews, ATM. See also Tony Buttitta and Barry Witham, *Uncle Sam Presents: A Memoir of the Federal Theatre, 1935–1939* (Philadelphia: University of Pennsylvania Press, 1982), and Susan Manning, "Black Voices, White Bodies: The Performance of Race and Gender in *How Long Brethren,*" *American Quarterly* 50 (1998): 24–46. Twenty-four of Gellert's FWP pieces for the "Negroes of New York" are collected and digitized at the Schomburg Center for Research in Black Culture, Manuscripts, Archives and Rare Books Division, the New York Public Library; scattered additional items from the "Negroes of New York" project are collected and digitized at the Beinecke Rare Book and Manuscript Library, Yale University.
77. Gellert, interview by Brown, October 22, 1976, Special Collections and Archives, George Mason University.
78. Gellert, "Negro Songs of Protest in America," *Music Vanguard* (March–April 1935): 3–14.
79. Conforth, 118, 127.
80. Gellert, *Music Vanguard* (March–April 1935): 4, 9, 8, 13, 11; Charles Seeger to Lawrence Gellert, December 24, 1934. Gellert Mss., Lilly Library, Manuscripts Department, Indiana University, Bloomington; on "Carl Sands" and the Composers Collective, see Reuss with Reuss, *American Folk Music and Left-Wing Politics;* Gellert on the word "protest" comes from Gellert interviews, ATM.

CHAPTER SIX: SCHOLARLY RIGORS

1. Lawrence W. Levine, *Black Culture and Black Consciousness: Afro-American Folk Thought from Slavery to Freedom* (New York: Oxford University Press, 1977), 246.
2. Dick Weissman, *Which Side Are You On?: An Inside History of the Folk Music Revival* (New York: Continuum, 2005), 26, 29, 28; Richard A. Reuss to Bruce Harrah-Conforth, December 31, 1984, Richard A. Reuss papers, Collection C6, Indiana University Archives, Bloomington.
3. Gellert interviews, Archives of Traditional Music (ATM), Indiana University, Bloomington.
4. Bruce Conforth, *African American Folksong and American Cultural Politics* (Lanham, MD: Scarecrow Press, 2013), 140, 163, 161, 160; Gellert interviews, ATM.
5. "Lawrence Gellert," *Wikipedia,* accessed December 2, 2015, https://en.wikipedia.org/wiki/Lawrence_Gellert.

6. I have borrowed "inventory of falsehoods," with permission, from Mat Callahan's valuable revisionist history of a different musical front, *The Explosion of Deferred Dreams: Musical Renaissance and Social Revolution in San Francisco, 1965–1975* (Oakland: PM Press, 2017).
7. Gellert interview, ATM.
8. Bruce Michael Harrah-Conforth, liner notes, *Nobody Knows My Name: Blues from South Carolina and Georgia, 1924–1932*, 33 rpm, Heritage HT 304, 1984, 1–2; Garabedian, "Reds, Whites, and the Blues: Blues Music, White Scholarship, and American Cultural Politics" (PhD diss., University of Minnesota, 2004), and Garabedian, "Reds, Whites, and the Blues: Lawrence Gellert, 'Negro Songs of Protest,' and the Left-Wing Folk-Song Revival of the 1930s and 1940s," *American Quarterly* 57 (March 2005): 179–206; Conforth, *African American Folksong*, 220, 236, 217.
9. My inventory of cross-matches between the Gellert collection in its parallel audio and print dimensions, the Gellert collection and parallels in the publications of folklore peers, and the Gellert collection and overlapping commercial blues from the 1920s and 1930s can be accessed through ATM. Additionally, I have prepared a document on the geography of Gellert's fieldwork that cross-references his publications and interviews.
10. Conforth, 46–51.
11. Texas Alexander, "Penitentiary Moan Blues," 78rpm, Okeh W401334, 1928; 10–17792, Side A2, ATM (issued as "Annie Lee" on Rounder 4013).
12. Sarah Haley, *No Mercy Here: Gender, Punishment, and the Making of Jim Crow Modernity* (Chapel Hill: University of North Carolina Press, 2016), 216, 232–34; "Dangerous Blues" issued on *Jailhouse Blues: Women's A Cappella Songs from the Parchman Penitentiary*, 33 rpm, Rosetta Records RR1316, 1987. Halpert, Herbert, and Mattie May Thomas. Dangerous Blues. Parchman, Mississippi, 1939.
13. Bruce Jackson, ed., *Wake Up Dead Man: Hard Labor and Southern Blues* (1972; Athens: University of Georgia Press, 1999), 126–28; Levine, *Black Culture*, 247, 481; and Lomax and Lomax, *American Ballads*, 18.
14. Irwin Silber, "Dubious," letter to the editor, *Mainstream* (July 1963): 61; John Greenway, *American Folksongs of Protest* (Philadelphia: University of Pennsylvania Press, 1953), 86.
15. Gellert interviews, ATM.
16. Howard W. Odum, "Folk-Song and Folk-Poetry as Found in the Secular Songs of the Southern Negro," *Journal of American Folk-Lore* 24 (July-September 1911): 267; John A. Lomax, "Self-Pity in Negro Folk-Songs," *The Nation*, August 9, 1917, 144–45.
17. Scarborough, *On the Trail of Negro Folk-Songs*, 227–28; Howard W. Odum and Guy B. Johnson, *The Negro and His Songs: A Study of Typical Negro Songs in the South* (Chapel Hill: University of North Carolina Press, 1925), 254–55; Newman I. White, *American Negro Folk-Songs* (1928; Hatboro, PA: Folklore Associates, Inc., 1965), 203, 385; John A. and Alan Lomax, *American Ballads and Folk Songs* (New York: Macmillan, 1934), 233; and John A. and Alan Lomax, *Our Singing Country: A Second Volume of American Ballads and Folk Songs* (New York: Macmillan, 1941), 282. Gellert, "Negro Songs of Protest," *New Masses* (January 1931): 16.
18. Gellert, *New Masses* (January 1931): 16; Gellert, *"Me and My Captain": Chain Gang* (New York: Hours Press, 1939), 16.
19. Howard W. Odum, "Folk-Song," *Journal of American Folk-Lore* (July-September 1911): 267–68; and Odum and Johnson, *The Negro and His Songs*, 252–53, and *Negro Workaday Songs* (Chapel Hill: University of North Carolina Press, 1926), 102, 106.
20. Gellert interviews, ATM.
21. Odum and Johnson, *Negro Workaday Songs*, 123; full Gellert transcription in the epilogue.
22. Odum and Johnson, *Negro Workaday Songs*, 105–6.
23. Odum and Johnson, *Negro Workaday Songs*, 115, 179.
24. Gellert, "Negro Songs of Protest," *New Masses* (November 1930): 11.

25. Dorothy Scarborough, *On the Trail of Negro Folk-Songs* (Cambridge, MA: Harvard University Press, 1925), 232. As a WPA folklorist, Herbert Halpert also collected a version from Euro-American folk tradition. See Herbert Halpert and Austin Harmon, "Stand, Boys, Stand," Maryville, Tennessee, 1939, Library of Congress, Washington, DC.
26. Gellert, *"Me and My Captain"* (1939), 7.
27. White, *American Negro Folk-Songs* (1928), 294.
28. Texas Alexander, "Work Ox Blues," 78rpm, Okeh 8658, 1928.
29. "Well on a Monday" in Gellert, *"Me and My Captain,"* 23–24, and in Odum, *Journal of American Folk-Lore* (July–September 1911): 293, and Odum and Johnson, *The Negro and His Songs,* 204, and Odum and Johnson, *Negro Workaday Songs,* 7, 75; "I Ain't Nothin' But Wages Hand" from a Gellert transcription in Bruce Michael Harrah-Conforth, "Laughing Just to Keep from Crying: Afro-American Folksong and the Field Recordings of Lawrence Gellert" (master's thesis, Indiana University, Bloomington, 1984), 212, and in Odum and Johnson as "Everybody Call Me the Wages Man," *Negro Workaday Songs,* 116; "Lice in Jail" in Gellert, *Negro Songs of Protest,* 22, and "The Cryderville Jail" in Lomax and Lomax, *American Ballads and Folk Songs,* 138–43; and "Cap'n Got a Pistol" on *Negro Songs of Protest: Collected by Lawrence Gellert,* 33 rpm, Rounder 4004, 1973, and in Lomax and Lomax, *American Ballads and Folk Songs,* 49–52.
30. Conforth, 160.
31. 10–17803, Side A4; 10–17802, Side B1; 10–17809, Side B1; 7–2222, Side A1; 7–2237, Side B1; 10–17853, Side A1, ATM.
32. 10–17829, Side A2, ATM.
33. 10–17825, Side A1, ATM. It may be the same female voice interacting, this time, with Gellert on 10–17805, Side A2, ATM.
34. 10–17811, Side A2, ATM.
35. 10–17802, Side A1 and A2, ATM.
36. Steven Patrick Garabedian, "Reds, Whites, and the Blues" (PhD diss., 2004); Conforth, liner notes, *Nobody Knows My Name;* "Nobody Knows My Name" 10–17830 Side A1, "Lawrence Gellert, ca. 1920s-1940s," ATM.
37. James Gellert, interview by author, September 10, 2002; Bob Neidich, email message to author, September 7, 2002; John H. Cowley, "Don't Leave Me Here: Non-Commercial Blues: The Field Trips, 1924–1960," in *Nothing But the Blues: The Music and the Musicians,* ed. Lawrence Cohn (New York: Abbeville Press, 1993), 267–68.
38. Liner notes and sleeve notes, *Negro Songs of Protest: Collected by Lawrence Gellert,* 33 rpm, Rounder 4004, 1973. The 1973 Rounder album was a reproduction of an earlier album prepared on the Timely label that was pressed in a limited run and never commercially distributed. I reviewed a copy of the original recording along with the back cover notes at the Library of Congress. See *Collection of Lawrence Gellert: Negro Songs of Protest,* 33 rpm, Timely TI-112, 1972. Recorded Sound Reference Center, Library of Congress, Washington, DC. Though the actual disc labels for the Timely release show the copyright date 1972, Gellert correspondence with Library curators from the mid-1960s suggests that, in fact, the album and notes were prepared earlier. As Timely was an independent leftwing music label started in the 1930s, the circumstances of the original recording remain murky. In 1965, however, it seems that Gellert was looking for an institution, in this case the Library of Congress, to distribute the 1,000 copies of the album he had in his possession. Lawrence Gellert to "Curator, Music Division, Library of Congress," November 19, 1965; Rae Korson (Head, Archive of Folk Song) to Gellert, November 30, 1965; Gellert to Korson, October 29, 1966; Korson to Gellert, November 4, 1966; and Gellert to Korson, November 12, 1966. Lawrence Gellert, "Corp. Subject," Folder 1, American Folklife Center, Library of Congress, Washington, DC. Both Mark Pumphrey, of the Polk County Public Library in North Carolina, and Michael Taft, of the Library of Congress, were of great assistance in this research.
39. Conforth, *African American Folksong,* xvi, 45–46.

40. Conforth, 56; Lawrence Gellert, "Draft Proposal," Gellert Mss., Lilly Library, Indiana University, Bloomington.
41. Northeast Document Conservation Center, "IRENE Tested on Aluminum Discs," https://www.nedcc.org/audio-preservation/irene-blog/2014/05/09/aluminum-disc/, accessed June 23, 2018; Michael Jay Biel, "The Making and Use of Recordings in Broadcasting before 1936" (PhD diss., Northwestern University, 1977); and Erika Brady, *A Spiral Way: How the Phonograph Changed Ethnography* (Jackson: University Press of Mississippi, 1999).
42. "The Duck Yas-Yas-Yas," 7–2141, Side B1, and 7–2256, Side B1, and "Tell Me Woman Blues" 7–2202 Side A1. See "Lawrence Gellert, ca. 1920s-1940s," ATM.
43. "Songs of Protest," *Time*, June 15, 1936, 51.
44. Alan C. Graves, "The Presto History Page," http://www.prestohistory.com/Presto.htm, accessed June 23, 2018; Gellert interviews, ATM. See also George J. Saliba, "High-Fidelity Instantaneous Recording," *Journal of World Communication: Communication and Broadcast Engineering* (January 1936): 11–13.
45. Cowley, 268; and see Debora G. Kodish, liner notes, *"Folk-Songs of America": The Robert Winslow Gordon Collection, 1922—1932*, 33 rpm, Library of Congress AFS L68, 1978. Kodish mentions Gellert specifically.
46. Lyric transcription from Kodish, liner notes, 21. For the original audio of Gordon's field recording of "Let's Got To Bury" performed by Reverend A.G. Holly in 1925, visit https://www.loc.gov/folklife/Gordon/sideAband9.html; the Gellert items are 7–2211, Side A1; 10–17831, Side B1; and 10–17835, Side B1, ATM.
47. Conforth, 89–91.
48. See Faith Berry, ed., *Good Morning Revolution: Uncollected Writings of Social Protest by Langston Hughes* (1973; New York: Citadel Press, 1992); Jonathan Scott, *Socialist Joy in the Writing of Langston Hughes* (Columbia: University of Missouri Press, 2006).
49. Levine, *Black Culture*, 29, 205–6. For more on this Price example, lynching, and blues protest, see Adam Gussow, *Seems Like Murder Here: Southern Violence and the Blues Tradition* (Chicago: University of Chicago Press, 2002), 59–65. In Gussow's subsequent *Beyond the Crossroads: The Devil and the Blues Tradition* (Chapel Hill: University of North Carolina Press, 2017), the author explores further dimensions of blues protest beyond overt lyricism. His incisive analysis broadens the perspective to account for a "strain of insurrectionary indirection" and "plausible deniability," and he makes the necessary point that "the black audience had historically shown its preference for witty double entendre" over "overt protest." This interpretation works from a similar premise of Black agency as does that of Levine and Gellert. Moreover, the concept of "plausible deniability" can additionally account for the gaps and disjuncture between protest and non-protest content even in a single song text from the Gellert collection. *Beyond the Crossroads*, 124, 127, and chapter 3, *passim*.
50. Levine, 29, 196, 207; Simone qtd. in Levine, 200. African American folklorist Willis Laurence James also reported examples of communal re-creation, in which traditional songs were rewritten with labor organizing themes, in *Stars in de Elements: A Study of Negro Folk Music* (Durham, NC: Duke University Press, 1995), 96, 153.
51. Gellert interviews, ATM; H. Howard Taubman, "Negro Folksongs: New Genre Dealing with Everyday Life Produced, Particularly in South," *New York Times*, July 5, 1936, X5.
52. Gellert, preface *Negro Songs of Protest*, n.p.
53. Gellert interviews, ATM.
54. "Way Down South/In Atlanta, Georgia" 7–2266, Side B1 and 10–17855, Side B1 (issued on Rounder 4004). Additional print to audio overlap in *Negro Songs of Protest* include "How Long, Brethren?" to 10–17803, Side A3 and A4 and Side B4 (issued on Rounder 4013); "Says I'm Boun'" to 10–17845, Side A1 (issued on Rounder 4013); "Lice in Jail" to 10–17793, Side A1 and A2; "Pickin' Off De Cotton" to 7–2172, Side B1; "Where Wuz

You?" to 10–17812, Side A1 and 10–17813, Side B2; "Lay Down Late/Cold Iron Shackles" to 10–17847, Side A1 and 10–17851, Side B2 (issued on Rounder 4004); and "If You Catch Me Stealin'" to 10–17808, Side A2 (issued on Rounder 4013). Other songs in the book can also be matched to parallels in the collections of established peers. Though the verses do not match up to Gellert's "Sistren an' Brethren," Scarborough has a song, "O-O-Oh, Sistren an' Bred'ren" in *On the Trail of Negro Folk-Songs* (189); Levine reports in *Black Culture and Black Consciousness* that a version of Gellert's "Preacher's Belly" was collected in New York City (326); as noted in my introduction, a version of Gellert's "How Long, Brethren?" titled "My Father, How Long?" is compiled in *Slave Songs of the United States* from 1867 (93); a verse of Gellert's "Oh Mah Kitty Co Co" shows up in Scarborough's transcription of "Ain't It Hard?" in *On the Trail* (228); lines from Gellert's "'Cause I'm a N——r" are included in Odum and Johnson's item "Everybody Call Me The Wages Man" in *Negro Workaday Songs* (116); and, as we have already established, a parallel of Gellert's "Let's Go to De Buryin'" was collected by Robert Gordon in the 1920s.

55. "Atlanta Town" as "Negro Got No Justice," issued on Rounder 4004. "Two Hoboes" can be paired to 10–17800, Side B2 and 10–17799, Side A1 (issued on Rounder 4004); "Early In The Morning" (which is a version of "The Midnight Special") to 10–17836, Side A2; "Look Over Yonder" to 10–17808, Side B1; "Steel Got to Be Drove" to 10–17846, Side B1 (issued on Rounder 4004); and "I Hear Danger Singing" to 10–17831, Side A1. "Bossman Sammy" to 10–17841, Side A4 (Gellert sings); "Work Ox" to 10–17799, Side B2 (Gellert sings); "Captain Don't You Think" to 10–17799, Side A2 (Gellert sings); "Corn Pone" to 10–17805, Side A2 (Gellert sings); and "Well on a Monday" to 10–17799, Side B3 (Gellert sings). Additionally, several of the items in the book overlap with songs in the collections of others: lyrics from "Look Over Yonder" in Gellert are included in Levine's *Black Culture and Black Consciousness* (214); "Squirrel on the Long" in Gellert appears as "I Ain't Free" in Odum and Johnson's *Negro Workaday Songs* (71); "Corn Pone" in Gellert appears as "Better'n I Has at Home" in Odum and Johnson's *Negro Workaday Songs* (85); "Well on a Monday" in Gellert appears as a stanza in Odum and Johnson's *Negro Workaday Songs* (7); and "Captain Did You Hear 'Bout" has some lines in common with "Po' Laz'us" in Lomax and Lomax, *Our Singing Country* (345).

56. Gellert, *"Me and My Captain,"* 8–9.

57. "Negro Got No Justice," Rounder 4004.

58. Conforth, 122, 63–64, 123, 159.

59. Conforth, 215, 121, 94; Gellert, "Negro Songs of Protest," *Mainstream* (February 1963): 23–24; Gellert, "Four Negro Songs of Protest," *Music Vanguard* (Summer 1935): 69; Gellert, "Sharecropper," *New Masses* (April 1936): 16.

60. Gellert, "Do Lak Alabamy Boys," *New Masses* (May 1933): 15; Conforth, 91; and Robin D. G. Kelley, *Hammer and Hoe: Alabama Communists during the Great Depression* (Chapel Hill: University of North Carolina Press, 1990), 53.

61. Conforth, 92–94; Gellert, "Scottsboro," *New Masses* (May 1933): 16; Gellert, "Georgia Work Song," *New Masses* (May 1935): 10; "He-I-Heira" in Odum and Johnson, *Negro Workaday Songs*, 92–93.

62. Gellert, "Belinda," and "Stan' Boys Stand," *New Masses* (November 1930): 10–11; Conforth, 62; "Belinda" field recordings on 7–2156, Side A1, and 10–17805, Side A1, ATM. Additional cross-matches from the early articles are "Diamond Joe," *New Masses* (November 1930): 11, on 7–2172, Side A1; "Picking Off De Cotton (Ain't Dat De Truff)," *New Masses* (January 1931): 16, on 7–2172, Side B1; "Oh Mah Kitty Co Co," *New Masses* (April 1931): 6, on 7–2287, Side A1 and B1 (Gellert sings); "Set Down White Folks," *New Masses* (April 1931): 7, on 10–17805, Side B1 (Gellert sings); "Corn Pone, Fat Meat," *New Masses* (April 1931): 7, on 10–17805, Side A2 (Gellert sings); and "Work All the Summer," *New Masses* (May 1932): 22, on 7–2194, Side A1 and 10–17815, Side B1.

63. "Mr. Tyree" issued on Rounder 4004; Gellert interviews, ATM; John A. and Alan Lomax, and Unidentified Group of Negro Convicts, "I Promised Mr. Tyree," AFS 254

B1, Bellwood Prison Camp, Atlanta, Georgia, December 11–12, 1934; "Gonna Leave from Georgia" issued on *Nobody Knows My Name,* Heritage HT 304; Bruce Bastin, *Red River Blues: The Blues Tradition in the Southeast* (Urbana: University of Illinois Press, 1986), 64–67. Bastin also speculates about the identities behind another item in the Gellert collection, "Gonna Leave from Georgia." He wonders if the guitarists and singer on the recording may have been the popular Atlanta group the Star Band. For more on protest, the Lomaxes, and Gellert, see John Cowley, "Shack Bullies and Levee Contractors: Bluesmen as Ethnographers," in *Songs about Work: Essays in Occupational Culture for Richard A. Reuss,* ed. Archie Green (Bloomington, IN: Folklore Institute, 1993), 134–62.

64. John A. Lomax and unidentified prisoner, "We Don't Get No Justice in Atlanta," AFS 263 B3, State Prison Farm, Milledgeville, Georgia, December 15, 1934; lyric transcription in *Our Singing Country,* 313–14, in "Outlaws" section of songs.

65. In the Gellert archive at ATM, see 10–17846, Side A1; 10–17839, Side B1; and 10–17844, Side B1. For a Lomax print cross-match, see "Pauline" in *Our Singing Country,* 402–4. There sounds to be additional overlap between recordings from this Lomax field trip and the Gellert collection. Such cross-matches are an avenue for future research.

66. Ronald D. Cohen, ed., *Alan Lomax: Selected Writings 1934—1997* (New York: Routledge, 2003), 9–11; "Po' Farmer," in Lomax and Lomax, *Our Singing Country,* 280–81; John Szwed, *Alan Lomax: The Man Who Recorded the World* (New York: Viking, 2010), 36–37.

67. Szwed, 37.

68. Szwed, 38–39, 141.

69. Szwed, 228; Alan Lomax, *The Land Where the Blues Began* (New York: Delta, 1993), xviii, 459–79; *Blues in the Mississippi Night,* CD, Rykodisc RCD 90155, 1990; and Alan Lomax, "I Got the Blues," *Common Ground* (Summer 1948): 38–52.

EPILOGUE: FREEDOM SONGS, SIXTIES REVIVALISM, AND THE TRAGEDY OF WHITE DENIAL

1. Alan Lomax, Woody Guthrie, and Pete Seeger, eds., *Hard Hitting Songs for Hard-Hit People* (1967; Lincoln: University of Nebraska Press, 1999), 12.

2. Lomax, Guthrie, and Seeger, *Hard Hitting Songs,* 365–66.

3. Samuel Charters, *Walking a Blues Road: A Selection of Blues Writing, 1956–2004* (New York: Marion Boyars, 2004), 132.

4. Charters, 136–38.

5. Lawrence Gellert, *Negro Songs of Protest* (New York: American Music League, 1936), 9.

6. Charters, 136–39.

7. Charters, 132.

8. Musicologist Susan McClary has deemed blues not just the essential Black roots music, but the essential twentieth-century roots music generally; R. A. Lawson has usefully termed blues the "counterculture" music of Jim Crow. I have written on the politics of the blues elsewhere. See McClary, "Thinking Blues" in *Conventional Wisdom: The Content of Musical Form* (Berkeley: University of California Press, 2000), 32–62; Lawson, *Jim Crow's Counterculture: The Blues and Black Southerners, 1890–1945* (Baton Rouge: Louisiana State University Press, 2010); and Garabedian, "'It Don't Make Sense': Willie Dixon, the Blues, War, and Peace," *Peace & Change: A Journal of Peace Research* 40, no. 3 (July 2015): 287–312. For key studies that have shaped my thinking, see James Cone, *The Spirituals and the Blues: An Interpretation* (1972; Maryknoll, NY: Orbis Books, 1991); LeRoi Jones/Amiri Baraka's *Blues People: Negro Music in White America* (1963; New York: Quill, 1999); Paul Garon, *Blues and the Poetic Spirit* (1975; San Francisco: City Lights Books, 1996); Angela Y. Davis, *Blues Legacies and Black Feminism: Gertrude "Ma" Rainey, Bessie Smith, and Billie Holiday* (New York: Vintage Books, 1998); Adam Gussow, *Seems Like Murder Here: Southern Violence and the Blues Tradition* (Chicago: University of Chicago Press, 2002); Reiland Rabaka, *Civil Rights Music: The Soundtracks of the Civil Rights Movement* (Lanham, MD: Lexington Books, 2016); Brian Ward, *Just My Soul Responding: Rhythm and Blues, Black Consciousness, and Race*

Relations (London: University College London Press, 1998); and the book and CD series by Guido van Rijn starting with *Roosevelt's Blues: African-American Blues and Gospel Songs on FDR* (Jackson: University Press of Mississippi, 1997).

9. Samuel Charters, *The Poetry of the Blues* (New York: Avon, 1963), 152; Paul Oliver, *Blues Fell This Morning: Meaning in the Blues* (1960; New York: Cambridge University Press, 1990), 272–73; and Pete Welding, liner notes, *News and the Blues: Telling It Like It Is,* CD, Columbia CK 46217, 1990.

10. Paul Oliver, *Screening the Blues: Aspects of the Blues Tradition* (1968; New York: Da Capo Press, 1989), 256–61; and *All You Need Is Love: The Story of Popular Music,* directed by Tony Palmer, 1976.

11. Samuel Charters, *The Country Blues,* rev. ed. (1975); Samuel Charters radio interview with Don Swaim, "Wired for Books," http://www.wiredforbooks.org/samuelcharters/, accessed March 29, 1984; and Steve Cushing, *Pioneers of the Blues Revival* (Urbana: University of Illinois Press, 2014), 44–46.

12. Steven C. Tracy summarizes the lines of scholarly debate over blues protest in *Write Me a Few of Your Lines: A Blues Reader* (Amherst: University of Massachusetts Press, 1999), 339–41. I address the subject in Garabedian, "'It Don't Make Sense,'" *Peace & Change: A Journal of Peace Research* 40, no. 3 (July 2015): 287–312.

13. Jeff Todd Titon, "Reconstructing the Blues: Reflections on the 1960s Blues Revival," in *Transforming Tradition: Folk Music Revivals Examined,* ed. Neil V. Rosenberg (Urbana: University of Illinois Press, 1993), 222. David Evans issued his own early intervention in revivalism with "Demythologizing the Blues," ISAM Newsletter 29 (Fall 1999): 8–13.

14. Garon, *Blues and the Poetic Spirit,* 199–200.

15. George M. Fredrickson, *The Black Image in the White Mind: The Debate on Afro-American Character and Destiny, 1817–1914* (New York: Harper and Row, 1971), 109.

16. Grace Elizabeth Hale, *A Nation of Outsiders: How the White Middle Class Fell in Love with Rebellion in Postwar America* (New York: Oxford University Press, 2011), 7, 3, 87.

17. Hale, "Hear Me Talking to You: The Blues and the Romance of Rebellion," in *Beyond Blackface: African Americans and the Creation of American Popular Culture, 1890–1930,* ed. W. Fitzhugh Brundage (Chapel Hill: University of North Carolina Press, 2011), 239–58.

18. Steve Cushing, *Pioneers of the Blues Revival* (Urbana: University of Illinois Press, 2014), xxiii, xxi; and Titon, "Reconstructing the Blues," 235. As Garon has pointed out, a body of "meta-criticism" is starting to take shape in the field, with intensive full-length studies that "focus on blues criticism as much as blues itself." Paul Garon, review of *Robert Johnson: Lost and Found* by Barry Lee Pearson and Bill McCulloch, and *Escaping the Delta: Robert John and the Invention of the Blues* by Elijah Wald, *Living Blues* (March/April 2004): 116–17; Pearson and McCulloch, *Robert Johnson: Lost and Found* (Urbana: University of Illinois Press, 2003); Wald, *Escaping the Delta: Robert Johnson and the Invention of the Blues* (New York: Amistad, 2004); Benjamin Filene, *Romancing the Folk: Public Memory and American Roots Music* (Chapel Hill: University of North Carolina Press, 2000); and Marybeth Hamilton, *In Search of the Blues: Black Voices, White Visions* (London: Jonathan Cape, 2007). An additional "meta" study that works in this interventionist mode is John W. Work, Lewis Wade Jones, and Samuel C. Adams, Jr., *Lost Delta Found: Rediscovering the Fisk University—Library of Congress Coahoma County Study, 1941–1942,* ed. Robert Gordon and Bruce Nemerov (Nashville: Vanderbilt University Press, 205). See also Adam Gussow, *Beyond the Crossroads: The Devil and the Blues Tradition;* Karl Hagstrom Miller, *Segregating Sound: Inventing Folk and Pop Music in the Age of Jim Crow* (Durham, NC: Duke University Press, 2010), and Ulrich Adelt, *Blues Music in the Sixties: A Story in Black and White* (New Brunswick, NJ: Rutgers University Press, 2010).

19. Stephen Petrus and Ronald D. Cohen, *Folk City: New York and the American Folk Music Revival* (New York: Oxford University Press, 2015).

20. Stanley Cohen, *States of Denial: Knowing about Atrocities and Suffering* (Malden, MA: Polity Press, 2001), 22.

21. David R. Roediger, ed., *Black on White: Black Writers on What It Means to Be White* (New

York: Schocken Books, 1998); Cohen, *States of Denial*, 49. As a leading figure in critical whiteness studies since *The Wages of Whiteness* in the 1990s, Roediger has been highly praised and highly targeted by proponents and opponents of the field. For Roediger's own contemporary assessments, see the new edition of *The Wages of Whiteness: Race and the Making of the American Working Class* (New York: Verso, 2007), with a new preface by Roediger, and *Class, Race, and Marxism* (New York: Verso, 2017). Roediger's point of stress is that critical whiteness studies is an expression of historical materialism, with roots and branches that grew out of radical Left activism and Marxism. As Roediger intends it, critical whiteness studies is part of an intersectional anti-capitalist project.

22. Guy and Candie Carawan, eds., *Sing For Freedom: The Story of the Civil Rights Movement through Its Songs* (Montgomery: NewSouth Books, 2007); Kerran L. Sanger, *"When the Spirit Says Sing!": The Role of Freedom Songs in the Civil Rights Movement* (New York: Routledge, 1995); William G. Roy, *Reds, Whites, and Blues: Social Movements, Folk Music, and Race in the United States* (Princeton, NJ: Princeton University Press, 2010); and Petrus and Cohen, *Folk City*.

23. For the most astute comparative study of the singing movement of the 1930s versus the 1960s, see Roy, *Reds, Whites, and Blues*.

24. Rounder 4004, 1973; Gellert, "Negro Songs of Protest," Federal Writers' Project Negro Group Papers, Folder 32, Box 2, Beinecke Rare Book and Manuscript Library, Yale University. This item is clearly out of place in the Federal Writers' Project papers, as it dates from a latter period of Gellert's life.

INDEX

Adomian, Lan, 22, 84, 104, 158, 160
Adventures of a Ballad Hunter (J. A. Lomax), 90–91, 197–98n60
African American Folksong and American Cultural Politics (Conforth), 11, 130–31
African American protest and white denial, 53–80; denial, defined, 4–5; denial of Black agency and Gellert's credibility questioned, 135–38, 181; protest construed as self-pity, 54, 56, 57–68, 77–78, 92, 192n13; resistance construed as new, 68–80; romantic racialism by white researchers, 5–6, 53–54, 66–68, 74, 77–78, 179–80; "white man" cycle of song lyrics and, 29–34. *See also* Gellert controversy
African American vernacular protest music: "freedom songs" and, 180–81; Gellert's access to, 35–38; Gellert's methodology and mission, 42–46; Gellert's political views and, 42, 46–52; Tryon, 25–27, 38–42, 187n27. *See also* blues music
Afro-American Folksongs (Krehbiel), 69–70, 92
"Ain't It Hard—To Be a N——r?" (song), 41, 61–65, 68, 142–44
Alan Lomax: Selected Writings 1934–1997 (R. Cohen), 169
Alan Lomax: The Man Who Recorded the World (Szwed), 170
Alexander, Alger "Texas," 139–40, 147, 152
Alexander, Michelle, 4
Allen, William Francis, 3
American Ballads and Folk Songs (Lomax & Lomax): leftwing folksong revival and, 81, 86, 88–89, 94, 103–4, 106; parallels to Gellert's songs in, 142, 147–48, 196n33; reviews, 197–98n60
"American Folklore and Left-Wing Politics, 1927–1957"/*American Folk Music and Left-Wing Politics* (Reuss), 10, 82, 120–21
American Folksongs of Protest (Greenway), 9, 124–25, 128–31, 142
American Music League, 19, 104, 174
American Negro Folk Songs (N. I. White), 54, 70, 71, 74–80
Ames, Russell, 9, 123, 129
"Angelo an' a Thousan' Mo" (song), 105
"Angelo Herndon" (song), 163
Angola State Penitentiary, 93
Archives of American Art (Smithsonian Institution), 50
Archives of Traditional Music (ATM, Indiana University): Conforth's research at, 10–11; Gellert's field recording discs archived at, 12, 21, 27, 139, 148, 150–52; Reuss's interviews archived at, 12
Aristocrat Records, 199n14
Asch, Moses, 122
Asheville (NC) Citizen, and Gellert, 23–25
Astor, Nancy, 25
"Atlanta Town" (song), 160–62
"Atlanta Town/Negro Got No Justice" (song), 167–68
ATM. *See* Archives of Traditional Music
"Atom Bomb Blues" (Gellert, song), 114
At the Hands of Persons Unknown (Dray), 57

Baez, Joan, 7, 9
Baker, Nancy Kovaleff, 105
Baldwin, James, 135
Barracoon (Hurston), 186n8
Barry, Phillips, 155
Basie, Count, 112–13
Bastin, Bruce, 11, 167, 206–7n63
"Baton Rouge" (song), 163
Beitler, Lawrence, 197n57
Belafonte, Harry, 117, 200n33
"Belinda" (song), 165–66
Bellwood (prison), 167
Benedict, Ruth, 124
Beyond the Crossroads (Gussow), 205n49
Big Road Blues (Evans), 11
Big White Fog (Ward), 108–9
"Big White Folks," 26, 187n27
Bilbo, Theodore, 113, 115, 116, 199n14
Black Culture and Black Consciousness (Levine), 12, 33, 68, 135–36, 155–56

Black Image in the White Mind, The (Fredrickson), 5–6, 177–78
"Black Man and White Ladyship" (Cunard), 15
Black Marxism (Robinson), 57
Black on White (Roediger), 180
Black Samson (prisoner), 90–92
Blackwell, Francis Hillman "Scrapper," 3–4
Blitzstein, Marc, 84
"Blues' Angry Voice, The" (Charters), 173–74
Blues Fell This Morning (Oliver), 11
blues music: blues revival research, 172–81; commercial "race records," 3, 55; Gussow on blues protest, 205n49; McClary on, 207n8; meta-criticism of, 208n18; white music collectors of, 6–7. *See also* leftwing folksong revival; *individual names of artists; individual names of music collectors; individual names of songs*
Boas, Franz, 74, 123
Brazil, Wayne, 73–74
Briggs, Cyril, 48
Brooklyn Daily Eagle, Gellert's work for, 22, 24
Broonzy, Lee Conley "Big Bill," 171
Browder, Earl, 107
Brown, Sterling: on African American songs of protest, 55, 72, 126; Gellert's work praised by, 8; "Negro Character as Seen by White Authors," 79–80; on "New Negro Renaissance," 54; travel with Gellert and Cunard by, 15–21, 31–32
Bukharin, Nicolai, 84
Burnett, Chester "Howlin' Wolf," 31

Cantwell, Robert, 8, 11
"Cap'n Got a Pistol" (song), 147
Cap'n You're So Mean (Gellert, album), 130
Carr, Leroy, 3–4
Charters, Ann, 173
Charters, Samuel, 109, 173–76, 177
Chavkin, Samuel, 188n42
Chicago Defender, on lynchings, 43
Child, Francis James, 88
Civil Rights Congress (CRC), 43, 112–14
civil rights movement: anticommunism and, 113; blues revivalism and, 178–79; folk revivalism intersected with, 123; "freedom songs" of, 180–81; "Tent City" encampment (Tennessee), 116
Cohen, Norm, 130, 136
Cohen, Ronald, 11, 87, 169, 179
Cohen, Stanley, 4–5, 179, 180
Cohodas, Nadine, 39–40
Coleman, Louis, 34, 104–5
Collection of Lawrence Gellert (Gellert, album), 123, 184n25
Common Ground (periodical), Alan Lomax published in, 171
communism, 108–34; anticommunism and, 7, 109, 113, 117, 122, 129, 198n2; civil rights movement and protest songs, 180–81; Conforth's criticism of Gellert, 109, 130–34; cultural left and postwar containment, 108–12; Cunard on, 16; folksongs vs. songs of protest, 120–30; Gellert's political views, 6–7, 46–52; Gellert's postwar music collecting, 112–20; *Hammer and Hoe* on, 34; Hughes and, 1–2; "outsider" America and, 7; sympathies of Alan Lomax, 196n36; Third Period (1928–1935) and transition to Popular Front, 81–85, 94–103, 106–7, 196–97n40. *See also* Communist Party USA
Communist International, Sixth World Congress of (1928), 84
Communist Party USA (CPUSA), 7; on African American "self-determination," 101, 111; American Music League, 19, 174; Composers Collective, 84, 97, 104, 106, 134; *Daily Worker,* 22, 52, 104, 105, 119–20, 188n42; Franklin Roosevelt backed by, 107; International Labor Defense, 34, 104; *Negro Liberator,* 104–5; Popular Front policy of, 81–85, 97, 102, 103, 106–7; SCU, 38, 127, 164; Silber and, 119; Workers Music League, 84, 97, 104
Conforth, Bruce: coaching allegation of, 137–38, 148; dating of Gellert's field recordings, 150, 151, 154; as Gellert authority, 10–11; Gellert's collecting questioned by, 109, 130–34; on Gellert's name changes, 23–25; on Gellert's protest songs, 139; Gellert's songbooks critiqued by, 162–65; on "no parallels" allegation, 142; research archives of, 10–11, 185n32; Reuss's warning to, 136; on timing of Gellert's recordings, 25, 27
Conrad, Earl, 35, 43, 44–45, 114–16

Copland, Aaron, 84
Country Blues, The (S. Charters), 172, 176
Country Joe and the Fish, 176
Courlander, Harold, 122, 123
Covarrubias, Miguel, 123
Cowboy Songs and Other Frontier Ballads (J. A. Lomax), 66
Cowell, Henry, 84
Cowley, John, 11, 150–51
Crisis, The (NAACP), *Negro Songs of Protest* (Gellert) reviewed by, 21
Cultural Front, The (Denning), 12, 82
Cunard, Nancy: *Negro: An Anthology*, 15, 16, 19, 44, 50, 126, 165; possible recording of, 149; travel with Gellert and Brown by, 15–21
Cushing, Steve, 178–79

Daily Worker (Communist Party): "Folk Songs of the South," 188n42; leftwing folksong revival and, 85, 104, 105; "Nat Turner," 119–20; on *Negro Songs of Protest* (Gellert), 22, 52
Davis, Benjamin, Jr., 104–5
Davis, Francis, 11
"Death of Harry Sims, The" (A. M. Jackson), 97
Degeyter Club (New York City), 84
Dell, Floyd, 47
"Demythologizing the Blues" (Evans), 208n13
denial. *See* African American protest and white denial
Denning, Michael, 12, 82, 113
"Do Lak Alabamy Boys" (song), 163, 164
Domination and the Arts of Resistance (Scott), 34
"Don't You Give Me No Cornbread" (song), 144–45
Dorson, Richard, 123
"Double Meaning in the Popular Negro Blues" (G. B. Johnson), 55
Drama Fortnightly, 26, 28, 189n5
Dray, Philip, 57
"Dubious" (Silber), 118–19, 201n60
Du Bois, W. E. B., 15, 35, 53, 67, 69, 76–77
"Duck Yas-Yas-Yas, The" (Tampa Red), 151–52
Dunaway, David King, 10, 11, 82, 125
Dundes, Alan, 129
Dunson, Stephanie, 56
Dylan, Bob, 7, 9, 31

Eastman, Max, 47
Echo (aluminum disc company), 151
Eisler, Hanns, 84
Equal Justice Initiative, 57
Evans, David, 11, 56, 130, 136, 208n13
"Everybody calls me the Wages Man" (song), 147

Fay, William (Gellert's pseudonym), 116–17
Federal Bureau of Investigation (FBI), 117
Federal Dance Theater (New York City), 50
Federal Music Project, 85
Federal Theatre Project, 108–9, 132, 133
Federal Writers' Project, 132
Ferris, William, 11, 129, 136
Filene, Benjamin, 33, 65–66, 85, 87–88, 93
Finkelstein, Sidney, 112–13
"Fishin'" (Gellert), 113
Fitzgerald, F. Scott, 24, 25
Folk City (Petrus & R. Cohen), 179
Folklore Center (New York City), 117, 176
"Folks Are Real Friendly Down Here" (Fay [Gellert]), 116
"Folk-Song and Folk-Poetry" (Odum), 60–63
"Folk Songs of the South" (Chavkin), 188n42
Folkways Records, 117, 119, 122
Ford, James, 16, 49
Fortune magazine, on socialism, 82
Frank, Leo, 191n42
Frank, Richard, 99–100, 101, 102–3
Fredrickson, George M., 5–6, 53, 66, 177–78
Freedom Singers, 9
Freeman, Mort, 117
Freeman, Penny Gellert, 13–14
"Frets and Frails" (Young's column, *Sing Out!*), 117, 118

Garland, Jim, 96
Garon, Paul, 10, 11, 177, 208n18
Garrison, Lucy McKim, 3
Gellert, Adolph (father), 22, 186n12
Gellert, Catherine (mother), 22
Gellert, Cecelia "Billie" (sister). *See* Neidich, Cecelia "Billie" Gellert
Gellert, Donald (nephew), 13
Gellert, Ernest (brother), 25, 47, 186n12, 190n31

Gellert, Hugo (brother): Communist Party and, 111; Hugo Gellert Papers, 50; *Karl Marx' 'Capital' in Lithographs,* 190n31; Lawrence Gellert's disappearance and, 13; Lawrence Gellert's music collecting and, 46–47; prominence as artist, 21, 22–23
Gellert, James (nephew), 13
Gellert, Lawrence: collected material as "verboten," 31, 41–42, 55, 138, 188n42; commercial recording work of, 45; as compared with the Lomaxes, 89–92; death/disappearance of, 12–13, 185n34; family history and Hungarian emigration, 22–23, 25, 186n11; FBI investigation of, 117; field archive of (Indiana University), 12, 21, 27, 139, 148, 150–52; friction with Alan Lomax, 136–37, 197n51; on his work, 1, 4; mental health of, 22; name variations/invented history/pseudonym of, 23–25, 116–17, 188n36; newspaper work of, 22–25, 43–44, 45, 50; recording media used by, 27, 31, 139, 148–52, 154, 158–60; Reuss's interviews of, 10–12, 184n22; Rockefeller Foundation grant, 8, 50, 112; scholarly research on, 10–14, 185n32, 203n9; "sing fest" fundraiser, 27–30; travel with Brown and Cunard, 15–22. *See also* Gellert controversy; Gellert's early music collecting; leftwing folksong revival; *Negro Songs of Protest* (Gellert)
Gellert, Otto (brother), 13, 22, 23, 186n11
Gellert, Theodor "Ted" (brother), 13, 22, 23, 186n11
Gellert, Tom (grand-nephew), 13
Gellert controversy, 108–34, 135–71; coaching allegations, and 137–38, 148–49; Conforth's criticism of Gellert, 109, 130–34; cultural left and postwar containment, 108–12; dating of field recordings and, 149–57; folksongs vs. songs of protest, 120–30; Gellert's postwar music collecting and scrutiny, 112–20, 135–36; "no parallels" allegation and, 142–48, 167–71; overview, 9–10; perception of entire archive as protest songs and, 138–42; print transcriptions and audio back-ups, 157–66; white denial of Black agency and effect on, 135–38, 181
Gellert's early music collecting, 35–52; access to Black vernacular protest music, 35–38; methodology and mission of, 42–46; political influence on, 42, 46–52; "sing fest" as gateway to, 27–30; Tryon as adopted home of, 25–27, 38–42; "white man" cycle of song lyrics, 29–34
gender chauvinism: Scarborough and, 70; toward white female vernacular musicians, 196–97n40
Georgia State Prison Commission, 44
"Georgia Work Song (He-i-Heria)" (song), 165
Gillette, William, 25
Gold, Michael, 16, 50, 105, 134
"Gonna Leave from Georgia" (song), 206–7n63
"Goodnight Irene" (Lead Belly), 7
Gordon, Robert Winslow, 131, 139, 153–55
Grateful Dead, The, 31
Green, Archie, 125
Greenway, John, 9, 124–25, 128–31, 142, 183–85n21
Gunning, Sara Ogan, 172, 201n56
Gussow, Adam, 11, 205n49
Guthrie, Woody, 7, 128, 129, 172–73

Hale, Grace, 7, 12, 178
Haley, Sarah, 140
Halpert, Herbert, 124, 137–38, 140, 148
Hamilton, Marybeth, 33, 70, 72
Hammer and Hoe (Kelley), 12, 34
Handcox, John, 128, 129, 172
Handy, W. C., 8, 16, 24, 50–52
Hard Hitting Songs for Hard-Hit People (Silber), 172–73, 179
Hemenway, Robert, 133
"Here I Am in Dis Low Down Jail" (song), 163
Herndon, Angelo, 134
"Herrenvolk democracies," 66
Herzog, George, 16, 123, 124
"Hesitation Blues" (song), 156
Hirsch, Jerrold, 33, 66, 67
Holiday, Billie, 106
Honey, Michael, 128
Hopf, Alice. *See* Lightner, Alice
"How Long, Brethren?" (song), 2–4, 11, 41, 168
"How Long, How Long Blues" (Carr & Blackwell), 3, 11

How Long Brethren (Tamiris), 50, 132
Hughes, Langston: FBI investigation of "subversives," 198n2; Gellert's postwar collecting and, 109, 126, 133; Gellert's work praised by, 8; Hurston and, 74, 80; *Negro: An Anthology* and, 15; *Negro Songs of Protest* (Gellert) foreword by, 1–2; as "red" poet, 155
Hugo Gellert Papers (Smithsonian Institution), 50
Hurston, Zora Neale, 14, 16, 74, 80, 123, 133, 186n8

"I Am a Union Woman" (A. M. Jackson), 96–97
"I Been Pickin' and Shovelin'" (song), 150
"I Got the Blues" (A. Lomax), 171
"I Hate the Capitalist System" (Gunning), 201n56
"In Atlanta, Georgia" (song), 124
Indiana University. *See* Archives of Traditional Music
Industrial Workers of the World (IWW), 83
"infrapolitics," 33–35
International Labor Defense, 104
"I Promised Mr. Tyree" (song), 166
Israel, Boris, 49
"I Went to Atlanta" (song), 144–45, 163

Jackson, Aunt Molly, 96–97, 101, 105, 172, 196–97n40
Jackson, Bruce, 141
Jackson, Mahalia, 9
James, Thelma, 125
Jazz: A People's Music (Finkelstein), 113
Jerome, V. J., 49
Jim Crow America (Conrad), 43, 45, 114–16
Jim Crow Guide to the U.S.A. (Kennedy), 187n27
"Jim Crow in Khaki" (Gellert), 45, 112
Johnson, Guy B.: denial by, 127, 136; "Double Meaning in the Popular Negro Blues," 55; *JAF* on, 123; *Negro: An Anthology* and, 16; *The Negro and His Songs,* 32–33, 54, 70, 73–74; *Negro Workaday Songs,* 54–55, 60, 70, 73–74, 144, 165; parallels to Gellert's songs, 79, 142, 144–45, 149; references to Gellert by, 123; *The Story of American Folk Song,* 10
Johnson, Hall, 21–22
Johnson, James Weldon, 73
Journal of American Folklore (*JAF*): Gellert referred to by, 122–23, 130; Odum published in, 56, 144
Journal of Negro Education, Brown published in, 79–80

Karavan Trading Company, 22
Karl Marx' 'Capital' in Lithographs (H. Gellert), 190n31
Kelley, Robin D. G., 12, 34, 100–104, 128, 164
Kennedy, Stetson, 187n27
King, Martin Luther, Jr., 113
Kingston Trio, 7
Krehbiel, Henry Edward, 69–70, 92, 139

labor unions. *See* communism
Lawson, R. A., 11
Lead Belly (Huddie Ledbetter), 7, 93–94, 117, 172, 196n36
leftwing folksong revival, 81–107; Black music in, 85–88; Communist Left and, 81–85, 94–103, 106–7; conventional dates of, 107; eras of (1930s–1960s), 7–10; Gellert's rise and fall, 103–7; Lead Belly and, 93–94; political climate of 1930s and 1940s, 81–82; postwar collapse of movement, 110–12. *See also* communism
"Let's Go to Bury" (Gordon), 153–55
"Let's Go To De Buryin'" (song), 153–55
"Levee Camp 'Holler'" (song), 89–90, 147
Levine, Lawrence W., 12, 33, 68, 72, 135–36, 141, 155–56
Library of Congress Archive of American Folk-Song: Alan Lomax and, 86, 110, 112; Gellert's correspondence with, 204n38; Gordon and, 153; Halpert's recordings and, 140; Handcox's songs documented by, 128; leftwing folksong revival and, 86, 88, 90, 106; Odum's and Guy B. Johnson's recordings and, 142
"Lice in Jail" (song), 147
Lieberman, Robbie, 11, 86
Lightner, Alice (Hopf), 25, 26, 36, 151, 189n3
Lightner, Clarence A., 26, 36
Lipsitz, George, 82
Locke, Alain, 15, 73, 74

Lomax, Alan: *American Ballads and Folk Songs,* 81, 86, 88–89, 94, 103–4, 106–7, 142, 147–48, 196n33; Archive of American Folk-Song and, 86, 110, 112; Conforth on, 131; critical reception of Gellert vs., 103–4, 106–7; dating of Gellert's recordings and, 153, 167; Dundes on, 129; FBI investigation of "subversives," 198n2; folk boom of 1960s and, 120; friction with Gellert, 136–37, 197n51; Greenway on, 129; *Hard Hitting Songs for Hard-Hit People* and, 172–73, 179; *JAF* on, 123; Lead Belly controversy and, 93–96, 117, 196n36; leftwing folksong revival and Black vernacular song, 86–88; legacy of, 8, 10; *Negro Folk Songs as Sung by Lead Belly,* 86, 93; *Our Singing Country,* 86, 110, 142–43; OWI and, 110, 112; parallels to Gellert's songs, 142–43, 147–49, 167–71; protest songs collected by, 139; Young on, 118
Lomax, John: *Adventures of a Ballad Hunter,* 90–91, 197–98n60; *American Ballads and Folk Songs,* 81, 86, 88–89, 94, 103–4, 106–7, 142, 147–48, 196n33; Conforth on, 131; critical reception of Gellert vs., 103–4, 106–7; dating of Gellert's recordings and, 153; denial by, 33, 54, 56–60, 63–68, 71, 77, 78; Greenway on, 129; *Hard Hitting Songs for Hard-Hit People* and, 179; *JAF* on, 123; Lead Belly controversy and, 93–94, 117, 196n36; leftwing folksong revival and Black vernacular song, 86–88; legacy of, 8, 10, 53; *Negro Folk Songs as Sung by Lead Belly,* 86, 93; *Our Singing Country,* 86, 110, 142–43; parallels to Gellert's songs, 142–43, 147–48, 167–71; protest songs collected by, 139; Young on, 118
"Look Over Yonder" (Gellert, song), 117
Lornell, Kip, 11
Lott, Eric, 57
Love and Theft (Lott), 56–57
"Lynchers Are Not Born" (Gellert), 113
lynching(s): of Leo Frank, 191n42; Levine on, 156; "Lynchers Are Not Born," 113; in Monroe, Georgia, 43–44, 114; statistics (1880s–mid-1940s), 57; of Thomas Shipp and Abram Smith, 197n57
Macbeth (John Houseman & Welles), 132
Mainstream (periodical), and Silbert's criticism of Gellert, 118–20
March on Washington, 9
Margolis, David, 13
Margulies, Max, 52, 84
Masses & Mainstream (periodical): "dialogues" by Fay (Gellert), 116; "Fishin'," 113; "Lynchers Are Not Born," 113
Mazzanovich, Muriel, 40
McCarthy, Joseph, 7
McClary, Susan, 207–8n8
McClendon, Rose, 133
McCue, Michael, 38
"Me and My Captain" (Gellert): allegations about Gellert's credibility and, 143, 146–47, 158–63; publication of, 8, 21
"Me and My Captain" (Gellert, song collection), 117
Meeropol, Abel, 197n56, 105–7
Memphis Slim, 171
Milledgeville (prison), 168–69
"Mill Mother's Lament, The" (Wiggins), 95–96
Mississippi Sheiks, The, 31
Monroe, Bill, 31
Moore, Richard B., 48
Mother Wit from the Laughing Barrel (Dundes), 129
"Mr. Tyree" (song), 167
Mules and Men (Hurston), 74, 186n8
Mullen, Patrick, 53–54
Music Union (Moscow), 1–2
Music Vanguard (periodical), Gellert published in, 21, 133–34, 163
"My Father, How Long" (Garrison), 3–4

NAACP, 21
Naison, Mark, 11
Nashville State Penitentiary, 90
Nation, The, and "Self-Pity in Negro Folk-Songs" (J. A. Lomax), 56, 58, 63–65
National Textile Workers Union (NTWU), 95
National Urban League, 21
"Nat Turner" (song), 118–20, 123, 129
Negro: An Anthology (Cunard), 15, 16, 19, 44, 50, 126, 165
Negro and His Songs, The (Odum & G. B. Johnson), 32–33, 54, 70, 73–74
"Negro Character as Seen by White Authors" (Brown), 79–80

"Negroes of New York" (Gellert), 202n76
Negro Folk Songs as Sung by Lead Belly (Lomax & Lomax), 86, 93
"Negro Got No Justice" (song), 160
Negro Liberator, and leftwing folksong revival, 104–5
Negro Playwrights Company, 109
"Negro Revolutionary Music" (R. Frank), 99, 101, 102
Negro Songs of Protest: defined, 183n9; folksong revival eras (1930s–1960s), 7–10; Gellert on his work, 1; Gold and terminology for, 50; "sing fest" as gateway to, 27–30; "white man" cycle of song lyrics, 29–34. See also *Negro Songs of Protest*
Negro Songs of Protest (Gellert): Gellert's methodology and mission for, 42–46; on "How Long, Brethren?," 2–4; Hughes's foreword to, 1–2; leftwing folksong revival and, 81, 88, 93–95, 103–4, 106; Lomaxes' reference to, 110; preface to, 35, 157; publication of, 19, 52; questioned as communist propaganda, 109, 116–19, 121, 123–34; reviews of, 21–22, 156–57; "Work All the Summer," 31. *See also* African American protest and white denial
Negro Songs of Protest (Gellert, album), 130
"Negro Songs of Protest" (Gellert, article series), 165
"Negro Songs of Protest: North and South Carolina and Georgia" (Gellert), 16
Negro Workaday Songs (Odum & G. B. Johnson), 54–55, 60, 70, 73–74, 144
Neidich, Bob, 13
Neidich, Cecelia "Billie" Gellert, 13, 186n11
Neidich, Irving, 13, 22
Nelson, Scott, 12
New Jim Crow, The (M. Alexander), 4
New Masses (periodical): on *American Ballads and Folk Songs,* 103–4; Gellert on press credentials from, 115; Gellert's earliest transcription in (1932), 30–31; Gellert's early work for, 50; Gellert's "Negro Songs of Protest" moniker and, 134; Gellert's notes-with-songs annotations in, 126; Gellert's work for, 21; "Jim Crow in Khaki," 45, 112; leftwing folk revival and, 91, 94, 98, 99, 103, 105, 106; on lynchings, 44, 190n23; *Mainstream* merger with, 113; "Negro Revolutionary Music," 99, 101, 102; on *Negro Songs of Protest* (Gellert), 22; "no parallels" allegation and, 143–45; print transcriptions/audio-back-up by Gellert and, 163–65; "Songs of the Negro Worker," 98–99; "Talk in Monroe," 112; "What Is Jazz?," 112
New York Folklore Quarterly, on folk-protest songs, 125
New York Times: on *American Ballads and Folk Songs,* 106; on *Negro Songs of Protest* (Gellert), 21, 157
New York World, Gellert's plans to work for, 24
Ney, Lew, 196n36
Niles, E. Abbe, 51, 191n41
Nobody Knows My Name (Gellert, album), 11, 150
"Nobody Knows My Name" (song), 150

Odetta, 9
Odum, Howard: dating of Gellert's field recordings, 156; denial by, 59–63, 65–67, 68, 70, 71, 73–74, 79, 127, 136; "Folk-Song and Folk-Poetry," 56, 60–63; Gellert's association with, 188n45; *JAF* on, 123; legacy of, 54–55, 123; *The Negro and His Songs,* 32–33, 54, 70, 73–74; *Negro Workaday Songs,* 54–55, 60, 70, 73–74, 144, 165; parallels to Gellert's songs, 142, 144–45, 147–48; protest songs collected by, 139; *The Story of American Folk Song,* 9
Office of War Information (OWI), 110, 112
"Oh Lawdy Me, Oh Lawdy My" (song), 169
Oliver, Paul, 11, 175–76, 177
On the Trail of Negro Folk-Songs (Scarborough), 54, 70–74, 79, 145–46, 205–6n54
"O-O-Oh, Sistren an' Bred'ren" (song), 205–6n54
Opportunity (National Urban League), 21
Ottley, Roi, 133
Our Singing Country (Lomax & Lomax), 86, 110, 142–43
"Overheard in Fayette County" (Fay [Gellert]), 116

Parchman Penitentiary (Mississippi), 140–41
Parish House (Episcopal Church, Tryon, North Carolina), 28–29
Parks, Rosa, 113
Patterson, William L., 113–14
Patz, Etan, 13
Pearson, Barry Lee, 178–79
"Penitentiary Moan Blues" (A. Alexander), 139–40
Peter, Paul, and Mary, 7, 9
Petrus, Stephen, 179
"Pickin' Off De Cotton" (song), 186n9
Pioneers of the Blues Revival (Cushing), 178
Poetry of the Blues, The (S. Charters), 175
Polk County (NC) News, Gellert's work for, 22–25, 28–30
Porterfield, Nolan, 196n36
Presto Recording Corporation, 36–37, 148, 150, 152, 154, 158–59
prisons and prisoners: Gellert's music collecting and credibility, 139–40, 149, 167; leftwing folksong revival and, 86–87, 89–93; as source of music collecting, 37, 44, 51
"Protest and Irony in Negro Folksong" (Ames), 129

race relations: African American protest and white denial, 67–68; civil rights movement, 113, 116, 123, 178–81; denial and romantic racialism, 5–6; Gellert's methodology and mission, 42–46; lynchings and, 43–44, 57, 113, 114, 156, 191n41, 197n56; Scottsboro Boys and, 12, 16, 46, 118, 127, 134, 163, 201n59; sexual assault as subject of songs, 140–42; "whiteness" and, 180, 209n20
"Racial Repertoires among Blues Performer" (Ferris), 129
"Ragged Hungry Blues" (A. M. Jackson), 97
"Reconstructing the Blues" (Titon), 177
"Record Reviews" (N. Cohen), 130
Red Channels, 198n2
Red River Blues (Bastin), 11, 167
Red Song Book (Workers Music League), 97, 106
Reed, John, 47
Resettlement Administration, 85
resistance as new. *See* African American protest and white denial
Reuss, Richard A.: on dating of Gellert's recordings, 156; on Gellert and Alan Lomax, 136–37; Gellert on popularity of protest songs, 49; Gellert's responses to controversy, 120–21, 124, 125–27; on Halpert, 138; interviews of Gellert by, 10–12, 184n23; leftwing folk revival and research of, 82–83, 86, 97, 103, 106, 107, 194n6; on "no parallels" allegation, 142; on print transcriptions and audio back-up, 158, 159; on "sing fest," 27
Reynolds, Horace, 197–98
Riegger, Wallingford, 84
Rijn, Guido van, 11
Robeson, Paul, 109, 133, 187n27, 198n2
Robinson, Cedric, 57
Rockefeller Foundation, 8, 50, 113
Roediger, David R., 12, 180, 208–9n21
romantic racialism, 5–6, 53–54, 66–68, 72, 77–78
Roosevelt, Eleanor, 174
Roosevelt, Franklin, 107, 110, 111
Rosenberg, Neil V., 8
Ross, Nat, 49
Rounder Records, 130, 150, 160, 181, 184n25, 187n21, 204n38
"Run, N——, Run" (song), 71–72

Sanders, Lynn Moss, 73
Scarborough, Dorothy: on *American Ballads and Folk Songs*, 106; denial by, 54, 70–74, 79, 136; legacy of, 123; *On the Trail of Negro Folk Songs*, 54, 70–74, 79, 145–46, 205–6n54; parallels to Gellert's songs, 142, 145–46, 148; protest songs collected by, 139
Schatz, Philip, 98–99
Schomburg, Arthur, 15, 133
Scott, James C., 34
"Scottsboro" (song), 163
Scottsboro Boys, 12, 16, 46, 134
"Scottsboro Boys" (song), 118, 127, 201n60
Seeger, Charles, 84, 85, 104, 134
Seeger, Pete, 7, 13, 84, 120, 172, 173, 198n2
Segal, Edith, 114
self-pity, protest construed as. *See* African American protest and white denial
"Self-Pity in Negro Folk-Songs" (J. A. Lomax), 56, 58, 63–65, 80
"Sharecropper" (poem), 163–64
Sharecroppers' Union (SCU), 38, 127, 164

Sharp, Cecil, 131
"Shoot That Buffalo" (song), 144–45
Siegmeister, Elie, 22, 84, 117, 158
Silber, Irwin: Gellert criticized by, 109, 118–24, 129, 135, 142, 201n60; *Hard Hitting Songs for Hard-Hit People,* 172, 173, 179; as *Sing Out!* editor, 9
Simone, Nina, 38–40, 156
"sing fest" (1926), 27–30
Sing Out! magazine: Gellert and postwar controversy, 114, 117–18, 121, 122; Gellert mentioned in Young's column, 176; Silber's role at, 9
"Sistren and Brethren" (song), 41, 105–6, 162, 163
"Sitting on Top of the World" (The Mississippi Sheiks), 31
Slave Songs of the United States, 3–4, 69
Smethurst, James, 12
Sobel, Mechal, 12
Social and Mental Traits of the Negro (Odum), 66
Socialist Party, 83
Solomon, Mark, 12, 103, 107
"Songs of the Negro Worker" (Schatz), 98–99
Souls of Black Folk, The (Du Bois), 35
Southern Folklore Quarterly, on Gellert, 124, 138
Southern Road (Brown), 16, 19
Spivak, John, 16, 44
"Stagolee" (song), 170
"Stand Boys Stand" (song), 42, 145, 166
"Steel Got to Be Drove" (Gellert), 117, 121
Story of American Folk Song, The (Odum & G. B. Johnson), 9–10
Stowe, Harriet Beecher, 5
"Strange Fruit" (Meeropol), 105–6
"Strong Men" (Brown), 16–18
Student Nonviolent Coordinating Committee (SNCC), 9, 117
Szwed, John, 11, 169–71

Take Your Choice (Bilbo), 115
"Tales of One Time I'shman, Told by Southern Negroes" (Fay [Gellert]), 117
"Talk in Monroe" (Gellert), 112
Talmadge, Eugene, 114
Talmadge, Herman, 114–15
Tamiris, Helen, 50, 132
Thomas, Lorenzo, 19
Thomas, Mattie Mae, 140–41
Thompson, Stith, 123, 125
Tibbs, Andrew, 199n14
"Tie-Tamping Chant" (song), 142
Timely (record label), 184n25, 204n38
Time magazine, on Gellert, 2, 4, 21
Titon, Jeff Todd, 177, 179
"Told My Captain" (song), 41, 143–44
"Tom Dooley" (Kingston Trio), 7
Tracy, Steven, 11
Tryon, North Carolina: "Big White Folks" of, 26, 187n27; as Gellert's adopted home, 25–27; Simone and, 38–40; Tryon Colored School in, 39–40
Tryon (NC) Daily Bulletin, Gellert's byline in, 23, 24
Tuskegee Institute, 57
"Two Hoboes" (song), 160
Tyree (prison guard), 167

Unemployed Councils, 99–101

Vining, Seth, Sr., 23–24
"Voice of Your Man in Service, The" (Pepsi-Cola), 45

Wages of Whiteness, The (Roediger), 208–9n21
Wald, Elijah, 11
Walking a Blues Road (S. Charters), 173–75
Wallace, Henry, 110, 120
Ward, Theodore, 108–9, 198n2
Ware, Charles Pickard, 3
"Way Down in Old Virginia" (song), 71
"Way Down South" (song), 19–21, 158–59, 186n9
Weavers, The, 7
"We Don't Get No Justice in Atlanta" (song), 168
Weed, E. J. (character in song), 162
Weigel, William "Bill," 26, 27, 28, 32, 36, 37, 189n5
Weissman, Dick, 11, 110, 136–37
Welding, Pete, 175–76
Welles, Orson, 132
"Well on a Monday" (song), 147
"Went to Atlanta" (song), 41, 174–75
"We Shall Not Be Moved" (song), 99–100
"What Is Jazz?" (Finkelstein), 112
"When He Gits Old—Old An' Gray" (song), 60–61
When We Were Good (Cantwell), 8, 11

Which Side Are You On? (Weissman), 137–38
White, A. L., 37–38
White, Newman Ivey: denial by, 54, 70, 71, 74–80, 136; legacy of, 123; parallels to Gellert's songs, 142, 145, 147, 148
white scholarship on African American music. *See* African American protest and white denial; *individual names of researchers*
white supremacy. *See* race relations
Wiggins, Ella May, 95–97, 101, 105, 172, 196–97n40
Wilgus, D. K., 123–24, 127, 158–59, 162
Williamson, Sonny Boy, 171
Wills, Bob, 31
Wilson, Teddy, 112–13
Wolfe, Charles, 11
"Work All the Summer" (song), 30–31, 42, 91
Workers Music League, 84, 97, 104
Workers Song Book No. 2 (Composers Collective), 106
"Work Ox" (song), 42, 146–47
"Work Ox Blues" (A. Alexander), 147
Works Progress Administration, 132, 150
Wright, Richard, 109, 133

Young, Israel "Izzy," 13, 117–18, 122, 176